SECRETS OF SUCCESS
A PLAN BOOK FOR MAKING IT IN THE 1980'S

by J. Nebraska Gifford
Melvin B. Shestack and
the editors of
Gallery Press

Photographs by
J. Nebraska Gifford

A WALLABY BOOK

PUBLISHED BY POCKET BOOKS NEW YORK
PRODUCED BY GALLERY PRESS INC.

POCKET BOOKS, a Simon & Schuster division of
GULF & WESTERN CORPORATION
1230 Avenue of the Americas, New York, N.Y. 10020

ISBN: 0-671-79121-4

First Wallaby printing March, 1980

10 9 8 7 6 5 4 3 2 1

WALLABY and colophon are trademarks of Simon & Schuster.

Printed in the U.S.A.

To Hal and Emmy.
With love and gratitude.

ACKNOWLEDGEMENTS

We wish to thank Don Myrus and Unitron Instruments, Inc. (Photo Division) for the excellent advice and the use of Sigma interchangeable lenses, Bronica ETRS-medium format SLR camera, and Metz Mecablitz 40 CT-4. We certainly would advocate the use of this fine equipment to anybody looking for the "secrets of success" in photography. Susan Smyth of Cricketeer, Inc. proved to be a generous helpful friend, as did Marcia Katz of Gordon of New Orleans and Dorothy Kalins, editor of *Apartment Life*. This book could not have been completed without the counsel of Eric Protter and Ed Ernest and our heartfelt appreciation goes to Nils A. Shapiro, who not only held our hand through it all, but whose splendid suggestions always proved worthwhile. A special three cheers goes to Elaine Oxenberg and to William Muschel and Abraham Michaelson, whose patience and understanding allowed us the time to be successful; and last but not least, to Arie Kopelman, who gave us boxing lessons.

CONTENTS

INTRODUCTION

The title of this book is wrong.

There are no *secrets* of success. Many of the key ingredients that go into the achievement of career and personal goals are well known to most people: careful planning; training and experience; a willingness to learn from others; the courage to overcome disappointments and setbacks; a commitment to working as long and as hard as necessary . . . and the ability to be honest, not only with others, but with *yourself*.

Being pointed in the general direction of success, however, is not enough; if that were all it took, the top of the heap would be far more crowded than the bottom. And you can bet that's not the case!

What's needed is not a pointing finger, but a *shove*. And that is why this book is so important to any man who is serious enough about wanting to reach the top.

What you will get in these pages are not generalities, but *specifics*. Not theories about what steps *should* work for you, but practical proven techniques that *are* working for some of today's most respected people in public and business life.

If two of the not-so-secret "secrets" of success are *careful planning* and *being honest with yourself,* you'll be thankful for the special self-analysis quizzes that the authors have placed at the start of each section.

If it is essential that you be *willing to learn from others,* think how much you will benefit from meeting 24 enormously successful men and women and hearing directly from them the most valuable advice they can offer. Here are those introductions, in the form of personal interviews conducted exclusively for this book, to help you.

If you question whether you will have *the courage to overcome disappointments and setbacks,* then take comfort and inspiration from the experiences of others who were in your shoes—and made it!

But real success means more than simply working your way up the business ladder and earning a great deal of money. It relates also to the *quality* of your personal lifestyle, the degree to which you can enjoy the results of your efforts . . . and, indeed, your ability to manage your own finances for long-term protection and security. Here again, the authors have called on leading consultants for advice that will help to make your success more complete and enduring.

Woven throughout this wealth of information is a single thread: the development of your *success attitude*. It may well be the most important benefit you will take away from "Secrets of Success," for once you have gained that positive feeling about yourself others will sense it and respond in ways that open ever-widening doors of opportunity for you. It is, after all, a fact that *success breeds success.*

Mel Shestack and J. Nebraska Gifford share that success attitude. They followed their own advice in bringing this book from an original idea to its present publication. The proposal they submitted many months ago reflected careful planning, solid research on the need for such a guide, a commitment to whatever time and effort might be necessary to do the job right, and an honest appraisal of how their own expertise ought to be complemented with others' experiences in the form of interviews.

Their confidence paid off. As editor and publisher of a magazine that succeeds by understanding the needs of today's young men, I bought the idea. Pocket Books bought it, too. The result is in your hands.

And its real success is up to *you.*

Nils A. Shapiro
Editor and Publisher, Gallery Magazine

WELCOME TO THE 1980s

NOBODY can totally predict the future, but the 1980s will probably be one of the most challenging decades of the 20th century. The reason is encapsulated in one word: *limitations*. In no other period, at least in recent history, have Americans been forced to live and work with such severe restrictions. Just the very word, "energy," is enough to make the most obstinate man realize that times, indeed, are changing—and not in the way Bob Dylan figured in his celebrated song of the 60s. Traditional American concepts are being questioned; the earth has its limits, it seems, and so does man.

Contrary to popular belief, the great American economic growth doesn't seem to have brought us more leisure time. "Americans are working more and more," economist Lester Thurow writes in the *Harvard Business Review*, "with fewer and fewer hours at home." Just a few years ago, Sunday was a "dead" day for business—only a few food stores and a drugstore or two would remain open.

"Now fully 25% of the work force is employed on Sundays," notes Thurow. "Shopping centers are hubs of activity. Many plants are open seven days a week, despite the energy crisis." Thurow denies that the present energy crisis represents a significant "turning point" in economic history. Energy, he says, has stopped becoming cheaper. It now simply costs more to live and everybody will have to earn more money to keep pace with costs. To accomplish this, we will have to work harder. Economist John Kenneth Galbraith worries that salaries will not keep up with the inflation, and that there will be less opportunity for experimentation because it will be too costly.

"If there is any word that is being used to characterize the 1980s," says Queens College management professor Dr. Arthur Witkin, "it is limitations, and to work within limitations, you have to be more careful, you have to plan more carefully. It doesn't mean you can't take risks, it is just that the risk has to be more carefully studied, before you take that chance."

The 1980s will offer as much opportunity for the ambitious man as any earlier period. But success will have to be approached within the parameters of the world condition. During a very prosperous period, more people may be able to make it big. When there are limits imposed, it takes planning, cleverness, intelligence, and pride . . . and a determined attitude.

Interestingly, the current generation of young men seems to have already grasped the realities of their future lives. Professional seers agree that among the vast majority of college students and recent graduates, *ambition* is no longer a dirty word. Gone is the look of the "rube" which symbolized the dress of the sixties, and part of the seventies. People still want to "hang loose", but they want to do it with style. While Frye boots remain a part of the wardrobe, they share closet floorspace with Bally shoes and English imports. Tie sales are way up. The catch phrase of the sixties was "drop out." In the eighties it is "join." Fraternities have made a big comeback in college.

"If it means wearing a grey flannel suit so my life will be easier, fuller," the president of a student council told us, "then by God, I'll wear the tie." We have travelled from coast to coast, north and south, talking to young men — and some older ones, too. They share in common the desire to want to know *how to make it* — and *fast*. Not long ago, students asked, "How do I get ahead without sacrificing my individuality?" Now they want to know, "What kind of suit does the president of General Motors wear?"

This isn't as crass as it may seem to be; the same student is also likely to be interested in ecology, peace, and the brotherhood of man. But he has learned that the best way to get your ideas across is to be successful. People *listen* to successful men.

WHAT YOUNG MEN WANT TO KNOW

On a recent Public Broadcasting System TV show about investing, the director of a major mutual fund was asked about the young men he meets. "Funny thing," he remarked. "I've been a trustee of a university for a long time, so I come into contact with a lot of young men. Five years ago I couldn't even get to talk with them. Now they come to me."

The show's moderator interrupted. "For investment advice?," he asked.

"More than that," the mutual fund expert explained. "They want to know the ropes. How to get ahead. How to insure success. They want to be somebody. They want money. They want at least a little power, and all the perks that go with it. They don't want to make too many mistakes getting there, either. They want a better life — and they want it young."

The moderator asked, "Specifically, what do they ask?"

"Everything. How to look. What kind of attaché case to carry. What kind of haircut is necessary. Everything, and they want to do it right."

"Isn't that being conformist?," the moderator questioned.

When the moderator accused the new generation of surrendering to conformity, the mutual fund executive denied the accusation. "Just because they want to look right doesn't mean they don't bring ideas and imagination to their work. It's just typical of a generation that realizes it's easier to work up new things wihin a traditional mold. Nobody's against change. They are just in favor of success.

"And why shouldn't they be? As a result of my success, I've been paid attention to by my local board of education. If I was a dropout and came to the meeting in dirty khakis and matted hair, who the hell would listen to me? And I've convinced them to teach music in the schools as part of a regular curriculum. That's what success does for you. My Lord," he concluded, with obvious satisfaction and enthusiasm, "SUCCESS IS JUST ABSOLUTELY GREAT!"

"Success is just absolutely great."

It's a fantastic feeling *to know you have made it* . . . that you've set a goal and achieved it. Your success is solid proof to one and all that you are not only a *winner*, but that you've worked long and hard; that you are someone special. *Losing* is not a word we will use often in this book. It is not a condition anyone should contemplate. You can accept a setback grace-fully, but the thing to do is keep punching, *never give up.* (There are times when it is wise to change your strategy—but that isn't the same thing as losing.)

Haven't you wondered why some people you know are fantastically successful while others of apparently equal ability just seem to be plodding along—working hard, but getting nowhere?

Well, success is often a matter of attitude.

Success is a matter of style.

It's also a matter of discipline. And sacrifice. You don't go anywhere in this world of ours without giving up a little; maybe just some free time. But the results of success are worth it.

All of us have some kind of native ability; few really successful people are geniuses. Most are just a little above average but have learned how to use what they've got in order to get somewhere.

When you know your limitations, there are no limitations.

We know two young men who graduated a few years ago from a pretty good business school. They were both willing to start at the bottom. Both gave lip service to ambition. Both felt they had a lot of talent in their chosen field. Both managed to get hired in executive training programs in large corporations.

Carl was the one who had a straight A average in school. Warren graduated with B's—but he had to work harder than Carl who seemed to be the more natural student. At this writing, Warren is being considered for a promotion to brand manager, a stepping stone to a vice-presidency in his firm. Carl appears to be stuck in the research department of his company, where his academic aptitude serves him moderately well. But, while he can make a decent living, the job is a dead end as far as advancement is concerned.

Both Carl and Warren started in the mail rooms of their respective companies. Carl came to work in jeans and a rock-and-roll T-shirt. There were no official dress regulations in the company. He was clean and gener-ally neat. Carl's attitude was that it was foolish for him to buy any new clothes or spend any money on dry cleaning when all he did was sit in the mail room and sort packages. He figured he would start looking like an executive when he was promoted to the next phase of the trainee program.

Warren had a different strategy. He came to work *looking* like an executive, wearing a conservative suit, a white shirt and tie.

Warren *looked* important.

Carl looked just like the full-time mail room boys.

Warren didn't get in deep conversations with top management, but with his *attitude* and *style* he couldn't help but be noticed.

Warren's attitude said to everyone: "I am a mailroom *executive*, and I won't be here long." Carl wasn't noticed at all, despite the fact he did his work easily and well.

A small thing, perhaps—but it is those small things which comprise the secrets of success. Has Warren given up any individuality or creativity by dressing like an executive? We don't think so. What Warren was trying to do was to insure his success, and was doing what he felt was absolutely necessary to insure it.

13

Can reading a book insure success? Of course not. Success comes from your own inner attitudes. What we can do with this book, however, is help you from wasting valuable time. We have studied the business habits and lifestyles of hundreds of successful men, and women, for some time — observing how they do things, and why. From synthesizing the aggregate experience of all these very successful people, we've come upon a number of obvious similarities; an amazing number of ideas and attitudes they have in common. We offer these ideas so that you can assimilate them into your own plan for getting ahead. We will save you a lot of valuable time wasted in experimentation.

A Few Words About Originality, Creativity, Individuality, Conformity, Imagination, The Business World And John Keats

One of the most prevalent fears among young people starting out is that they will have to sacrifice their individuality once they get into the business world. At this point, we'd like to assure you that such is not the case. Creativity and individuality have very little to do with how you look or dress.

John Keats was one of the most brilliant, imaginative poets who ever lived, creating metaphors and images which have rarely been matched. Yet his poetry, his originality, his brilliance, all were contained within the rigid discipline of accepted literary standards. His most fantastic similes are generally thought to be found in his sonnets. The sonnet, of course, is a poem of exactly fourteen lines, usually in iambic pentameter, in a definite rhyme scheme; sort of a "grey flannel suit" of poetry, you might say. Yet within these limitations, within these confines, Keats was able to produce the most original poetry·of his lifetime; work which has lasted hundreds of years. Keats knew the secrets of success.

All of us are different, of course, and it is the differences among us that make us interesting and colorful. But we are also much more alike than we choose to believe — at least if we are goal oriented. You don't necessarily have to agree with all the customs, beliefs and principles that people live by. But it will certainly help you to know by fact and example how the majority of achievers make it.

You bought this book because you're interested in yourself as an achiever. And you know who you are . . . right?

Wrong.

Most of us only have the barest idea of who we are, what we want, and how to go about getting it. Of course, we have some feelings about it. But come on. Can you sit down and write one paragraph about yourself, and where you want to be, as a private person and business person five years from now?

If you were a reporter assigned to interview *you*, could you sit down and write an honest, no-holds-barred, bottom-line profile of yourself? Remember, it's a proven adage of successful business that any problem can be solved if the facts are known. Truth is the best weapon with which to win the first battle.

Dr. David Kahn, a noted New York psychologist you'll meet later in this book, tells his patients, "*All facts are helpful in the long run.*"
Successful people don't fool themselves.

14

PART I:

SOCIAL SUCCESS

TAKING INVENTORY OF YOURSELF

"IT was my first big assignment," a Cleveland merchandising executive confided to us. "My firm had bought a chain of stores and I was put in charge of improving sales. But I couldn't seem to communicate with the employees of the company; there was no way I could get through to them. It was as if a force field was between us.

"The first thing I did, as a trained merchandiser, was to take inventory of the stock of the stores. I wanted to know about every piece of merchandise . . . which ones moved and which ones didn't. And it was then that I got the idea about myself. I had the technical capabilities needed to run the business, but somewhere in my emotional makeup there was a big gap. A gap big enough to prevent my making a success of the operation, because of my problem with people.

"So I used my business training on my own psyche. I decided to *take inventory of myself*. I did, and discovered that what I called my 'shyness' manifested itself as hostility toward my co-workers. Speaking in sales terms, as soon as I saw that shyness was not a product that 'moved,' I was able to take hold of myself. I just sat down, told the sales manager that I was a shy person . . . not a snob . . . and my troubles began to diminish."

Before we get into the details of planning for success, it is necessary for you to take inventory of yourself, to discover who you are so that you know what tools you have to work with. Remember, no one but yourself is going to see this — so be *honest*. A cardinal rule of successful people is that they are honest with *themselves*. Just look around at your friends and acquaintances and see how many of them are hamstrung in their personal and professional lives because they fool themselves.

We know an exceptionally bright man who has known nothing but failure because he cannot accept the responsibility of admitting error. It's *always* the other person's fault. We know another young man whose personality is so abrasive that he has already lost three jobs. When he gets fired, it's always the fault of the company. "They can't accept my honesty with customers," he says, almost with pride.

He is quite good in his field, and he's managed again to get another job. But his friends, justifiably, fear yet another disaster, because he still refuses to be honest with himself and is paying the consequences. Think about it; is this a problem *you* have?

Most of us, happily, don't have deep-seated neuroses and have the ability to change our habits. Or, if not, we can sometimes use our idiosyncracies to our own benefit.

We have come now to our SECRETS OF SUCCESS INVENTORY QUIZ. It is a marvelous test, because all you have to do to get a high score is answer all the questions *honestly*. There are no grades. The results come from re-reading the answers. You will have a quick and valuable readout on yourself . . . your likes, dislikes, fears, ambitions, eccentricities, talents, shortcomings, tastes, personality. If you find a question terribly difficult to answer, maybe that's an area you have to explore even further. It doesn't matter whether or not, for example, you are a great athlete. If athletics give you pleasure, they are worth pursuing. But if a game of golf is a terrifying experience for you, you may never be successful at it. So drop it. Or, at least, don't count on it in your arsenal of success weapons. There *are* other ways to make that sale or sign that deal.

Ask yourself this question, right now: WHO AM I? Most of us answer it this way: "John Smith," or "Bill Jones." That's a copout, because we are all lots of things. When I asked a successful young friend, Tom, who he thought he was, he answered: "I'm Tom . . . . I'm a man. I'm a husband. I'm a father. I'm a sales executive. I'm a student (he was taking two night courses). I'm a squash player. I'm a football fan. I'm an American. I'm a brother. I'm an uncle. I'm a veteran. I'm a skier. I'm a Californian. I'm an Irish-American. I'm a Catholic. I'm a Republican. I'm a fan of Barbra Streisand. I'm a Jaycee. I'm a bird watcher. I'm a day person."

If we're going to want to use all the parts of us . . . and we are all men of many parts . . . then we must know what those parts are!

We've provided the following test to help you make a quick study of yourself. Take it right now.

YOUR PERSONAL SUCCESS INVENTORY

Are You Ready For Success?
By Gail North

What does success mean to you?

To some it means recognition—strong visibility in their chosen professions. To others it means acceptance—an invitation into more opulent levels of living. It could mean financial abundance, international leadership, public recognition, or even a guarantee of the love of beautiful women. No matter what the personal implication, we all agree that success is the forerunner to a life style that is full, rich, and extremely gratifying.

It's been said that "you can have anything as long as it's within the context of your own potential." Successful people know that this context represents the full range of possibilities inherent within themselves. So, for the moment, we'd like you to consider yourself a pioneer; you're going to explore your territory—your context—and find out: where you stand in your life; how you view yourself, from your integrity to your intuition; your passion for status; your personal style. You're going to ensure that you're ready for success!

Professional marketers agree that before they can achieve coveted astronomical sales figures for a product they have to know the territory—and know it well! What kinds of customers live there, what do they want, what are they willing to chance? You're in the success business now. You are a product, and you need to know how *you* function, how *you* think, how *you* feel, what parts work *for* you and what parts work *against* your chances for the success you want.

Beginning with a basic honesty with yourself, answer all of the following questions with a sharp eye on your own bottom line. Be prepared to retain both the points that illuminate your *strongest* features and the points that trigger your *weakest* thrusts. The two extremes are important: they will lend the support you need as you shape your Personal Success Inventory.

Are Your Dreams And Desires Being Secretly Thwarted?

We all know about the fear of success — it's that catch-all cop-out for keeping the status quo. Yet, it's an important concept to consider. Fear can be a basic "negative persuader" hidden inside your psyche, but begging to be exorcised so that you can go on with your life. You may hear yourself saying, "I want, I want...," but if that secret fear mechanism is activated, your anxiety level may be working *against* solid achievement. Most successful people have a built-in anxiety receptor; they know when it's being triggered, but learn how to manipulate it and how to quickly re-establish their immediate goals.

There are two basic negative persuaders you must be familiar with when dealing with success anxiety. They show up in these forms of self-doubt:

1. Success — is it compatible with my image of myself?
2. Success — will it force me to use the full range of my personal power?

The first results from your personal conditioning — the image you were fed in childhood by parents, siblings, friends. You may be caught in an old script which is now obsolete, but lingering. The second deals with the natural strengths you may be hiding within an old, worn-out self-image. Both are important considerations to investigate. Once you establish what you're struggling against, your options for success are wide open.

On a separate sheet of paper, answer *all* of these questions. Write as little or as much as you want, for each.

Success —Is It Compatible With My Image of Myself?

SOCIAL QUIZ

1. Does the idea of your own personal success exhilarate you?

2. Did your parents prepare you for success? How?

3. Were you given positive or negative inspiration regarding your personal ambitions?

4. Were your parents' aspirations for you compatible with your own secret ambitions?
   a. What did they want you to become?
   b. What did you want to become?

5. Did you feel emotionally swamped by their expectations of you?
   a. Did those expectations cramp your personal vision of success?
   b. Did you feel resentment, perhaps guilt, over their demands?

6. Were your parents' expectations too high?
   a. How did that make you feel? Inept? Fraudulent? Challenged?
   b. How did you react to their demands? Passive acceptor? Aggressive denier?

7. Were your parents' expectations too low?
   a. How did that make you feel? Guilty over your own ambitions? Resentful at not being recognized? Stifled by invisibility?
   b. How did you react to their demands? Passive acceptor? Aggressive denier? Secret achiever?

8. Whether their expectations were too low or too high, do you today often feel that you're not moving — that you're caught in a slum mentality? Are you always putting yourself down?

9. If you continue to deny your own expertise, is it because you are harboring a secret perversity?
   a. Does a private inner voice tell you that you've won when you've failed?
   b. Whom have you beaten?
   c. Do you understand that the best revenge against your "negative persuader" is for you to live well?

10. Do you think of yourself as a rebel or an outlaw as a cover for not moving ahead, achieving?

11. Can you separate out the information you were fed in the past from what you would like in the present and in the future?

12. Can you give up the past, let go of the old scripts, celebrate your own desires, and make success a compatible image with yourself?

Who Are Your Heroes And Where Do You Stand?

You see them every day and are probably curious about how they got where they are. Now that you've established what's been holding you back on a psychological level, you're ready to look at them more closely. Think about the people with well-defined images of success. How do you feel about them? How do you feel with them? What would you like to know about them? You may want to begin observing these people in action, watch how they behave in different situations.

The following quiz will help you to define where you stand with models of success and how you feel about yourself in that role.

1. There's at least one person in your life who captures the aura of success. Who is it?

2. What are the visible qualities you most admire?
   a. Appearance?
   b. Social ease?
   c. Friends, associates, women?
   d. Financial status?

3. What are the invisible qualities you most admire?
   a. Integrity?
   b. Personal power?
   c. Self-esteem?

4. How do you feel in the presence of successful people?
   a. In the right milieu?
   b. Like an outsider?
   c. Envious?

5. Do you jump right in and try to explore how they got where they are?
   a. Do you engage them in conversation?
   b. Do you listen to what they say and how they say it?

6. Do you avoid contact with these people?
   a. Pretend they aren't there?
   b. Speak to everyone but them?
   c. Secretly diminish them to make yourself feel okay?

7. Can you use the qualities you observe in these people as models for yourself?

8. There's at least one person in your own life with whom you are a success. Who is it?

9. How does your own personal power manifest itself with this person?

10. Use the following checklist to obtain a good measure of how you behave with that person:
    a. Do you initiate conversations?
    b. Do you generate ideas?
    c. Do you create the ambience you want?
    d. Do you disagree with points that are made?
    e. Do you believe your opinions are valid?
    f. Do you insist on being heard?
    g. Do you listen to what is being said?
    h. Do you feel trusting enough to be resilient, to change your opinion when you're proven wrong?
    i. Do you sometimes act with impertinence or even audaciousness?
    j. Do you use your sense of humor?
    k. Do you take conversational risks?
    l. Do you feel you can be yourself in all of your positions?
    m. Do you act with strength and courage?

11. If you've answered yes to these questions, you may have to begin to act as your own role model! Can you acknowledge your own abilities?

12. Can you imitate your own behavior and transfer it into the business or professional arena?

13. Can you stand being your own hero?

Now read over your answers. You may be surprised at some of the results, because you haven't focused on this before. Write down a list of the answers which bother you, and think about them.

We're not through.
Read your answers very carefully; they are things you already know about yourself—but seeing them on an "inventory sheet" paints a clearer

WHAT HAVE YOU LEARNED?

picture of your persona: your likes, dislikes, ambitions, fears, strengths. *You are a man of many parts.*

Here is another exercise that follows the quiz. It's not a totally original idea. It's the first thing the instructor asks his students to do in a number of success courses now offered by universities, especially in their night schools. These courses have caught on not only because most of us want to learn to be successful, but because *they work.*

Assume you are a reporter given the assignment of interviewing yourself. The City Editor has told you: "Find out what kind of person the guy really is . . ."

In these "success courses," the students read their personal profiles to each other and discuss them, which can be embarrassing. But *you* don't have to worry about grammar or writing style. It isn't going to be published. Nobody is going to see it. You don't have to hide anything—because it's for your eyes only. Just put it all down.

As an example of a personality profile, here is one written by a 24-year-old recent college graduate who is in the training program of a major real estate corporation.

Paul Carter is 24 years old. He graduated from Arizona State at Tempe with a B.A. in Political Science. He just finished his Master's in Business Administration at the University of Kansas. He maintained a B average throughout his scholastic career. He managed an intra-mural soccer team. He plays squash once a week, reluctantly. He is five feet ten inches tall and weighs 200 pounds. He could lose some weight. Paul wears suits to work, but prefers to lounge around in jeans and sneakers. Paul listens to jazz and rock; his favorite singers being Linda Ronstadt and Billy Joel. He likes old Duke Ellington records. He didn't read one novel last year, but did finish about five non-fiction books—including the Book on Running (he never started) and Richard Nixon's memoirs. Paul thinks he is shy. He is embarrassed by his thinning hair (a family trait). He is unmarried, and currently uninvolved. He lives with two roommates in an apartment house in Kansas City. He watches TV. He subscribes to the Wall Street Journal. Paul has almost $4,000 invested in stocks. He hopes to have a seat of his own on the Stock Exchange someday; or if not, at least a responsible position with a major firm. Paul drives a 1973 Buick Riviera. His travels, except for a trip to Hawaii with his parents as a teenager, have been confined to the American Southwest.

Now, few of us are psychiatrists; but we *are* capable of learning a good deal about Paul Carter by simply "reading between the lines." And Paul can learn a lot about himself from his own profile. For example:

1. He tends to be a bit disorganized. The facts he wrote are presented in a haphazard way.
2. He is not totally firm in his ambition. He gives himself an out—cautious.
3. He worries about his thinning hair and burgeoning waistline. It isn't the hair or waistline which will hinder his success—many, many bald fat men are marvelously successful. It's *worrying* about it that can be counter-productive.

4. It's more fun for him to be involved in sports as an administrator than as a participant.
5. Clothes aren't really important to him.

Now, these are just five, off-the-top-of-your-head opinions about Paul Carter. A serious student could devise an entire psychological profile from it. We're only interested in it from a success standpoint.

Paul appears to be intelligent and wants to get ahead. However, he suffers from a bit of confusion as far as his self-image is concerned. In order to succeed, you *must* have a positive self-image. And you can build that by getting to know your "real" self.

According to noted psychiatrist Dr. Theodore Isaac Rubin, "None of us is in complete contact with reality. Some of us are not in contact at all." Dr. Rubin believes that, to the extent you can "validate reality" (i.e., be realistic about things), you have a phenomenal asset. "Functioning in the real world," Dr. Rubin writes, " is a corollary and prerequisite for the good economic investment of emotions, energy and time." He feels that if we know in which areas we tend to be more realistic and in which we lean toward the fantastic, we own some very valuable information.

Dr. Rubin feels it is imperative for a person to know his assets and limitations, as well as the areas needing growth and development. "Being aware of your assets gives you the opportunity to use and develop them and to raise your self-esteem," Dr. Rubin writes. Dr. Rubin advises everyone who is looking for success in life to examine these eight areas:

1. *People* — Are you too trusting, too stand-offish, too naive?
2. *Money* — Is it being utilized in *your* behalf, realistically, or does money dominate you?
3. *Self-preservation* — What is destructive to you and what is constructive? How often do you set yourself up in life ... get into jeopardizing situations? Do you fall into uneasy financial situations? Do you involve yourself in emotional attachments which always result in unhappiness?
4. *Timing and Placing* — Do you put yourself in the right place and right time? (Dr. Rubin feels that, if you do, it is no accident; it comes from a need for self-preservation and self-gratification.)
5. *Time* — You must be realistic about time. Are you cognizant of the time it really takes you to do things? Do you have patience? Do you give up easily, if it looks like a long haul? Dr. Rubin asks, "Can you put off immediate satisfactions but continue in immediate involvements, in order to arrive at larger achievements later on? If so, you have some very important assets, indeed."
6. *Temptations* — Which ones can you resist? Which ones can't you resist? Can you deal with temptation at all?
7. *Deceptions* — Where do you deceive yourself? Do you rationalize yourself out of everything? Unless you stop kidding yourself, you are doomed to NO success.
8. *Optimism* — You must mitigate setbacks, pain and depression with *hope*. Don't think that positive thinking is just media hype. Dr. Rubin insists that "people can grow and change."

Using information learned about yourself from the quiz and profile, make up an asset chart. It can be a ready reference on your climb up the success ladder. It needn't be fancy, just as comprehensive as possible. Many extremely successful executives use some variation of it to work out solutions to various kinds of problems.

ASSETS	LIABILITIES	NEED TO IMPROVE
Strong voice	Tend to procrastinate	Nervous gesture
Good Intellect	Careless with	with finger
	details	on ear.
		Write
Neat		thank-you
Come to		notes.
work early		Finger nails

Just divide a sheet of paper into three parts, with these headings: Assets; Liabilities; Need to Improve. Remember, you will be the only person to see this—so be brutally honest. Then, once in a while, check on yourself. It's an easy way to see where you are going, how you are improving. If you do this once a month for a year, you'll discover how well, or how poorly, you are handling your liabilities.

INTERVIEW *"You've got to know how to cope with failure ..."*

MORTIN GOTTLIEB:

When Anita Loos told Helen Hayes that Morton Gottlieb rode his bicycle through miles of New York traffic each morning on his way to his office, the great actress shuddered. "Isn't it dangerous?" she asked. Ms. Loos smiled. "How would a Broadway producer," she replied, "know when he's in danger?"

It's called having *chutzpah*, and Gottlieb says he can't think of a successful man he knows who doesn't have at least a little bit of it.

Broadway producer Gottlieb certainly can be considered an authority on the vicissitudes of success. In one of the most uncertain professions in the world, he's managed to produce a series of smash hits: "Sleuth," "Same Time Next Year," and "Tribute," among the most recent. "You have to know how to cope with failure," Gottlieb warns, "when every project means taking another chance. You have to be fairly masochistic and have *chutzpah* at the same time."

Originally indigenous to New York and derived from the Yiddish, *chutzpah* is not accepted by colloquialists as a solid American term. Humorist Leo Rosten defines *chutzpah* as "that quality enshrined in a man, who, having killed his mother and father, throws himself on the mercy of the court because he is an orphan." In other words, a bit of *presumption mixed with nerve and audacity*. The ability, therefore, to take risks.

Although Gottlieb claims that "anyone can be a producer," his own experience proves otherwise. "I have always wanted to be successful," he admits, but he worked at his profession slowly, with strong goals in mind. "You must have tenacity," Gottlieb says. He also feels that "it is a

24

danger to succeed too early." At a recent Yale seminar where he addressed senior students, the questions dealt more with *how fast* the students could become successful, than how proficient they could become. That's looking at things backwards. "If you achieve based on experience," he advises, "you accumulate a certain frame of reference. You build cement blocks. A solid foundation."

A Yale graduate, Gottlieb's apprenticeship in the theater began as a press agent. He further continued training as a company general manager for a series of notable producers, including Gilbert Miller and the American Shakespeare Festival. With his final goal always in mind, he mastered the fiscal matters so necessary to his profession. Gottlieb says he can't stress too strongly that setbacks shouldn't discourage anyone. He insists, "Opportunity comes more than once."

It never occurred to Gottlieb that he might fail. "Push and tenacity," he says, referring to keys to success. "And knowing not to give up." Gottlieb's favorite theatrical adage is, "You've got to keep the store open." If you're going to keep yourself available to success opportunities, however, it is imperative to have confidence in your own ability to handle those opportunities when they do show up.

Gottlieb also believes that success comes more easily if you have social ease. "Not false charm," he says, recalling a "marvelous course we all had to take at Erasmus Hall high school in Brooklyn.

"We learned how much to tip. Even how to ask for a date. We had a little improvisational theater in the class. We even learned how to read a menu." Gottlieb said it seemed unimportant at the time, but knowing these things makes life less complicated. "You can act with less hesitation." Knowing those things frees you from unnecessary worry.

The true mark of success, according to Gottlieb, is being able to not only survive in your chosen field but to keep improving. He mentioned the actors John Gielgud and Ralph Richardson, who are at least in their late 70s and perform every night. "That's the mark of success." Gottlieb exclaimed. "They are better than ever." He smiled. "That's the way we should all be, getting better all the time. What other way is there?"

HOW TO BE POPULAR

*"Popularity can make you
more effective both as an
achiever and as a person ..."*

THERE was a TV series a few years back set in a Los Angeles high school. One of the episodes dealt with the adventures of a transfer student from a midwestern school who embarks on a campaign to break through the wall of indifference he meets during his first days at the school. We don't remember the character's name, but let's call him Steve.

Any newcomer to an established group, whether school or office staff, will find cliques already formed and social circles already in action. Once Steve realizes that it is indifference, not hostility, that he is facing from the other students, he embarks on a campaign of recognition. And that's what popularity is, by the way—*recognition* and *admiration* on the part of friends and colleagues.

Many people are liked, yet aren't necessarily popular. But Steve is a clever kid. He finds little things to help himself be noticed: a girl is carrying an unwieldly load of books through the hall, so he takes the books, and helps her; when somebody's car won't start he is the first to help push, but doesn't make a big thing about it and leaves when the car starts.

When he is having trouble in math, he stops the best math student in the hall and compliments him. "You're really terrific with that math stuff, Smitty," he says. "I'm so far behind, I don't think I'll ever catch up. You couldn't spare a half-hour after school, could you?" The good math student, flattered, offers help, and Steve's first real friendship with another boy in his class takes root.

At that point, Steve is on his way to becoming popular. While watching the TV show we thought how clever the character was in being able to insinuate himself into a closed society without generating any rancor. His personality invaded the class as a nutrient, rather than as a missile. Little by little, the other students began to take to him; they didn't even realize that he hadn't been there a long time.

Steve checks out who are the class leaders, and focuses his campaign on them—with little things, quietly. But as he earns acceptance and the affection of his fellow students, his faculty advisor is very concerned. "You've only been at the school two months," he chastises, "and you're already running for public office." He shakes an admonishing finger at Steve and warns, "Life isn't a popularity contest, you know."

The teacher's advice may have been well-meant, as are a lot of bromides we grow up with, but often they are founded in myth. The truth of the matter is that in our world, being liked *is* what most of us want. It isn't necessarily a disease nor a psychotic compulsion. It is a natural desire. And the people who are relatively popular often succeed more easily than people who aren't. A recent study conducted by the University of Rochester Graduate School of Management and Business Administration shows that an inordinate number of the top ten executives in Fortune 500 companies held some kind of elective office in either high school or college. "School offices are generally filled by students who are very popular," reports University of Rochester spokesman James S. Peck. "Our study shows that once a person reaches the top, his idea of popularity might diminish (i.e., the emphasis he places on it). But on the way up, it seems to be a valuable tool."

It may be true that no one gets to be chairman of the board on popularity alone. But neither can the rude, crude, insensitive man blame his standstill in business on a poor choice of fathers-in-law. Knowing how to keep people happy and liking you is getting to be almost as important to success as work and talent. Some people may derogate the idea, but it is a fact that popularity is an asset highly prized in our society. We Americans like to read about popular people (just look at the success of *People* magazine and all its imitators), and we often seek to emulate them.

There are still those among us who like to believe that being a nice guy conflicts with getting ahead either socially or in the business world. No, it certainly isn't the end-all. But, like correct dress and manners, a degree of popularity can make you more effective as a person and as an achiever; even (heaven forbid) if it isn't natural and you use it as a cover. Besides, popularity also makes your social life a lot more enjoyable.

Can *anyone* be taught to be popular? As with development of most skills, the essential ingredient is the willingness of the student to learn.

The option of your becoming more popular depends in large part on *you*. If you want to stay home and work on mathematical theory so that you can offer the world a new way to trisect an angle, it probably doesn't matter if anyone likes you — or if you like them. But most of us aren't scientists or artists or great novelists. So if you want to get ahead and enjoy an active, exciting life — a tremendously profitable life — you had better start learning to like people.

A cardinal rule of popularity, according to Burt Reynolds, who is one of the most popular people in Hollywood — with men as well as women — is "to like people without worrying if they are going to like you in return." Reynolds told us that, "Like everything else in achieving success, popularity necessitates an attitude. What you say to yourself is, 'I am a nice guy. I like people. I want them to like me. I have no intention of working them over.' I look for the good things in my friends and associates, not the bad, and concentrate on that."

Reynolds also says, "*Unless you have a pretty good opinion of yourself you're not going to have an easy time making friends.* It's amazing how people pick up on things, and *it's your opinion of how you perceive yourself that gives others the clue on how to think of you.*"

The best way to learn anything in this world is to *observe*. You obviously have a friend or business associate who is very popular. Watch him. See what he does when he comes into the office, or enters any room. What does he do at lunch, at parties? Listen to his conversations with other people. If you weren't bright and aggressive and anxious to succeed, you wouldn't be reading this book — so assume you're pretty observant, too. And there is an even better way: *Ask.*

You will find that most successful people have a strong sense of security; they will be pleased you asked them for advice, and will offer it willingly.

How to Sell Yourself the First Time Around

Don't let anybody tell you that it isn't necessary to impress people. Ask any salesman—successful salesman, that is—about the need for selling yourself and you'll be told that it is imperative to impress a client, and quickly.

Do you remember the book, *The Hucksters*, by Frederick Wakeman? It was made into a movie with Clark Gable and Sidney Greenstreet. Gable joins an advertising agency and meets his client, the president of a soap company, played by the corpulent Greenstreet. A number of executives are sitting around a conference table, looking to Greenstreet, who is chairman of the board. He stands up, commanding the collective attention of his staff. He opens his mouth to speak; instead, he makes a terrible gargling sound, and expectorates—yes, spits, on the table. Everyone is horrified. Greenstreet smiles. "None of you will ever forget that," he says confidently. "That's what packaging is. A first impression which nobody will ever forget."

There, are however, other ways to create a first impression. One of the real secrets of success, according to Clifford Grodd, president of Paul Stuart, Inc.—one of the world's most successful men's clothing stores—is knowledge not only of who you are, but also of *how you come across.* "You can be an off-the-wall character," he says. "That's one of the great things about living in this country. But if you are off-the-wall, you have to know you pay heavy consequences for it."

First impressions, like manners, are apt to be taken as a key to a man's character. "It may be a foolish criterion," Grodd agrees, "but what else has a potential date, friend, employer, host or hostess to judge by in this frenetic world? A man who wears yellow shoes with two-inch thick soles and double-knit bell bottoms might not be a freak. The man whose hair isn't washed or who insults people at their first meeting may not be a terrible person. A man who wears a cowboy hat (and isn't a Texan) might not be a cornball. But the people he meets may not stick around to discover the truth hidden by his off-beat behavior.

Perhaps the best general guide in this area is a quotation from the great Lord Chesterfield, who advised his son to take great care to act "like the reasonable people of your own age, in the place where you are."

SUCCESS WITH WOMEN

"A man may have rough edges in business and get away with it, and with his dealings with other men. And he might make a lot of money. But in the changing values of the 1980s, no man can be considered totally successful unless he can be a friend, colleague—as well as a lover—of women. It was hard enough in the 1930s, 40s, and 50s. Supposedly it got easier in the 1960s. And the 70s. I don't think so. Men still have to work at man/woman relationships as hard, if not harder, than any other area of their lifestyle ..."

—Cary Grant

"There is no man who doesn't have some difficulty in dealing with women on a one-to-one relationship, and that includes me, Warren Beatty, John Travolta. Everybody. But that doesn't mean you don't keep trying. That's the answer. You try. Women know it if you're trying, and that's half the battle."

—Burt Reynolds

"I asked a Vietnamese friend why after centuries of following their men, the Vietnamese woman now walks ahead of the man. He said that there were many unexploded land mines since the war..."

—David Butler,
Newsweek Senior Editor

"The best of women are those who are content with little..."
—The Ayatolla Khoemeini

"Whether women are better than men, I cannot say—but I can say they are certainly no worse..."

—Golda Meir

"A woman has to be twice as good as a man to go half as far..."
—Fannie Hurst.

If one of your friends tells you he has no trouble dealing with women, he is lying. Almost all surveys about the alleged new relationships between men and women indicate that today's man views himself as willing to accept the "new woman"; he understands the justice of equal salary for an equal job; he is able to let her pay the restaurant check; and he will lecture on the virtues of liberated women as better lovers. Still, with all this self-professed change of heart, very few men admit to having no trouble in establishing relationships with women. Conversely, women seem to have equally as hard a time establishing relationships with men.

This, despite the fact that almost every person we interviewed about the importance of man-woman relationships to their ideas of success, stressed how high on their list of priorities it was.

There is evidence to the effect that men who become successful in business also have more successful dealings with women, namely long-lasting marriages. A survey reported in *The New York Times* pointed out that top management executives in major companies were better able to have stable relationships with women.

Although divorce is more common in higher echelons of business than it used to be, it is still below the average in middle-management levels. "Bad relationships with women can impede your progress," says business psychologist John Wardel in an interview in *U.S. News and World Report*. "They cause tensions which you bring to the job. A man can climb the ladder to the top, only to slip and fall because those tremendous pressures emanating from the home diminish his capabilities on the job."

HOW MEN AND WOMEN CAN GET ALONG BETTER

Nancy Evans

Dr. David Kahn

Nils A. Shapiro

A Gallery Relationship Seminar

"Sometime in this century," the late Margaret Meade wrote, "men and women will begin to learn that it is possible for them to get along with one another." Of couse, that has been the historic problem. And it undoubtedly is one of the most difficult "secrets of success" to master. It necessitates the greatest possible understanding on the part of all of us. To investigate the subject, the editors of this book invited a panel of experts including the celebrated psychologist, teacher and author, Dr. DAVID KAHN; NILS A. SHAPIRO, editor and publisher of *Gallery* Magazine and NANCY EVANS, a writer and co-author of *How to Get Happily Published* who is presently working on her own book about the problems of young men and women. The moderator of the discussion was MELVIN SHESTACK, co-author of "Secrets of Success."

SHESTACK: Here's a line from an article that appeared in *Madamoiselle* Magazine — it generated more mail than any other. "Why Aren't These Nice Men Married Yet?" It didn't talk about marriage per se, but rather why women and men today — especially those in their thirties — have so much trouble getting along with one another. And they do. Among our friends — unmarried and married — the major topic of conversation after we've been together a while inevitably turns to relationships and why they don't work.

DR. KAHN: I'm sure a number of your patients have that problem: "Why can't I meet somebody? Why can't I get along? I'm a good looking, attractive man. I go to a party, I go home alone. What is wrong? The *Mademoiselle* article says essentially that women don't really — in spite of what you read and hear — want an open, full relationship. The author says that women want all the privileges of equality, but none of the obligations.

EVANS: And that's why men aren't married to them.

SHESTACK: Apparently men can't handle it at the moment. The world has changed . . . at least in urban centers. Letitia Baldridge tells us, "In business, treat your female colleagues as colleagues and treat all other women as women." Use the old fashioned idea. So why this problem? The problem of meeting and getting along has probably been with us for all time.

SHAPIRO: I also think you're talking about different kinds of men. I was brought up in a time when chivalry was *de rigeur*; the equality movement didn't really get moving until I was well into my adulthood. Happily I've been able to use the equal relationship as one that has advantages for me, and I'm enjoying my life even more now because of it. But many men in their late thirties or forties don't have the same professional opportunity to be around women all the time as I do. Instead, they're being told that everything they were brought up to feel was wrong. Now, that's one kind of man. On the other hand, you have the man who is, say, eighteen to thirty-four; he was brought up at a time when the women's movement for equality was so much a part of his environment — so much of his growing up — that he doesn't even have to think twice about it. I think . . . You think he thinks twice?

KAHN: I don't think there's any difference in those men.

EVANS: I don't either. The younger group may be more expressive about their feelings and know the code words of liberation, but I think that when push comes to shove they have many of the same problems as the older men. Which figures since how you behave has more to do with the way in which you are raised than with the age in which you live.

KAHN: Nothing helps. People just learn more ways to be destructive to each other. Relationships are no better today than they ever were, and they probably never will be .mm even with all the self-help books on how to relate, and how to be warm and how to be open. That's the real problem.

SHAPIRO: Are you saying it's not really man-woman relationship that's the problem? That it's man-man and woman-woman, or people-people?

KAHN: Most people don't seem to get along with each other. Partly because they don't get along with themselves. People appear to treat themselves as harshly as they treat others. How can we help others with their needs when we can't take care of (or even know) our own?

SHAPIRO: That certainly complicates the problem, doesn't it?

EVANS: Are problems more complicated now? They seem to be more convoluted.

KAHN: No, they're the same as ever. Except that now we have airplanes, and we didn't have them before: we have skyscrapers and we didn't have them. But the kinds of things people do to each other are the same.

SHESTACK: Even though the world's a little different? When I was, say, twenty-five years old, the thing to do was get married as soon as possible. All my friends were getting married; we all made bad marriages; none of my high school friends are married to the same women they were married to.

KAHN: That's happening now, too.

EVANS: But I think there has been a real change. Perhaps it may be true for only a minority, but I feel I am one of that minority. By the time I graduated from college it was not mandatory that you be engaged on graduation day, whereas a few years before I graduated — at least for the women's and men's colleges on the East Coast — there was a chain reaction among friends to get married. By my time, we weren't getting married.

KAHN: Whether people get married later or earlier, they still don't get along. It doesn't make any difference. It really isn't a black picture at all. It's just reality. If you have the wrong expectations of what a relationship is, and if you're using the relationship (and everybody's pretty self-serving, you know), to fulfill your own needs, the same thing is going to happen. In spite of the feminine movement, or whether you have prohibition or you don't have prohibition, or whether you wear mini-skirts or you don't wear mini-skirts — you put two people together and what happens? And what will happen in the Eighties? The same thing that happened in the Thirties and the Twenties. What makes you think that people can get along better in the Nineties than in the Forties?

SHESTACK: Maybe it has something to do with women having a little more confidence. My youngest daughter, for example, thinks in terms of going into medicine as a scientist. It never dawns on her to be a nurse. Never. She always talks in terms of being a doctor. That has nothing to do with it?

KAHN: No, I don't think so. I have many successful patients, both men and women — they make a lot of money and have good jobs, yet they don't seem to function well in close relationships. So, if a woman gets a good job and gains occupational self-fulfillment, she may still not be able to get along with men. Where do you get the idea that if you're successful you get along better with people? You eat better, you have silk sheets and you have a house in the country, but your close relationships are likely just as bad.

SHESTACK: Many of the people we've interviewed for this book agree that, to be successful, you have to be able to get along with people. I don't know if this crosses over, but what these people have said is that what helped them to become successful is having a relationship with someone of the opposite sex. Not necessarily being married, but being able to have a long and lasting relationship. Now, there is a contradiction here.

EVANS: I think one of the problems is this: Once upon a time it was the man who, after graduation, went out and worked; and his commitment to work was the motivating force during his twenties and thirties. The woman's primary commitment was to relationships and to the family. Nowadays, more and more, you've got the woman coming out of school with the kind of commitment to work that only a man had before. And that means you've got women terribly involved in their work at a time when they traditionally were concentrating on their personal lives. So you have men and women moving down parallel tracks. The self-confidence I see in my women friends does help them to work much more effectively and in a large part it springs from success in their work. But sometimes it works against them in trying to build a relationship. The confidence a woman has can be threatening to some men. And there's this paradox: it seems that the more successful a woman becomes, the less men there are around. The comment I hear consistently is, "Why can't I find a man just like my women friends? Men who have those characteristics I value so much in my women friends?" In other words, a man she can feel comfortable with and who will feel comfortable with her—all of her.

KAHN: Women don't get along very well with each other. People don't seem to get along well with each other.

EVANS: I know you believe that. I don't.

KAHN: What I see is many people living in quiet desperation, and some live in noisy desperation. But nothing much has changed in terms of the way people deal with each other. We're the same. People don't relate any differently, whatever movements there have been, or scientific change—air conditioning, or electric blankets, or homes in the country or cars. Sure, society's changing, science is changing, we've gone to the moon. But people can't get along any better across the breakfast table. Let me make a comment: there's probably more damage done every day as a result of what people do to each other—demean each other, manipulate each other, use each other—than all the damage the Nazis did and all the wars in the world have done. But people don't pay much attention to that.

SHESTACK: We all agree that there's a problem, and the problem may have been with us since time began . . . except all of a sudden now we do a lot more writing and talking about it. There's hardly a periodical that doesn't have at least one article on relationships, because we all want to be able to get along with our fellow man.

SHAPIRO: I wonder if one of the problems is expectations. Each of us feels that everyone else is getting along, because we don't know what *their* problems are. So we feel, "Gee, look at all the married people; look at all the happy people— how come I can't make it? Perhaps one of the best things we could do for anyone would be to say "You're not alone." If you wake up in the morning and ask "Why did I ever get married? I really wanted that girl I saw in the store last night. If only I were single." Then you start resenting the person who's with you. But if you know that other people have the same feelings—that it's a common one—you come to expect less from yourself or the situation you're in. Maybe then you'd be more satisfied with the situation.

EVANS: And you'd be more willing to work at it. If it's not perfect, why not work on the imperfections on the relationship?

KAHN: "Work" on a relationship? Good intentions are not enough—we don't yet know what to "work on." What, exactly makes relationships fall apart? My patients come in and they say, "How can I get a good relationship and not get hurt?" And I say, "You can't." Part of the price, if you love a canary or a plant or a dog or a person, is that you're vulnerable. And these people want to get into relationships without getting hurt. They think a good relationship is a "nice" relationship. You show me a couple married forty years who never had a fight, and I'll show you a couple who never had a relationship.

EVANS: So what's the ideal for all these wonderful, working couples?

SHESTACK: A lot of it comes from television and things like that.

KAHN: How can you make a commitment to someone to love them forever? I don't even know what is going to happen tomorrow. I may not make it through the day. What expectation is there that I will love her forever? I don't even love some of the things I loved two weeks ago — food, or books or anything. Where does that kind of idea come from? Everything changes: people die; depressions come; airplanes crash. One other point: we see that some people are taller and some are shorter, some are fatter and some are thinner. We understand individual differences. I'm not a good football player and other people are. What makes you think that most people have the same capacity for love, for empathy, for relatability? What makes you think that everyone really has it, and that if you teach them how to do it they'll be able to do it?

SHAPIRO: Relationships are more than intense love. Sometimes that can go and come, and peak, and come again. It's the same with friendships. You really get involved with them. You work with a friend in an office, become close and then he gets a different job. It's a kind of semi-divorce. You're sort of separated. You maintain a friendship with that person. You see him occasionally, you invite him for dinner. But men and women who are lovers don't seem to be able to do that once they've split.

KAHN: Many people hold on to relationships after the meaning is gone. Through the force of habit they hang on to "friends." For example, year after year they invite these "friends" for Thanksgiving dinner though they may no longer have anything in common. Such people are not strong enough or aware enough to say, "He doesn't meet any of my needs anymore, and I don't meet his, so let's call it quits. It was good while it lasted." So they go on and on with these foolish consistencies.

SHAPIRO: There will always be one or two friends you keep. Certain people just stay friends for whatever reason — they may have emotional ties, or some kind of sentimental tie.

KAHN: Well, sometimes to grow, would be to outgrow your friends.

EVANS: But you can retain friendships. Sometimes you drop out of each other's lives. And later you may come back at a time when you make a match again.

KAHN: If you're not too busy, or if you need something.

SHAPIRO: Well, in addition, each of us has certain basic needs. And just like pieces in a jigsaw puzzle, one piece will fit and all the others won't. There are certain people you meet in your life — men or women — whose nature, whose personality traits fit your needs. And what we're really looking for, after all, is to satisfy our needs in any relationship. We use people — I don't mean that in a nasty way — but we do *use* them to satisfy our needs. Then there are those few with whom we can retain long-lasting relationships.

EVANS: The trick is in knowing our needs.

SHAPIRO: Now we're getting to the heart of it.

KAHN: You've said everything correctly except one thing: *lasting*. If I take a girl as a friend, the basis on which I pick her should be knowing who *I* am. Very frequently we say, "Oh, I didn't know her well enough." Never true. You didn't know *yourself* well enough. If I know who I am, then I know what to pick for food, for vacations, for sex. But I wouldn't want to pick anybody who isn't what I want, and then try to change her. That is the biggest waste of time in the world. So the trick is to know who you are. Most people don't even know very much about how to please themselves, or to meet their own needs.

EVANS: Or they have some image of what they want.

KAHN: So you see a girl and she fits the image of society; she's got big breasts and blonde hair—whatever the ideal is. But that's not picking based on your own needs. Another important point: If you really get down to who is your friend, and who it is you love and whom do you enjoy having sex with, *it's not the person —it's how you feel about yourself when you're with the person*. I've never loved a woman: I loved how I feel about myself when I'm with that person, and that's why I think she's so great. She's very unimportant. She's a catalyst for me. When you say, "I love Charlie," what you mean is "I feel a certain way about myself when I'm with Charlie." Charlie doesn't do it; Charlie is relatively unimportant.

SHAPIRO: Then you're saying that no marriage can really work, except on the basis of "what do I get out of it?"

EVANS: A nicer way to put it is that the people you like to be with are people with whom you're funny and smart with, and who bring out the best in you.

KAHN: And with whom you feel good about yourself. Do most marriages work? If as many buildings collapsed as do marriages, we'd call out the National Guard. Marriages happen not to work very well.

SHESTACK: Do you think there should be a new system?

KAHN: I don't know.

SHESTACK: The fact remains that, for most middle-class young men you get your job with IBM or with International Harvester, and you think "Gee for me to go up in this firm, it's important to have a wife. Everybody else is married; I'm going to do it." It's going to happen, it's going to keep happening. I don't think society is going to change that quickly. We want—we *like* to be together. Most people don't want to go against the mores of society. They give a lot of lip service to it, but they basically end up doing what is expected of them.

KAHN: A fellow making love to his girl in Poughkeepsie or upper Sandusky is doing about the same thing as the fellow in New York, who has seen the same movies and read the same books. You play with her here, you touch her here, then you take her out and buy her a present and do things for her. This is a social phenomenon; it has nothing to do with the individual. In a sense, we are all amateurs at relationships. We play out the scripts that have been taught to us — roles — we have learned a series of set responses and try to squeeze these into our human interactions —whether they fit or not.

SHESTACK: People do things when they are told by society to do it. If Halston were to shit on somebody's head, others would wear it as a hat.

SHAPIRO: Now let's be practical. The importance of this *Secret of Success* book is that it offers practical advice for those who want to be successful. We're not going to change the nature of men and women. What we should address ourselves to now is the formula for accomplishing that. To the extent that we can produce one, the kind of formula that would work best to obtain and retain a successful man-woman relationship. One point was made very well by Dr. Kahn: in order to be able to begin a positive relationship, you have to first understand and know yourself and know what your own needs are. Only then will you know what to look for in a woman who will help you feel good about yourself. Now, with that as a starting point, why don't we see what other kinds of things we can do to make the best of what has been painted as a very bleak picture in the future of relationships? A man could, of course, choose to remain a bachelor.

KAHN: Even if he chooses to remain a bachelor, he's going to have a series of relationships. Life is a series of relationships.

SHESTACK: Consider how it affects the success of his life in other respects. If the Presidency of a certain corporation is available, the Board of Directors will likely choose a man who is "happily married with a family" over one who is not. They will call on the man who seems to be more stable.

KAHN: However, he may not be the best worker.

SHESTACK: True. But wearing a grey flannel suit with a burgundy tie gives the appearance of being conservative and responsible. In business, one would perceive me that way. I might not have any talent whatsoever, but chances are I would be the one selected for a job, whether that is fair or not. The essence of this book is to tell people in the democratic capitalist society how to succeed. And one way it to "play the game."

KAHN: One of the ways to be successful is to know yourself; then you have to know the games society plays . . . and you have to play them to win. But neither of these assure intimacy and closeness.

SHAPIRO: How do you know the games that women play? Are they playing a new game today?

KAHN: No, it's the same game; and the men are playing the same game.

SHAPIRO: Well, there must be some opening, some door, that could start people off so that they could share some happy moments together.

KAHN: One of the doors would be *not* to go into anything with preconceived notions of how it's supposed to be. When you try to force the situation to fit your preconceived notions, you get disturbed by the fact that they don't fit.

SHESTACK: Most people don't. But they still want to have a degree of success in life. And that has to be done within the limits of *reality*. Self-actualization may be an impossible dream. It's never there. The Grand Canyon is actually a big hole in the ground; it's what we make of it that is real to us. We must have some kind of system in which to live and work, otherwise we're going to flounder. But most people are going to get married.

SHESTACK: Nancy what do you think are women's preconceived notions of men? You've obviously gone out with a number of men in the last several years.

EVANS: I think the problem of "categorization" is one of the biggest stumbling blocks in meeting someone initially. For example, he's wearing a suit, so you assume he must be a responsible kind of man. In reality he might be the biggest baby on the block. So, because he may be wearing a three-piece suit, and you've been raised to think you should be with somebody who's wearing a three piece suit, you may mistakenly choose to go out with him instead of with the guy who may not look the part but who in fact may be the better emotional match.

KAHN: I think what Nancy is saying is that we get programmed: the Princeton man keeps looking for the girl who looks like the Wellesley or Vassar girl. He may find a different beautiful and warm girl but she is OUT. There is no way he's going to bother with her, because of his conditioning.

He is locked into his belief system.

EVANS: Yes, and I think you've got to go through a few of those stereotypes in order to learn.

KAHN: Nancy's right about this. One of the ways you could perhaps better find what you call success is to get deprogrammed. R. D. Laing says that the stone age mother and father hand down to their mother and father who hand down to their mother and father notions that make children half-crazed imbeciles by the age of fifteen—with high IQs if possible—and under the guise of love we do people the most violence. So you get programmed with all this stuff about sex and money and mink coats and the right places to go, and to be "honest" and not lie. A few of my patients come in and say things like, "I did everything my parents told me. I was Miss Goody-Twoshoes. I was perfect, and I ended up in a mental hospital." What we're trying to teach people to be like is not what people are like at all. And so begin the facades. By the way, La Rochefoucauld said something like this about marriage. "Two people get married, and the smarter one convinces the dumber one they've got a thing going, and they both convince society."

SHESTACK: Well, again I have to take a pro-marriage stand. It's a system that seems to work for most people. It gives you a unit from which to work.

KAHN: I would like to ask you what works as *badly* as marriage? Marriage works hardly at all. I'm not against marriage, but it just doesn't work. The number of divorces—the number of people who stay married who would like to get out of it, but can't afford to because they have kids, etc.—what do you mean when you say marriage works?

SHESTACK: But all relationships have a tentative life. Why do we expect perfection in relationships? Sometimes entering into a kind of partnership and working as a partnership makes life a lot better.

SHAPIRO: Let's define "working" in terms of relationships, and use marriage as an example. What benefits does one get out of marriage?

EVANS: Rather than limit this to marriage, let's talk about long-term relationships.

SHESTACK: People seem to want desperately long-term relationships.

KAHN: For the wrong reasons. Some people give more care to the selection of an auto than to the selection of a mate.

SHESTACK: That's one of the things that some of the successful people interviewed in this book have said—that you should mate for life, but then you should put time into choosing a wife. A man will want an equal as a golf partner, and an equal as a business partner. But he'll pick some idiotic blue-eyed blonde to spend the rest of his life with.

EVANS: See the type casting! "An idiotic blue-eyed blonde."

SHESTACK: Actually, I'm on your side. But I think that most men are programmed, and they're still going to get married. There's a force that says sometime in most young men's lives they're going to enter into marriage. Some people more successfully than others.

KAHN: True, most people do marry, and while some people marry for "love," many marry to get out of the house, for financial gain, for prestige, to be taken care of, etc., etc. How many people have you heard say, "I married my mate because I felt that I could grow through a relationship with him or her."?

EVANS: Mel, you used the word "partnership" before, and I think that is more appropriate to what I'm thinking of in terms of a long-term relationship.

36

SHESTACK: My wife and I know three successful marriages out of the many people we know. They're all partnerships. They're all people who share. They can argue and hate each other, but somehow they work together and somehow work it out.

KAHN: Well, if you're willing to make all kinds of compromises with yourself you can get along with anybody.

SHESTACK: But compromise is the way most things work.

KAHN: I know one very good marriage, and the thing that holds it together is that they both hate the same things. But they don't have much going between them. You take two people who get married; they move in, unpack the gifts, and send out all the little thank-you notes. Then one cold winter they find themselves sitting in their apartment with each other, with nothing much to say. In these instances hope has turned into disillusionment and frequently boredom. Part of the reason these people fight is that it's the only way they can feel anything. Fights are very essential in relationships for people who don't know what else to do. The tearing apart is very essential to people who aren't self-actualized. Many of these negative and destructive interactions stem from the feeling that one has been let down by one's mate. It's a feeling of, "How could you treat me that way after all that I did for you." To a large extent, this comes about when one or both of the partners withhold the motives upon which his or her behavior is based. Partners give to each other without stating the expectations that lie behind the giving. For example, let's assume I give you a watch, and I don't tell you that in turn I expect you to invite me over to your house often — and then I give you the watch and you don't invite me, so I'm angry with you. If I had said to you when I first gave you the watch, "I'm giving you this watch, and I expect you to invite me over to your house every Saturday night," chances are you wouldn't take the watch. So most people go into relationships with very ulterior motives. And that's another reason why people don't get along: They don't advertise themselves very honestly.

EVANS: How can we help them to make their lives a little better?

KAHN: You start off with the premise that you're a fallible individual, and that your girl friend is a fallible individual, and neither of you will ever be anything else. That's the premise you have to start off with.

EVANS: And get rid of that "Prince Charming fantasy."

KAHN: All of that, but you can also be romantic. So you're fallible, you forget where your glasses are. Sometimes you even have a belly ache. Okay. You start out with the idea that change is the most constant thing in the world, and the person you marry, or go with, is going to change . . . though perhaps not as fast as you, or as slow. You start off with the idea that what you will become or do in the next moment cannot be predicted by me or anybody else. I might be going with a girl I love and care for, and yet another girl might be more exciting because of her newness, not necessarily because of her qualities. But I understand that. I understand that my girl gets jollies other places than from me; I don't feel that I should be upset if someone else is more fun at a party than me, and that she likes to be with him. So I give my girl space. I understand that the only way we can have anything that means anything is to permit her her own individuality and let her be what she is. And if she chooses to be with me that's good. I don't want anybody to be with me because she feels she has to be with me. I wouldn't want it that way. And I also know that if she leaves me, I can make it with someone else. But most people don't feel that way. They want to possess the other person; they want to control and manipulate them.

SHAPIRO: Practical person that I am, I've summarized some of the points we've been talking about. I'm trying to create a kind of formula to help the reader of this book begin to understand from all this. First, begin to know yourself, really know yourself—what your personal, individual needs are. Second, when you meet a woman, be sure that if you're going to have a long-term relationship, select as carefully as you possibly can, and carefully think through whether or not that person is compatible with what you know your needs to be.

KAHN: Which may change.

SHAPIRO: That's a very important point. Before we continue with this summary, is it your feeling, Dr. Kahn, that you should try to find a new woman if the one you've had is no longer compatible with your needs? Or, instead, should you attempt to have your present woman understand your changes sufficiently to see if she might change accordingly?

KAHN: Neither. When I change, I don't know what I'm going to be next. So, how can I spell out any of that? I don't know anything about the future.

. . .

SHAPIRO: Okay, but for the benefit of the reader of this book, for example, that a man has begun to know himself, and is very careful in his selection of a compatible mate. Once that commitment is made—and let's say that it's made in the form of marriage—a number of things happen over a relatively long period of time; let's say ten or fifteen years. There is a commitment; we now have a certain amount that the woman in this case has given to the relationship. Let's say they're 45-50 years old at that point, and the man changes. From the standpoint of fairness, if you have certain basic values in your life—one of which is to attempt not to hurt someone you have cared for, who's been good to you—even forgetting about children and the so-called responsibilities, there must be some kind of commitment to that person. And if a man begins to change, as is going to happen to many of the readers of this book, what do you do about that?

KAHN: Let's define "value." It might be that I hurt a person more by staying with her when I don't want to, out of sympathy, than I would by leaving. She won't want my sympathy, she wants me to care for her. So I'm not so sure, using your values, that you should stay with the woman.

SHAPIRO: Then, in your view, what should a man do as part of his successful life style, and social relationships?

KAHN: The question will be answered by a different approach. You understand that you are a process, not an object like a chair, and that the woman is a process. Processes change, and the most constant thing in the world is change. You start off with that premise about everything. Long Island is changing: the sand is being worn away. The letters in the attic are yellowing and fading. Everything changes. What makes you think you're going to be consistent? If I meet a girl, I've got to meet her as a process. This is Nancy the process; I am Dave, the process. I am not a table. Even a table changes in a hundred years; it warps. If you want me to go into a relationship thinking I'm an object to the other person and the other person is an object to me, then I'm stuck.

SHESTACK: Successful people are those able to hang in through unpleasant business situations. They don't quit. They stay. Is it not true in their personal lives?

SHAPIRO: It seems to me, what's coming out of this is that, of the four success areas—lifestyle; business; financial, and relationships—this last is the one for which there is almost no basic success formula. At least, that's what Dr. Kahn is saying.

KAHN: There isn't any. With all of the books written, including my own, we're not even scratching the surface. It's only recently we've even begun to try to study the subject of human relations. You can search for answers regarding the improving of human interactions in all sorts of experiences — marriages — swinging — transcendental meditation with gurus — marriage counselling, etc., etc., but in general, all have been ineffective in making relationships more meaningful or in bringing people closer together.

EVANS: What we've been saying is that at least you can try to think more clearly about relationships.f   SHAPIRO: That's just the point that I was starting to make. There are at least certain guidelines you can begin to come to.

SHESTACK: Nancy, what do you think men do wrong? What's the first thing you say when you don't go out with a man the third time? You're bored out of your mind, and you say this guy should be different. Are you really giving him a chance?

EVANS: That's one thing I try to be conscious of, yes. Not to reject somebody solely on the basis of my preconceived notion of what is appropriate for me.

KAHN: I have patients who never let anyone love them, because they never let anyone know them. And I think the greatest gift you can give to someone is to let them love you. Most people can't do that.

EVANS: By getting those expectations out of the way, you can allow yourself that freedom.

KAHN: Some men have the idea that to be loved is a great thing. The idea is to be in love. Being loved does you little good, yet everyone wants to be loved and adored. I like to be in love. That's what I can feel. I can feel *my* toothache. I can't feel *your* toothache. A lot of people love me; they adore me. I cannot feel their feelings — perhaps it's good for my ego. But it is only my love for someone that I can experience. I believe that most people are searching for someone to love them, rather for someone to love. As I mentioned earlier, we are amateurs in most of our beginning love affairs. We start off attempting to love a complex other person, without having much experience in loving simple things — like a flower, for instance.

SHESTACK: Most of us don't love anything. They only love what they are told to love in New York Magazine. It's the same with developing one's own tastes. Many people can't, so when they're told to stop loving it, they drop it. It's not a natural thing.

KAHN: Here's one other basic thing. Men want understanding from women. They want to be understood. They don't have any idea about giving understanding. They do not grasp the value to themselves and to others of giving understanding. In general, I find that my male patients are more set in their ways than my female patients. Their acquired roles are more crystalized. The male role in our society is an impossible one and to try to attain it causes much of the male insecurity. How can one be a good lover, a good provider, a great parent, a person ready to do battle and win, an understanding husband, a contributing member of society, etc., etc. Men trying to live up to such expectations are plagued by constant pressures, all of which, among other things, prevent them from entering into close relationships.

SHAPIRO: Feeling good about yourself is all you really ever have to do. You know that whatever happens, you're going to be alright.

KAHN: I don't need some pretty girl to determine whether I'm okay. Is that where my okayness lies? That if she loves me I'm okay, and if she doesn't I'm not. If I start off with that game, I am finished. I mean, my okayness is not determined by whether you like me, or whether this article gets published, or whether Nils ever talks to me again, because I don't base my okayness on the fact that I am approved of. I think I'm okay, even if I'm disliked. So I don't have any trouble. But do I have good relationships? No. They're stormy. They have all kinds of feelings in them. Sometimes I think I'm the luckiest guy in the world to have this girl, and sometimes I'd like to punch her. Your goodness of feeling about yourself has to be internal. It can't be based on externals, because if it is you're like a yo-yo. Up if they like you, down if they don't.

SHAPIRO: And that comes right back to the first point in my summary, which is: begin to know and appreciate yourself.

SHESTACK: One question that I would like to ask of everyone is, "What do you feel the 1980s will bring to the art of relationships?"

KAHN: What will relationships be like in the future? For the most part, like they are today! What needs to change first is the way people *think* about themselves and their interactions with others. It is highly unlikely that people will undergo the radical changes in their attitudes and values that could possibly lead to changes in the way individuals treat and deal with each other.

SHESTACK: But don't you think economics play a big part in this? Statistically, people can live together because it's cheaper — whether they're married or not. Older people, as well. Even unmarried.

SHAPIRO: But young people, too. The whole business of alimony is going to become more reasonable, to the point where it will be economically easier to change spouses.

KAHN: I also think that by the '80s we're still not going to raise men's consciousness. We've long held the idea that women are inferior, and I can't tell you how much this runs through my own thinking, because I was programmed that way. My girlfriend is smarter than I am, but when I want her to do something I tell her as though she were stupid. Because way back I was taught that way ... It's going to take a long time to change the attitudes that men have toward women.

SHAPIRO: But there are some people who are great to live with who might not be mathematical geniuses. You may find that they satisfy part of your life say, the physical, playing tennis — and you can find your intellectual gratification in other ways. Everything is imperfect. Then too, life is filled with long silences. There are times when nothing happens. It's wonderful for two people to be sitting in a room for two hours, not talking, and still feel the closeness and be happy that you don't *have* to talk.

KAHN: But when that happens today, the man or the woman asks, "Is something the matter, honey?"

SHESTACK: Nancy, do you believe that it's necessary to be in love with somebody? To have a relationship? You yourself? You yourself — do you look forward to the idea of marriage?

EVANS: I'm trying to get rid of the idea of evaluating every man one meets as a possible Mr. Right. I think the Mr. Right idea can only be destructive. But it's taken me a number of years to try to get that out of my head. It's a necessary part of growing up. You have to learn to eliminate what you don't want before you can start narrowing in on what you want.

SHESTACK: All our training in the 1960s dealt with instant gratification. Everything out there had to happen immediately. You are a product of that. That's when you went to school. Are you now able to give men *time*, so you can get to know one another? So many people are afraid.

EVANS: I also think men are terrified that a woman doesn't have time to go out with them. And now when asking for a date they say, "Could you possibly fit me into your schedule?" This turn of events is something new. But there are a lot of men and women who are both working, and you have to make time to have a relationship. You actually have to *plan* a time to have a personal life, or you could very well go through life without one.

SHAPIRO: Do you understand that when a man is involved with his job, he may suddenly have a meeting and have to cancel a date with you?

EVANS: So do I. That's the difference. *I* may have to cancel the date. I'm not always available, and that's something the man has to deal with. That new fact of life may frighten him. Because on the one hand he wants you to be this successful woman, and he sincerely does want you to be in the world out there. But on the other hand he wonders if you're going to be there when he needs you. And I have a similar problem: Is he going to be there when I need him?

SHAPIRO: I would imagine that one of the problems a man has when you cancel a date is determining in his own mind whether or not the reason you give him is the truth. He's wondering, "Is she just trying to let me off easy? She doesn't really have a meeting, but it's better than telling me she doesn't want to be with me tonight." That sort of thing.

EVANS: There is also the possibility of misinterpretation. So there's constant miscommunication that you've got to shake out every once in a while.

SHESTACK: What do you think a man should do to get rid of that? You meet a man at a party, you get into conversation, you're both in the same business. He says, "Hey, let's have lunch or dinner," and you think this might be the beginning of a relationship. He's a good-looking fellow, nice, smart. What do you expect? What do you look for? He's looking to get laid, number one. It's always there. So are you, in a certain kind of way. But aside for sexual things, what do you want?

EVANS: For one thing, not all relationships are as lovers. Sometimes you meet a man and from the very first you know you want to be friends.

SHAPIRO: I may be naive, but I feel that more and more men are beginning to understand—perhaps because of women's lib or equality—that the first thought doesn't have to be "I want to get laid."

EVANS: Also, people think it always has to happen on the first night. This is the instant gratification generation. But, in fact, it doesn't always happen.

SHAPIRO: I have friendships with several women. I began those friendships and cultivated them because I feel that they enhance my life. This is an area where sex takes no part. If men realized the friendships they can have with women, they'd be better off.

SHESTACK: Most men don't understand that women are just as scared as they are.

KAHN: I think men are more scared than women.

SHAPIRO: This may sound a bit crude, but it's a formula that works. When I was a kid and on my way to one of my first real interviews, I was afraid of meeting the President of that company. The fellow I was walking with said, "Why don't you picture him sitting on the toilet seat at home." I laughed, but when I walked into his office, I did that and it worked. I wonder if a man facing his first date with a particular woman should try to briefly visualize her sitting on the toilet seat at home. The fear might be gone, and you can get fun out of it from that point on.

As you have learned from reading this candid conversation, the most difficult kind of advice — even from experts — is that which deals with the historic battle of the sexes. The difficulty of the man-woman relationship has been the core theme of the wide majority of novels, movies, operas . . . even dinner table conversations. It provides the fuel for the thriving marriage counseling business: thanks to it, the "Ask Abbys" of the world are able to write advice columns five days a week in thousands of newspapers, and hundreds of books on the subject have been best-sellers.

If *you* have the answer to how men and women can get along in perfect harmony, then our advice is to stop everything else you are doing, and let everybody know what you know. We guarantee that you will not only make a fortune, but that you will become the most famous man on earth.

The authors of this book have been together for almost twenty years, most of them as husband and wife. Still, we don't know all the answers, and we have had as many problems as anybody else. We have, however, learned a few things that work for us, and we will share them with you. They are pretty basic for getting along in any relationship.

1. Don't presuppose virtues in others that you don't have in yourself.

2. Learn to listen.

3. Try to think about *giving* instead of receiving. Rather than think "What is my partner giving me?", try to think, "What am I doing for my partner?"

4. If you don't understand what your partner is trying to say, *ask*.

5. Don't be afraid to criticize. Conversely, accept criticism.

6. There are times when you *must* give in, even if it is against your better judgment. You have to weigh whether being stubborn on a given point is worth an entire relationship.

7. Work at your relationship the same way you attack other areas of your life. Set goals. Work hard.

8. Don't always expect happy endings. Life is fraught with problems. *Nobody* is problem free. Solving problems together is a good way to grow together.

9. Learn to accept your partner's idiosyncracies. It is very hard for people to change. If you are going to spend a lot of time with someone, then you are going to have to put up with some of what you consider to be his or her "nonsense." And your partner is going to have to put up with yours. You can discuss it. You can make promises that you will change. It probably won't happen. If you are 60% happy, then you are way ahead of the game.

10. Don't lie to each other. It's always better to have the facts. Remember what Dr. Kahn says, "All facts are helpful in the long run."

Truth is always the bottom line, and we live in a bottom-line world. Facing reality allows you to grow; in a relationship, as with most other things, you can generally work out a solution once you have the facts.

HOW CAN MEN BE MORE SUCCESSFUL WITH WOMEN?

"Most men don't listen. One of the problems with ambitious men is that they are resolutely single-minded. It's probably a symptom of their success and I understand it. But this single-mindedness, this keeping of their minds on their business all the time, isn't very pleasant when you are walking down the street with a man. The woman wants to look at the shops, the people. The man just wants to get to his destination. I am in sympathy with a man's goals, but there are times — when he is with a woman he likes — to forget about them for the moment, and just be himself. It will be good for him, and wonderful for the relationship ..."

—Sharon Edwards
former Motion Picture
Executive

"Probably men and women are equally at fault about this, but men I know seem to start with a pre-conceived notion about a woman, and the talking begins with that. They make an assumption and then don't ask questions about how you really feel about things. Many women friends of mine agree with me. Life with men would be better if they asked questions and then listened to your answers ..."

—Melanie Arwin
Commercial Artist

"Men still don't take women seriously. They pretend to, now that liberation seems to be an accepted word. I know a man who says, 'Some of my best friends are women,' but he hasn't the slightest idea of what women are all about. He's very bright but can't figure out why women drop him after a few dates. If he would take the time to *try* to understand them, even if it was difficult, the distances could be brought closer ..."

—Gay Bryant
Executive Editor
Working Woman Magazine

"The worst thing a man can do is to presume intimacy when he first meets somebody. That includes touching someone he just met, making any kind of sexual comment. Standing too close to her. Invading her body space. A good salesman gives a person space and time to make his sale. Gives the other person a time to consider. A bad salesman is too pushy. It's the same with men and women."

—Joyce Wadler
Columnist, *New York*
Daily News

"Many men don't have any sense of the history of what it is like to be a woman, having to have a life of all giving and not complaining. Women are now complaining. If men were more thoughtful, less competitive, less spoiled, I think we'd get along better ..."

—Sheila Samton
Designer

"Sexually, men have very little patience. They are in such a great hurry; they're so selfish and so afraid of nuance. It's as if they are terribly unsure of their ability and want to get it over with as quickly as possible, rarely considering the woman's needs. I don't mind being a sexual object, as long as I am considered very special, worth spending a lot of time with ..."

—Heather Tidyman
Gem Expert

"Men refuse to give up their options. Women are more inclined to concede. Relationships, at least serious relationships, demand commitments. Many men give lip service to commitment, but they want loopholes ..."

—Lindsay Maracotta
author of the best-selling
Sad-Eyed Ladies.

SOME THOUGHTS ABOUT LIBERATED WOMEN

A great deal has been written about the new woman. So be it. We are in total favor of her new state. But the fact remains that *most* women want to be treated as equals *and also* have the door opened for them, and have men stand up when they come into a room. If a man were to outrun Gloria Steinem for a seat on a bus, she would probably get as mad as any other woman. The man who can mix a sense of equality with a little old-fashioned courtesy will more often be successful with women.

We surveyed twenty very successful businesswomen. To a woman, they preferred to have the man pay for their meals, if he could afford it. If he can't, that's another story. "A successful man," one woman told us, "shouldn't ask a woman out unless he can pick up the tab—if it is a social occasion. For business, the situation changes drastically." (More about that later in this book.)

AN AFFAIR TO REMEMBER —OR FORGET!

What if you are married, or living with somebody, and want to have an affair with another woman? We won't sit in judgement here; much depends on how well you can handle it. There are some authorities who say it is very healthy. But there is a cardinal rule which most ambitious and successful men know: *Success demands sacrifice.*

The goal must come first.

Anything which clutters your mind or creates unnecessary tensions is counter-productive and should be avoided whenever possible.

This, of course, doesn't take into consideration human emotion. The genitals have no ambition other than to satisfy their immediate needs. The strongest men are weak in certain situations.

If you *do* falter in this area, *keep it as private as possible. Don't hurt anyone. Don't tell your friends.* Keep as close to the truth as possible. Keep it as far away from your career as possible. It is a good way to lose a job, a wife, the respect of your friends. The fact remains that, *while a lot of people may envy a swinger, nobody really respects him.*

DRINKING

Social drinking is part of American society. But nobody respects or admires a drunk. *Don't get drunk.* No woman can really tolerate a drunk, except possibly a drunken woman. Avoid drunken women like the plague. They can only do you great harm.

People are judged by their companions. Only private detectives in TV series are allowed a bunch of creepy friends. Successful men choose their friends carefully—and especially their women friends.

CHOOSING A WIFE

"If thou wouldst marry wisely, marry thine equal ..."—Socrates

George Bernard Shaw once said that it was a woman's business to get married as soon as possible, and a man's to keep unmarried as long as he can.

44

Times have changed. Men are getting married at an earlier age than women; especially goal-oriented men. There has been much written about the new singles generation. Fewer of these men get the good jobs than do married men of their same age. Most major companies prefer married executives because of a belief that married men are more stable, more able to handle commitment and responsibility. True or not, myths hang on, and ask any personnel director whom he will choose if two men are equally suited for a job. The married man will almost always get the position.

Most executives we talked to stressed the importance of marriage, even those whose marriages didn't work out. "I wish we could have made it work," one financial vice-president of a Philadelphia bank confided. "If a marriage is successful, it means peace of mind on the job. Now, half my time is spent trying to find a woman I can communicate with. I try to tell myself it isn't cutting in on my career, but I'm only lying to myself."

Richard W. Ogden, Vice president of Manufacturing for the Seminole Manufacturing Company in Columbus, Mississippi, and a frequent contributor to business journals, says that "marriage and career can be in eternal conflict, or you can work to create a harmony between them that will give your life richness beyond any expectations." In his excellent book, *How to Succeed in Business and Marriage* (Amacom, 1978) Ogden says that the "trouble with many people, and the reason that company ties have led to so many disastrous marriages, is that these astute, hard-driving, success oriented individuals have applied themselves to only one area — the job — without realizing that the same effort is necessary for a successful marriage." Ogden feels that marriage is the cohesive force of our business society. He stresses that marriage and a career are not only compatible, but necessary. He advises executives to work hard to make sure their marriages work. "You can live the good life," he says, by making sure that marriage and career goals pertain "to what is important to you and your wife."

Now this is going to sound very crass and undemocratic. It goes against the romantic tradition (which might not be such a bad idea, since the latter has helped catapult the divorce rate):

A man should choose his wife at least as carefully as he chooses his job.

A man chooses an equal as his golf partner.
A man chooses an equal as his business partner.
A man chooses an equal as his lunch partner.
A man chooses his equal to accompany him on a fishing trip.
A man drinks with his equals.
A man discusses his personal philosophy with his equals.
A man will go to the best architect and the most competent construction company, to build his house.
A man will shop around to buy a tennis racket.

But so many otherwise intelligent men choose beanbrained little wives with big boobs and super behinds. Then they wonder why they become bored as hell. The women get pregnant and the men are stuck either way: chained to an unhappy marriage, or committed to an expensive divorce. Divorce is expensive; there's no getting around that.

Two domiciles cost a hell of a lot more to support than one.

Ambitious man: *choose your wife carefully.*

1. Make sure your intended is *equally* as amibtious as you are. Both

for herself and for *you*. If your wife isn't in your corner, who will be? (Conversely, if you do marry a career person, know what you are getting into. You're going to have to like it.)

2. It's easier to make a go of it if both of you are of *equal* social and religious background. Of course, marriages between couples of dissimilar backgrounds can work; it is up to the individuals involved. But if you do marry someone similar in background to yourself, it is just one more stumbling block you don't have in your way.

3. Make sure you have *equal* (or similar) interests. If she hates golf, and you are devoted to it, you are in for a hard time, buddy. Make sure you know all *her* interests, too. People in love often dismiss sensible warnings. "I hate rock and roll and you adore it, but we'll work it out." You just might not. People don't change too easily; by the time most people marry, they are pretty well formed as people with deeply ingrained opinions and likes and dislikes.

4. Opposites may attract, but equals have an easier time of it. Marriage is a partnership; partners are in the *same* business. They have to think as much alike as possible, if they are to avoid going bankrupt.

5. Have *equally* strong sex drives. As we've said before, it isn't the only thing. But without it, watch out!

6. Have an equal desire to have, or not have, children — and both of you must be equally willing to sacrifice because of children.

7. Have an equal opinion about money — its importance, as well as its limitations.

8. Have an equal idea about what ambition is, and what it entails.

9. Feel equally as strong about each other emotionally.

10. This is of primary importance: It is easy to love someone — love has a lot to do with intangibles and genitals — but if you *like* each other equally you have a marvelous chance of success.

11. Set equal goals as to what the marriage should bring to you both.

12. Try hard — but both of you ought to know that sometimes one partner is "more equal" in some things than is the other partner, and it . . . well, *equals out* in the long run.

A WORD ABOUT DRUGS

Most success guides don't even mention them. But another one of those often ignored facts of life is that drugs are here; they've been with us a long time. Our advice would be simple: *don't use them.*

The genuinely successful man knows that real euphoria comes from within. But again, that is for the perfect man, and we are all merely *trying* hard to reach that perfection. *Avoid all hard drugs.* If you must smoke marijuana, do it with trusted friends. Don't do it in the office. Don't do it around people you don't know. Maybe it isn't harmful. That's immaterial. The fact is, most people in high positions are in late middle age. And *they* frequently view marijuana as harmful. Remember, they have the power to damage your career.

As for cocaine, we think it is dangerous.

It would surprise us if many real achievers in Fortune 500 companies snorted "coke."

HOW TO FIND A
STATUS SOCIAL
ACTIVITY

G IVING of one's time to worthwhile causes is one of the nicest and warmest of customs. Health organizations, museums, community theaters, refugee centers, homes for unwed mothers and a thousand other important charity organizations are able to exist because they are helped by businessmen and women who give freely of their time and expertise to make them run.

Working for a "cause" is also one hell of a good way to make your name known in your community and to help you get ahead in business. It's also a way to have a really interesting and upward mobile social life. And it can get your name in print in the most favorable manner.

There are very few top executives in Fortune 500 companies who don't also appear on the board of at least one worthwhile cause, be it the Red Cross, the Salvation Army or the Fund To Build a Botanical Garden for Middle City. Yes, charity is a worthwhile activity, and takes a lot of time. And we're not suggesting that you not do it directly from the heart. But the ambitious man *thinks*, and *plans* . . . so why not take the heart's goodness and turn it into a little personal achievement profit!

Many years ago, one of the authors of this book worked as an account executive in a large advertising agency in a medium-sized New York State community.

Times have changed, and today many of the most successful and professionally run agencies are now located in large cities throughout the country. But in those days, New York was still the mecca, the headquarters of advertising, and all of us grey-flanneled types were desperate to get to Madison Avenue, the advertising Olympics, where everybody was a contender.

Most of my contemporaries were as interested as I in landing a New York job; we read the classifieds in *Ad Age* and subscribed to the Sunday *New York Times* to study the account executive ads in that paper. We wrote letter after letter; most were unanswered. And there was a reason. None of us had worked for more than a year or two; we had no solid achievement. We couldn't show anything, not even an ad that we had written. We were well-dressed apprentices, doomed to a life of advertising obscurity in the hinterlands.

Then one of us—I'll call him Herbie—landed a job with J. Walter

Thompson. The biggest then, as now. What really floored us was that Herbie had been the most unlikely candidate for stardom of any of us. So we thought. That's how much we knew, and that's why Herbie today is executive vice-president of marketing for a conglomerate headquartered in Texas. When he comes to New York these days, it is in the company plane.

We always took Herbie with a grain of salt; young men have a streak of cruelty in them. Herbie was not gifted by nature with streamlining. He wasn't fat, but he was so constructed as to never give the impression of being sleek. He bought his suits at the same conservative men's store as the rest of us. His shoes were shined, he was well-groomed. But Herbie only attended a local community college. (He came from a family of six sons, all of whom are professional men, by the way — and all did it on their own.) He didn't have a specific talent. The rest of us prided ourselves on our ability as copywriters and idea men.

But it was Herbie who got the job, and we all learned a lesson. After work, we used to go to a place called the Treadway Bar to discuss the day's activities, gossip, contemplate our futures. We all were single. We all were Korean veterans. We all had college degrees from decent schools. We all were ambitious.

We all liked Herbie, and we asked him to join us every night, but he was always busy. He seemed always to have a meeting to go to for the March of Dimes, or a paper to write for the Police Athletic League. What really made us laugh was his involvement with the Committee For a Children's Zoo, an organization set up by local Jaycees to raise funds for a barnyard type zoo, which the city didn't have. "Where's Herbie?", we would laugh, over a bowl of pretzels in the Treadway. "At a goat auction," someone would say. And we'd double up with laughter.

But Herbie had the last laugh. He knew something we didn't know. And in a short time it became clear to us. One day there was Herbie's picture in the paper with the mayor, presenting a check for the first payment toward a children's zoo. His picture appeared in the social pages, in black tie, surrounded by debutantes at the first annual Children's Zoo Ball (now a major social event in the city where Herbie's career began). The story with the picture quoted a community leader, who also was the president of the largest bank, praising Herbie's organizational efforts in making the Zoo project a reality. Herbie was cited by the Jaycees as one of the ten most promising young men in the city. When the first chance for promotion came within the company, Herbie got the position; the memorandum which was passed around announcing the promotion mentioned Herbie's community spirit and intense sense of leadership. Within a short time after that, Herbie answered an advertisement in *Ad Age*. He had a very unusual resume to send off, complete with dozens of clippings from the daily papers about his activities, plus a copy of the memo from the boss citing his qualifications.

There's more: Herbie was no longer the butt of our jokes. But he still didn't come to the Treadway. His social schedule didn't allow for it. Mothers invited him to dinner to meet their eligible daughters (this was in the pre-liberation dark ages) and Herbie became quite glamorous as a man with an obvious future. Whatever he did with his nights, he certainly wasn't buying goats.

And we all learned a lesson which still works: *Pick an activity which can both help your career and help the community, and make you feel good to boot.* It doesn't much matter what it is; every charity or worthwhile cause has a star-studded board of directors.

1. Committees need work. Young men who are willing to contribute their brains and skills will gain ready acceptance.

2. It is a perfect place for a young man to exercise leadership ability. It is the young men who often have more time to do charity work. When you are a vice president of a business, it is your *name* the cause needs. When you are only a beginner in business, the cause needs your time and effort. It will not go unnoticed.

3. When looking for a cause to align yourself with, it is wise to find something you like. You have to live and work with it, so it is more fun to have a feeling for it. We know of somebody who became involved with a crippled children's committee, certainly a decent and worthwhile endeavor. But whatever the reason, this fellow, as good a guy as he was, couldn't spend time with actual crippled children. A fault? Maybe. But he couldn't and, therefore, was hindered in his growth with that organization. Instead, he changed his community cause to that of raising money for the local orchestra. He liked music and musicians, and he could give his all. So be sure to find an activity which suits your particular proclivities.

4. Don't promise what you cannot deliver—even if you mean well. If you say, "My job keeps me busy most of the time and I can only devote two hours a week to the activity," then you will be appreciated for the intensity of the two hours you *can* put it.

5. Don't be shy. Let them take your photograph.

6. Accept the dinner invitations. It is a way to meet new people. You never know when that connection will come in handy, or when you will be looking for another job and need a reference. A letter from someone who is not your immediate employer, but who has worked with you on an executive committee of a worthwhile cause, will be well received by a prospective employer.

7. Every committee of every cause—whether museum, health, or save-the-children, attracts the socially prominent young women of the city. (Even in today's liberated society, the lady bountiful has become the person bountiful.) They still come to meetings; charities and causes are *social* excuses to get out. Do the work, but you can have a lot of fun besides. And meet some very interesting people at the same time.

8. A word of caution. If you get involved in politics, that can help, too—of course. But if your company president is an ardent Republican, and you appear in the paper time and again as a professional Democrat, (or vice-versa) it's possible that nothing will happen. Then again, you might not get that promotion.

   This statement might be heresy. It *is* a free country. Nobody knows how you vote. But politics, like religion, is still controversial. Make very sure of your superior's feelings before you go off and support a candidate whom he dislikes intensely. Then, make your own decision about what to do, but be prepared to take the consequences. In nine cases out of ten, it will make no difference whatsoever. But most of us seem to work for Boss Ten. We believe in sticking to principles, but there's no need to stick them in someone's eye. A word to the wise . . .

INTERVIEW:

"To be successful, you have to be willing to make a commitment."

RICHARD C. AULETTA:

Ever since we've known Dick Auletta, he's not only had the *look* of success; he has also never promised that which he could not deliver. It has paid off. Fifteen years ago, he was a hard-working young man on the way up. At forty-one, and the even harder-working president of R.C. Auletta and Company, he's arrived. Dick drives a Rolls Royce (1964), has a Connecticut country house, and wears custom-tailored suits. His office wall is a huge bookcase filled with luxuriously bound (leather-and-gold) nineteenth century first-editions. His clients range from Dannon Yogurt to the Palace Restaurant (the most expensive, and one of the acknowledged greatest, in the world). Auletta is both public relations counselor and business strategist. (A number of his clients rely on him for company policy as well as corporate communications.) He has a firm belief that any successful man must understand not only how a business works, but how to address himself to current issues. "If you don't," Auletta warns, "the tide will pass you by."

Have you always concerned yourself with being successful?

"I always knew I would be successful. I grew up with the notion that if I swept streets, I would turn out to be the very best street sweeper. It's important to be special at whatever you do."

You are a very impressive dresser. Have you always been that way; or did you decide deliberately upon fastidiousness as a tool for achievement?

"I don't think it was a conscious decision. I have always been rather neat. As a kid I shared a room with my brother. I could always tell if he wore my clothes, because he never folded sweaters when he put them back in the drawer. I was the only kid I knew who hung up my shirts in the same way each time, and buttoned all the buttons."

What were your earliest influences?

"There were many, but I often think back to when I was in the army. A lot of the other trainees, and we had all been to college, more or less considered the professional soldiers beneath them. For some reason, I didn't. I was fascinated by them. They were good at things I wasn't good at. I learned that some people were more talented in certain areas than were other people; that sometimes you can't judge people by ordinary criteria. And I learned a lot about advancing myself in the service. Once I was put on a detail picking up cigarette butts under barracks. It was awful work and I thought: "I should be able to do something better than this." I went to the first sergeant and told him that I could do something more than pick up cigarettes. . If you have any recollection about life as a basic trainee, you know this was taking a chance. But he laughed and asked if I could make coffee. I could and did, and because of my taking that chance, the first sergeant got to know me and I eventually became C.Q. A good job. I also learned in the Army that you can push people only so far. That if you back someone into a corner, he'll be forced to strike back at you. A good lesson is knowing when to stop."

50

What makes you happiest —the most satisfied?

"Even when I started out I had a pretty fair notion of what would make me happy. The people I admired appeared to be very enthusiastic about what they were doing. I wanted a job that would not dull my enthusiasm; something I would look forward to doing each day. Also, a woman who would make me happy. I cannot think of anybody who has one without the other. At least, having a job I love and a wife to share it with has helped me keep my perspective. Even if I didn't progress any further financially, having the work to look forward to and the happy home—well, I wouldn't need any more. The houses, the Rolls. That's all make believe. Fun. But not imperative."

Can you list five qualities or things a young man needs to be successful.

"They overlap. But I'll try:

1. A willingness to work hard.
2. Got to have dreams.
3. Got to have talent.
4. Got to have integrity.
5. Got to have luck."

What do you mean by luck?

"Being present when an opportunity arises. Or for one thing, who you happen to get hooked up with in your jobs. Early jobs, anyway. Just look at the young people around Nixon. Their lives got turned around because they were associated with someone whose ethics they never questioned. That is where our colleges fail. We aren't taught ethics. Or how to judge people."

What sort of difficulties do you encounter as an executive?

"There are all kinds, of course. Business is not always a democracy; you have to make decisions that will affect some people adversely. And you have to have the toughness to be able to fire people. Just recently, I heard that someone was angry at me. I heard it secondhand. Something I had said. Actually, I was misinterpreted. But I called the person, confronted him with it, and in a few minutes I made peace. That's very important. It doesn't matter what you say or mean; what matters is the person's perception of it."

What are your own observations about the successful men you've met? What do they all have in common?

"It depends on how you define success. There are those few men who have a unique success and find inner peace and contentment. But in the broader sense, I think, to be successful you have got to be willing to make a commitment. In marriage. Business. Life. All the successful people I know, the great achievers, have this sense of committment. They also know how to use time. The most precious thing in the world is time."

What price do you pay for success?

"Sometimes, it gets very lonely."

THE ART OF CONVERSATION

"Conversation is a way of selling yourself and, ultimately, your product."
—Og Mandino Author of "The World's Greatest Salesman..."

"A good conversationalist is not one who remembers what was said, but says what someone wants to remember."

—John Mason

"Conversation means being able to disagree and still continue the conversaton."

—Dwight MacDonald

"The person who is a good conversationalist has a much better chance of being successful than one who is not."

—Henry Ford ("Advice to New Company Executives")

"I don't know one man at the top," says millionarie publisher Malcolm Forbes, "who can't hold his own in conversation, whether in business or just at a party. Being a good conversationalist means that you know something about life and are willing to share it."

The fact of the matter is that *everyone* is a little nervous when meeting new people, new situations. Conversation is a good way to allow yourself to relax in a new situation; small talk is like an aperitif, it is a pleasant and calm way to get on to the main course.

The way to become a conversationalist is through practice. *Talk to people* and *listen to them*; like every other fear, the horror diminishes with practice and confrontation. And, like anything else that bothers you, learning to conquer it is a major undertaking. At one time conversation was called an "art" because there were so many *don'ts* connected to it; it took an "artist" to discover a safe topic, an inoffensive topic. Today, anything is topical as long as you do it interestingly and with a modicum of good taste.

As you become a better conversationalist you'll develop your own rules, but here are some to start with.

1. *Key the subject to your listener.* Well applied, this primary rule will keep you from being either boor or bore. It means that the once-prohibited subjects of discussion—sex, religion, politics—are now acceptable if they will interest and will not embarrass any of your listeners. Remember, though, that the beautiful woman who likes to talk about very personal intimacies when you are alone may pretend Puritanism in the presence of other women ... and your locker-room buddy might be somewhat more inhibited in public.

You can tell dirty jokes to people whom you *know* like them. But watch yourself with women and strangers. You can argue politics and religion, *if* the others want to. But if you see that you are getting no response, back off quickly and change the subject. Most of us feel that a good argument makes a good conversation—but a *good* argument is still *impersonal* and *unemotional*. You can talk business if everyone at the table is shop-minded, or if the subject is interesting enough to the uninitiated. It means that you can talk about *yourself* if you are of phenomenal interest to your listener, but with anyone but your mother or lover, you'd better think about that "phenomenal" interest. Dick Cavett, one of the more noted conversationalists, says that "a bore is one who talks about himself when you want to talk about *yourself*." So see that your *I* has overtones of *you*.

The most wonderful or most accepted topic is *awful* if it is over your listener's head. Remember that it is as impolite to leave one of your group out of the conversation as it is to whisper to one person in front of another. That's probably why philosophers claim you can't have a decent conversation with more than one person; the talk necessarily seeks the lowest level.

"You can't ask, 'Am I boring you?' " Cavett advises. "Or, 'Does this embarrass you?' Your listener will be too polite to say 'yes' and the question itself is boring. And embarrassing." Cavett suggests that good conversationalists also *watch*. Even the professional good listener gets a glazed eye, or fails to ask interested, intelligent questions to encourage you. And whenever you are in doubt, *follow* — don't lead — the conversation.

2. *Take Your Turn:* This means, of course, no monologues. If ever you find that you have talked for three minutes straight, without question or comment from your listeners, you can be pretty sure that you are talking on a subject of interest only to yourself. Be aware of the drone in your own voice. We are all at fault here. Remember: If the others have nothing to contribute, what you have is a *speech*, not a conversation.

Taking your turn also means not interrupting when others are talking. There are two kinds of interruptions. The obvious one, interrupting the speaker in mid-sentence, is easy to avoid; just wait until the other has stopped talking before you start. For heaven's sake, don't ever ask "Have you finished?" You might as well say right out that he's a windbag and you thought he'd never run down.

The other kind of interruption, equally culpable, is often prefaced by "That reminds me . . ." or "By the way . . ." Such phrases usually signal a digression or an irrelevancy. When you interrupt another's train of thought, or send a discussion off into a tangent, you indicate that you are either stupid or rude, either unable or unwilling to stick to the speaker's point.

Even if everyone else observed these rules, telephones, doorbells and new arrivals will often conspire to interrupt you in mid-point. When you are interrupted, the politest thing to do is the hardest: shut up. Don't go back and finish a story — don't excavate a buried point — unless you are asked to do so. If a new listener has come along in mid-story, a polite someone else will brief him on the subject and ask you to go on. The polite newcomer will second the nomination; only then, with the briefest possible synopsis of what you said before, should you continue. If you are not given these cues, it may be because your story is not appropriate for the newcomer's ears, or because the situation has gotten beyond control; it's not always because your audience was bored. So if you get a chance to make your point later on, don't air your annoyance with a petulant, "As I was trying to say a little earlier . . ."

3. *Think before you talk and think beyond the subject at hand.* That's the secret of tact. The object is to avoid making anyone uncomfortable, unhappy or simply self-conscious — even unintentionally. Contrary to popular opinion, the opposite of tact is not truth. *The opposite of tact is just plain thoughtlessness.* Think before you tell a psychiatrist joke to someone who has just begun psychoanalysis; where one's emotions are

involved, a joke is not always a joke. Think before you fascinate a widow with war stories; she might be a war widow. Think before you talk gourmet talk to your plain-cook hostess.

Cavett has a rule: "Don't limp before the lame." The tough part is to remember who is "lame", and where, before you speak. You can't know everybody's sensitive spots, but you can guard against touching most of them if you cultivate the art of temporizing. Try not to be positive on subjects involving taste or opinion. "It seems to me . . ." and "There's a school of thought that says . . ." will get you into less trouble than "This is the way it is . . ."

Indicate, and learn to believe, that other viewpoints and other tastes are as valid as your own. Try not to be funny about subjects that others might, for personal reasons, consider very serious. Then you'll be fairly safe.

When you do blunder into an awkward situation, you can only say, "I'm sorry," or "I didn't know," and *go on* to another subject. Overlong apologies and involved explanations only prolong the mutual embarrassment.

4. *Respect others' privacy—and reserve a little for yourself.* The American habit of "interviewing" every new acquaintance is appalling to some. You have to place people a little, before you can know what conversational topic will interest them. But do it, if you can, by exchange of information, not by questions which might appear to be prying.

There's seldom any danger in a question like, "Do you play golf?" but more personal questions court a conversational tone which might embarrass you, if not your interviewee. What if you say, "Are you married?" and she says, "Not very." What if you ask, "Have you any children?" and she launches into an agonized account of why she has none. "Where did you go to school?" and "What do you do for a living?" seem innocent enough, but even they can be embarrassing. We once watched a salesman ask a customer, a very distinguished looking man in an Ivy League suit, where he went to school. It was the wrong thing to ask. The customer had dropped out of grade school, and was a self-made man—something to be proud of, to be sure, but he considered it an embarrassment and the question ruined a possible sale.

All such questions might have been safe in the bad old days, when "society" was stratified and people were more apt to be what they seemed. But then, of course, the questions were also unneccessary. Today, if you want to know those things about your new acquaintance, volunteer the same information about yourself . . . not as a recitation, but as part of a story or statement. Nine times out of ten, the new person will match your information with his own, but the option is his. If he thinks it's none of your business, or if he'd rather not be reminded that he never finished grade school (as in the case of the "Ivy League" customer) he can pass much more gracefully than if you were to ask the question outright.

With old acquaintances, similar restraint in question-asking is desirable. When you know a person well, the more reason there is to suppose that he'll tell you anything he wants you to know, so even your fishing should be relatively guarded, particularly on questions of money.

As to your own privacy, suit yourself within these two boundaries of taste:

    a. Don't burden casual acquaintances with your troubles. (There's something about cocktail parties that generates "confessions." Be careful.)

54

b. Remember that everything you say can be used against you.

There is something else to bear in mind: The person who is said to wear well is usually one who saves something of himself for his intimates.

5. *Be natural.* You've often heard that what you say and how you say it is a first impression give-away to your character and your background. But there's a sleeper in that cliché. It's worse to pretend to be something you are not than to be what you are without an apology.

No matter what other "advice books" say about "cultivated speech," a man's speech had best *not* be cultivated; it ought first of all to be natural. If it is not natural for you to sound like Helen Hayes, why try? On the other hand, if slang sits uneasy on your tongue, and your "a" is just naturally broad, why try to sound like Rocky Graziano?

This is not to discount the value of grammatical, articulate speech, nor to imply that you must say "boid" for "bird" just because that's the way you foist loined the woid. It's only to suggest that a natural "ain't I?" is sometimes better than uncomfortable, inconsistent, "am I not?"—and vice versa. It's to point out that a genuine, regional accent is more help than hindrance to a man.

It is true that, like the best manners, the best speech is the least noticeable speech — but you can count on this: an honest, unself-conscious way of speaking, be it ever so different from your listeners' way, is always less noticeable than an *affected*, unnatural "correct" way. Improve your grammar, your diction, your English usage if you can — but improve along the lines of your true self. Don't ape the fashionable phonies who speak as "they" speak.

Here's a bit more advice on the subject:

1. Don't correct another's grammar or pronunciation, not even indirectly.
2. Don't bother to say "stop me if you've heard this one," because no one will stop you, anyway.
3. Be careful with compliments. Give them in private. To compliment one person in front of another may be interpreted that there is nothing to compliment the other about. Receive compliments with grace, however. Nothing embarrasses a sincere and well-wishing acquaintance so much as to have his compliment disparaged, denied or argued. Women tend to be the greater offenders with false modesty, but men seem more often genuinely embarrassed by compliments.
4. Don't say "Huh?" or "What?" when you mean, "What did you say?" or "Sorry, I didn't hear what you said."
5. Don't use a lot of foreign words or phrases. (Unless it is second nature to you and your pronunciation is impeccable.)
6. Don't give second-hand opinions without crediting their source.
7. In business situations particularly, call her Miss or Ms. or Mrs. until she invites you to use her first name. With men, too — seems old fashioned, maybe, but it works.
8. In public, the best manners are the quietest. Try not to attract attention to yourself.
9. One last personal pet peeve of ours: When you begin with the phrase, "As far as," be sure to finish with "is concerned." Example: "*As far as* his manners *(are concerned)*, they are poor.

THE LOST ART OF CORRESPONDENCE

It is a lost art.

And this is what you should remember as a man on the way up, who understands the value of *rare* things. Because fewer and fewer people can write effective letters, those who can will be *truly valued*. And we're not kidding when we call it a rare talent. At a seminar run by the American Management Association, dealing with the abilities of the current crop of young executives, a universal complaint was that *even the brightest young men could not express themselves in writing.* (Just think —*If so many young men have trouble writing, and you don't, it means you have cut the odds.* You have a greater chance of getting ahead, both professionally and socially.)

Much of the problem can be traced to our rapidly deteriorating educational system; many books have been published on the subject of bad writing, some of them notoriously badly written. An entire generation of young people has been cheated of a chance for success, because they cannot write effective English sentences. This doesn't mean every one has to be a professional writer. But if you *can* write well, you are a big step ahead of everyone else, because a phenomenal part of business life in contemporary America deals with *written* communication.

Although most of your friends and colleagues will stare blankly if you bring up the subject of social communication (written), very successful people know all about it. We invited the president of a company we once worked for to a large party we were having; it was for the most part merely a courtesy. We didn't expect him to drive 40 miles from his suburban home to drop in to our place for a Sunday afternoon drink, but it was part of office protocol to extend the invitation.

We didn't expect a reply; it was a big open house. No RSVP was required. But this particular man wrote us a letter—just a few lines on his personal stationery thanking us for thinking of him. And the letter was in his own handwriting, which meant to us that this important and busy man took the time to respond to us. A fine courtesy; a thoughtfulness which was not forgotten.

The man in question had a deserved reputation as being more or less ruthless (though honest) in his business dealings. But actions tend to balance out impressions, and Mr. X, our former employer, was able to get away with a certain amount of excessive toughness in business by tempering it with thoughtfulness, courtesy and kindness. This was many years ago, and we *still* remember that letter. And that was during a period when social correspondence was still a recognized form of activity.

"There is nothing more pleasant than receiving a beautiful letter," says Letitia Baldrige, author of the *Amy Vanderbilt Complete Book of Etiquette*.

"It can inform, console, thank, express love or indignation. It can persuade, dissuade, congratulate, chide, cajole, inspire, or say very effectively, 'I'm sorry.' There is nothing within the range of human emotions that cannot be expressed by a reflective written word." Ms. Baldrige is saddened by the fact that the world of instant communications has made us so lazy that we are losing the ability to communicate our real selves to each other on paper. It is easy to communicate information via computers, but the computer cannot convey the emotions of the heart.

Also, take this into consideration: *It is easier to write our deep feelings than to verbalize them face to face or on the telephone.*

There is an executive in Los Angeles named Allen A. Arthur who never forgets any of his friends' birthdays. Just a one-line note on his unusual stationery. But those of us who receive this remembrance never forget old "triple-A" as his friends call him. He also generates a lot of business that way!

We'll give no rules, since this is a book about attitudes. But try to develop the attitude that it's important to write letters.

Never forget to thank your hostess after a dinner party. Again, just a line or two is enough. You won't be forgotten, because almost nobody else will do it. It only takes a few minutes and a first-class stamp.

Phone calls are fine, and immediate—but after you meet a woman you like and want to see again, a handwritten couple of lines telling her what a good time you had and that you would like to see her again will cut down a lot of the formalities.

You would like to do this sort of thing but don't have the time? Everything you have to achieve takes some time, some sacrifice. You're too lazy? You have a habit of *not* writing thank-you notes, or condolences? Well, that behavior obviously permeates every area of your life, and you're not going to achieve, buddy—unless you change, and now.

There was a time when etiquette demanded that personal notes be written on personal stationery, and we still think this is a good idea. However, most men beginning their careers aren't expected to have their own stationery. A sheet of white paper may be sufficiently correct, but it is preferable to use your company's stationery which, no matter how over-designed it may be, is accepted taste.

WHEN TO WRITE —AND HOW

Now, when should you write a social note? Most of all, that's up to you, and depends on the people you are dealing with. Again, writing social notes as a *habit* is an attitude you must develop, and we assume you have some common sense. This is not a primer, but a *guide*.

The 1980s promise to be a decade in which we must live within certain rules; inflation will diminish somewhat, but prices will still be high. Life will necessitate a great deal of planning. Historically, formalities are always enforced during periods of limitation. It helps us to accept those limits, to make a kind of game out of it. The 1930s were a very formal time. Life was hard—and people, even those with little money, worked out their lives according to rules. Take a look at pictures of boardwalks at Atlantic City shot during that period. Men wore ties in the summer, women wore dresses. Times were harsh; dressing up made the person feel better. Nobody is saying the 1980s are going to be as harsh as the 1930s. But we do perceive the forthcoming decade as years in which unreasonable behavior will be tolerated with less acceptance than, say, in the profitable Sixties. Those who can make use of such rules as courtesy and thoughtfulness will be the people who are most successful in the 1980s. Social correspondence falls into those rules, so we suggest you learn.

There is a way to make it easier. It will take an afternoon's space to complete it.

Write yourself some sample letters.

File them. And then use them as guides when you want to send one.

File them under: *Social Notes*.

Here are some examples for you to use as guides.

Palmyra Associates
4 GREAT JONES STREET, NEW YORK, N.Y. 10012

May 28, 1980

Dear Jack and Irene,

I owe you enormous thanks for last Sunday's lunch. I've really been busy lately, and the good food and excellent company was a marvelous antidote for a very tense week.

I hope I will be able to reciprocate shortly.

Sincerely,

Tom

Tom Johnson

Jules Siegel
Communication Design
222 WEST 23 NY 10011 [212] 243-3700

May 28, 1980

Dear Bill,

You were really great to come bearing gifts!

I'm very fond of Browning's poetry, and the book will bring me happiness on many birthdays in the future -- not only this one.

Thanks again.

Sincerely,

Tom

Tom Johnson

Leonard Oxenberg & Associates

Public Relations

May 25, 1980

Dear Tom and Alice,

I just wanted you to know how happy I was to hear that you are now the parents of a baby boy. I can hardly wait to see you and toast the event with champagne.

Congratulations, and good health and happiness to your son.

Sincerely,

Tom

Tom Johnson

365 West End Avenue
Apartment 502
New York, New York   10024

May 25, 1980

Dear Alice and Paul,

There is no question at all that you two are masters
at making your guests feel at home.   I can't tell you when
I've enjoyed myself more.   The weekend did wonders for my
spirit.

Thanks again.

Sincerely,

Tom

Tom Johnson

Creative Concepts   240 East 76th Street   New York, NY 1002

May 25, 1980

Dear Anne,

I've been looking forward to visiting your country
place for some time, and the very time you ask me I
can't come. We're having a stockbroker's convention
that weekend in Omaha.

I certainly hope you will invite me again.

Sincerely,

Tom

Tom Johnson

WACO AMERICAN

4 GREAT JONES STREET, NEW YORK, N.Y. 10012

May 25, 1980

Dear Lila,

I have just heard the sad news about the passing of
your father.

I know that words are superfluous in times like these,
but I still wanted you to know that you have my heartfelt
sympathy.

Sincerely,

Tom

Tom Johnson

59

PERSONAL STATIONERY

There is nothing like the authority of the printed word; your personal letterhead is an example. There are still some who claim that there is only one correct letterhead: the Tiffany style personal stationery. Generally, it is a very conservative engraved name on heavy, off-white paper. *Only* the name, no address. The address is to be handwritten by the person whose stationery it is. Now this may be "correct," but it is hardly necessary. Any business stationery will do for a man.

THE RETURN OF MANNERS
LETITIA BALDRIDGE

Watch most important men. They have a number of things in common, as you will learn by delving into the business section of this guide. But what is most universal is their knowledge of, and *use* of, good manners.

Happily enough for all of us, manners are making a comeback.

Etiquette is, as Letitia Baldrige says, a "starchy" word. Etiquette has to do with the kind of formal attire you wear at an afternoon wedding, and "how you unfold the napkin on your lap."

But real *manners* means being thoughtful toward others; being creative in doing nice things for others, or sympathizing with others' problems. There is nothing formal nor stiff about that.

It is a fact that the 1980s will bring us closer together. The city is making a phenomenal comeback; the energy shortage (which will be with us in one form or another during the declining days of the 20th century) means that more of us will live and work in closer proximity. Wichita is becoming more like Chicago or New York. Never has the need for manners been greater. "Having good manners," says Ms. Baldrige, "gives one a feeling of security in dealing with people." And leaders and achievers need to feel secure at all times ... or, at worst, give to others the *impression* of confidence.

Also, a boorish man—even a slightly boorish man—is simply less likely to be promoted. The denizens of "Animal House" may elicit laughs from their college-bred audience. But not one of those jokers will get good jobs, the best women, nor the great financial rewards life has to offer. The truth of the matter is that the boys in the more conservative fraternity house, who have neat haircuts and wear blue blazers, will be the people chosen by industrial recruiters and government, and get credit from banks.

Good manners are effective tools for getting ahead. Someone with excellent manners is *trusted* on first impression. And frankly, first impressions are often lasting impressions.

President of her own consulting firm, Letitia Baldrige Enterprises, Inc., "Tish" Baldrige brings impeccable credentials to the field of manners, stemming from her years in diplomatic life as an assistant to the American Ambassador in Paris and Rome and three years as Social Secretary to the White House during the John F. Kennedy administration. A former Tiffany & Company executive, Tish Baldrige is the editor of the 1978 version of the *Amy Vanderbilt Complete Book of Etiquette*, probably the best guide to contemporary living ever published and a book we strongly recommend to every young man concerned with success. It covers everything anyone ever comes in contact with, from what to wear at a Ukranian wedding to what presents to buy a friend who is marrying for the fourth time. We met with this gracious lady, and asked her views on manners for the successful man.

Has society changed enough for manners to change?

"Societies which prosper are always in the process of changing. And so do our customs of dealing with each other. In the business world, for example, life has been dramatically altered by the growing number of women in positions of responsibility. Men and women are searching for new guidelines on how to relate to each other in the office, at meetings,

61

or traveling together on business. So a new set of guidelines are in the process of being worked out now — still in the embryonic stages in some areas. We call them manners, and it becomes an accepted system of behavior through use. But basically, manners are just knowing how to behave, knowing how to say 'thank you', 'excuse me', and 'may I help you?' "

Exactly how have manners changed?
"The women's revolution is the big motivation for a change. It's forced men who were trained one way to change their thinking. Men are very unsure about how they should act toward women on an executive level — whether, for example, they should rise when a woman comes into the room."

Well, should men rise when women come into the room?
"It depends on how comfortable they feel not rising. There are those men who rise and extend their hand to everybody who comes into a room. I personally am a great exponent of 'pressing the flesh.' The handshake. It makes people feel good about themselves and you. It establishes a nice cheerful hello. But as a rule, I'd say that one doesn't have to stand for a colleague, a woman who works with you regularly. But one should always stand for a visitor from outside the office, and certainly for the chairman and president of the company."

How about opening doors for women?
"Men have traditionally opened doors for women, and many men still do because it is comfortable. But now I think the rule calls for whoever happens to be there first to open the door for others. Women are perfectly capable of opening doors."

Is there one rule all young men on the go should memorize about dealing with women in business?"
"Yes. Treat colleagues as colleagues, whether men or women. The real secret of success for a man (or woman) is the ability to relate to other people. It is terribly important to have a sense of humor, and to have an appreciation of other people's sense of humor. That's good manners, too."

What about calling a woman Ms.?
"Some women just don't like it. But they should inform friends and colleagues of that fact. I personally favor using Ms. before a woman's first and last names (Ms. Joan Smith) for a good reason. A logical one. The usage saves time. You don't have to research whether or not the woman you are addressing is married. After all, Mr. doesn't have any reference to marital status."

How about picking up the tab? Should a woman pick up the tab?
"Certainly, when it's her business turn. If a man and a woman dine together on business, they are not on a date. It is perfectly proper for the man to pick up the lunch tab on the first business meeting; but if she offers to pay the tab on the subsequent lunch, that's logical, too. And for goodness' sake, let her pay. Don't make her shove money to you under the table. Waiters are very sophisticated nowadays. They have become more used to women paying bills than are most executives whose bills are being paid. Remember, though. No one respects a man who is known

never to pick up a check. And similarly, in today's world, the same applies to women who never pick up a tab.

"The way to save embarrassment all around is to decide in advance who is going to pay. Of course, if a woman calls to invite you to a business lunch, she should pay the bill. When someone else is paying, it is nice not to order the most expensive thing on the menu. When a man is the guest of a women, he should follow her lead as to suggestions she makes on the menu."

What about lighting women's cigarettes?

"This is still considered a courteous act, but it is no longer considered ungentlemanly, in a business situation, not to light her cigarette."

What do manners really do for you?

"They're an asset — like having a portfolio of blue chips. A man who moves in the world with a sense of security, quietly polished, stands out in the crowd. What good is a superabundance of education and knowledge if a person doesn't know how to act in common, everyday situations?"

From your observation and experience, what are other factors in a man's success?

"Well, the successful man is extremely well organized. The successful man remembers things. He keeps notes, and he follows up on those notes. Most successful and dynamic men that I know keep their word. If they say they are going to send you something, they do. It is very bad manners to make wild promises; so many people do, unfortunately. Another factor in success is how one speaks, both in business and socially."

How one speaks?

"Yes, just listen to company presidents — at a cocktail party or in a business conference. The voice is very important. At a meeting one has to be able to project, to be heard by everyone at the meeting.

"I knew an otherwise very bright man whose career was nipped in the bud because he couldn't conduct a meeting in which he could be heard. His superiors continually had to ask, 'What?' and he didn't last long. A man should develop an assertive, self-confident voice, well modulated, so he can be understood and heard across a lunch table or in a boardroom. Self-confidence has to be projected in a voice. It is something that requires practice."

What about honesty? Is that considered good manners?

"Whatever it is, it is essential. Most successful executives I know are straightforward. Those who aren't may get away with it for awhile, but they always get caught and thrown off their pinnacles. And I should mention another thing. Success with family relationships."

Family Relationship?

"Yes. I think the majority of successful men have at least a minimal success in their family relationships. (The same goes for women.) It seems to go hand in hand. There are those, of course, who have been married six times, but they are rarer than newspaper coverage would lead us to believe. The very successful, who have made it on their own without having their fortunes handed to them by Papa, usually have a strong sense of family."

63

How about anger? Do successful executives you know blow up?

"It's considered ill-mannered to blow up, but let's face it. People do. Some of us are more 'human' than others. But apologies for the blow-up should always follow. Some of the greatest men I've known—actually worked for, like President Kennedy and Henry Luce, would really let loose with their tempers on occasion. But they always made up for it with their own kinds of apologies, and their staffs always understood the reasons for the temper shows. We were able to accept their blow-ups, because we understood why they had to happen. Better to let it all hang out on us, rather than the public. They always made up for it to us.

"The really great people I have known in life have been under the greatest of pressures. When they *can* keep their cool and handle their antagonisms and frustrations, they are to be admired and appreciated."

PART II:

BUSINESS SUCCESS

Someone once said that business is the great art of America — but it is an art that can be acquired. There is no doubt that business has once again captured the imagination of young Americans. Ten years ago, the business schools were advertising for students; some even closed. According to studies made in 1978 by the Department of Commerce, business is now the first choice of over half of America's college students — even if their majors were something more esoteric. New York University has a very popular series of seminars in which Ph.D's in liberal arts disciplines are learning to fashion their skills in the field of business. Other schools, especially in metropolitan centers, are following suit. "Success in business is an attitude," says Irvin Field, president of Ringling Brothers, Barnum & Bailey.

"If you have the right attitude," claims Ray Poelvoorde, director of Lippincott & Margolies, "half the battle is won. So many young men haven't the slightest idea of what life is all about."

Of course, no book can *make* a man successful in business — but it can offer ways to test your attitudes, to check on whether you are doing the right thing. Getting ahead is the name of the game, and to get ahead you should know a bit about yourself.

Here is another success inventory created by Gail North especially for SECRETS OF SUCCESS. Again, these "quizzes" are neither passed or failed. There is no correct answer. The questions are designed to make you think about yourself with regard to success. If you worry about jealousy, for example — especially about people being jealous about the good job you are doing — will that hinder your progress? Will you subconsciously hold yourself back because you want people to think you are a good guy instead of a successful guy? If you are tied into the "I must be a good guy" syndrome, you're in a lot of trouble.

Success —Will It Force Me To Use The Full Range Of My Personal Power?

1. Do you believe you have resources of personal power?
   a. How often are you haunted by the knowledge that you have it and refuse to use it?
   b. How often do you choose the passive role as a measure of safety?
2. Do you try to equalize your position in life with those around you?
   a. Do you pretend to be shyer than you are to be 'regular'?
   b. Do you refuse the admiration of others because it may elevate your position in the crowd?
   c. Do you shun the spotlight by employing mock modesty?
   d. Do you abdicate power to others in order to look 'fair'?
3. Are you worried about jealousy?
   a. Other people's jealousy toward you?
   b. Your jealousy toward others?
   c. How do you handle it?
4. Are you afraid of losing people if you become successful?
   a. Whom will you lose and why will they leave?
5. Do you ever think of yourself as acting out the role of the victim?
6. Hidden inside every victim is a powerful person wielding enormous amounts of power. What is your powerful person saying? How loud is that voice and how often do you hear it?
7. What are the benefits of keeping your power, your potential, your abilities locked up?
8. What are the benefits of liberating them?
9. What steps are you taking now to use your resources?
10. When you fantasize the future, where do you see yourself five years from now? Ten years? Twenty?
11. What's stopping you from making a beginning, now?

"It's the conceptualization that makes the difference ..." **INTERVIEW**

CHARLES W. CHILDS

Charles Childs believes it is important to utilize the "science of your own professional skills" toward the advancement of your career. His background is especially interesting. He was public relations director of the United States Navy recruitment campaign directed to minorities, was an editor of the original *Life* magazine, and an information officer for the Ford Foundation. Presently, as program manager in Union Carbide's corporate communications department, Childs represents that company's image in over two hundred communities where Union Carbide has production facilities. Childs has developed and guided a pre-packaged public relations system which plant managers with little background or training in public or community relations can implement with a minimum of effort. The program has worked exceptionally well.

"There's still a feeling that public relations means hobnobbing with celebrities and glad-handing," Childs complains. "That a P.R. man is somewhere between Josef Goebbels and a Hollywood publicist. I always hear public relations defined as 'indefinable'. Something against which a measure of performance or achievement cannot be applied.

"This is fallacious thinking. In actual fact, public relations is a science. It is made up of *evaluating*, on the one hand, and *execution* on the other; two words a career-minded executive should always keep in mind. Between these two polarities, comes the art or skill of conceptualizing.

"The skill, as I said, is the conceptual part, the way in which you creatively use your research and evaluation to solve the problem. How you mold the facts to solve the problem. This is the critical difference that makes for success, that separates the men from the boys. It is the *problem-solving device* that sets one plan against another, in terms of being the better plan.

"Now, how do you use this for yourself? It's all in attitude. Most of us put our thinking, and rightly so, *in behalf of the organization* which pays our salary. What you do is turn this concept to your own needs; when the situation arises, use your professional skills *in behalf of yourself*. Attack your own career problems armed with the same weapons you use professionally. With variations, of course, for your particular professional discipline, it can be reduced to a kind of three-box formula:

EVALUATION	CONCEPTUALIZATION	EXECUTION

"This formula can be applied to the problem-solving part, the job-hunting part, the advancement part, of almost any career situation. I was in a meeting recently with some colleagues. It wasn't our problem; we were asked to join in at the last minute, as spectators. In the course of conversation, an associate of mine was asked, out of the blue, how he would attack the particular problem. Instead of blustering through, he outlined some research steps that should be taken. He conceptualized some assumptions where he thought the evaluation would pay off, and was able to come up with a tentative solution on his feet. It didn't turn out to be the right concept, but he impressed everybody nonetheless.

"Companies need and will utilize people who understand the process that leads to a solution and the best way to do that is through evaluation, conceptualization and execution. It's something to keep in mind throughout a professional life."

WHAT WILL JOBS BE LIKE IN THE NEXT TEN YEARS

WHAT will life be like for an ambitious man in the 1980s? Early in 1979, a group of futurists, prognosticators and business executives—funded for this purpose by Phillip Morris, Inc.—met in Richmond, Virginia to discuss the future of work. Theodore J. Gordon, president of the Futures Group and chief engineer of the Saturn program for McDonnell-Douglas aviation company, told the conclave that the "family" of today should remain dominant as compared with alternate living arrangements which the popular magazines seem to feel are growing in popularity. Gordon says that there will be a rise in the birth rate toward the end of the 1980s, and perceptions about women's roles will change again, "possibly triggered by underemployment in the work force." He feels that child-rearing will become a leading profession, and that single-person households will disappear as the economic advantages of multiple-wage earner households become apparent.

Pollster Louis Harris claims that the political divisions beginning in the 1980s "are likely to be between those who advocate a higher and higher material standard of living, on the one hand, and those who feel that such a rise in material acquisition is less important and that the quality of human experience is far more important." The big news will be that old-time New Deal liberals and hard-line conservatives will discover themselves on the same team. Harris feels that we no longer will have economic determination as the chief control of our politics. "In the future, redistribution of the opportunities to partake of quality-of-life experiences, to join together in new common cause to enhance the living of life instead of simply redistributing wealth, is likely to be the focus of the American scene."

A notable change in the near future, according to William E. Bonnet, vice president for environmental assessment with the Sun Company, will be a reduction in the mobility of people. Transportation is fast becoming a much more expensive commodity. Bonnet doesn't think mass transit will necessarily improve, but thinks smaller cities and satellite complexes will develop around bigger cities. These smaller units will contain "all the elements of living—commercial, residential and industrial areas—in close proximity. People will tend to live much closer to their work."

Walter Hahn, a senior specialist on science, technology and futures research for the Congressional Research Service predicts that within the business office itself, the daily personal-interaction pattern is in the process of serious change. "Most of the printed-paper routines that consume so much time (and space) will be gone. Mail sorting, opening, will decrease significantly. Hahn says that the "paperless" office is something we will see sooner than we expect. "There will be fewer reasons to move around the office and the building; thus the social structure of business office itself, the daily personal-interaction pattern is in the process of serious change. "Most of the printed-paper routines that consume so much time (and space) will be gone. Mail sorting, opening, will decrease significantly. Hahn says that the "paperless" office is something we will see sooner than we expect. "There will be fewer reasons to move around the office and the building; thus the social structure of the office will change." Hahn wonders if office workers will suffer from the boredom and reactions in health and attendance we now see in automated manufacturing plants.

Although most of the futurists felt that we would have to live within stronger limits than we had before, and with fewer choices, William Lucy, secretary-treasurer of the American Federation of State, County and Municipal employees, says there will be no shortage of useful, productive work that needs to be done in this country. "The nation's housing stock is delapidated. Unrepaired railbeds are a barrier to adequate transportation. New energy systems are needed. We can train toward those needs, target our resources to them, use them to build the momentum for a new productive upsurge."

James O'Toole, associate professor of management at the University of Southern California graduate school of business, cites the *attitudes* of workers as becoming the central factors in national productivity. "In the industrial sector," he predicts, "uncooperative, recalcitrant and obstreperous workers can be automated out of the process of production—and productivity will rise as a result."

O'Toole is adamant in his conviction that the success or failure of the national enterprise rests on the willingness of individual workers to take responsibility for the quality and quantity of their work, to take initiative in those increasingly frequent situations that cannot be routinely handled, and to show a real interest in the welfare of customers, suppliers and fellow workers. Because of increasing balance of payment deficits and the declining dollar, O'Toole says that managers may no longer be able to afford to play golf on company time, and American workers will no longer be able to goof off or sabotage cars on the assembly line. O'Toole suggests that we will all have to work like hell in the 1980s and that it won't be such a bad thing. As for goofing off, he says, "the nation can only afford such behavior if it *doesn't* want oil, Bauxite, coffee, French wines and Japanese radios."

All the futurists seem to have fears—but most expressed hope, feeling that it will be a very challenging time. And that, all in all, there will still be lots of exciting positions and plenty of room at the top.

BEST JOB OPPORTUNITIES IN THE 1980s

Economists are predicting that the greatest job opportunities in the coming decade will be found in the area of the U.S. called "the sunbelt."

Kirkpatrick Sale, in his book, *Power Shift*, foresees the shift of *economic and political power* from the northeast to the "sunbelt", and cites a half dozen reasons for the region's growing influence:

Agribusiness (Growing, processing and marketing food.)

Defense Industry (There doesn't seem to be any let-up in the production of sophisticated weaponry; if anything, it is on the increase.)

Technology (Most of the new high-technology centers have been built in the sunbelt states. Can you name one sophisticated technical manufacturing operation recently introduced in New Hampshire?)

Oil (No comment needed here.)

Real Estate (If you had owned a good-sized parcel of land in Arizona in 1949, for example, and sold it in 1969, you could likely have retired on that deal alone. And the boom hasn't stopped. There's that whole big desert . . .)

Leisure (People in the sunbelt area spend as much money on play as they do on housing and industry.)

Writing in *Money* magazine, Joseph Coyle points out that "to round out the list, three other sectors ought to be added: government; chemicals, and the sweep of supportive services needed to keep the boom *healthy* (doctors, dentists, medical technicians), *wealthy* (bankers, stockbrokers), and *wise* (teachers, although here the demand still has not caught up with supply even in the biggest boom cities).

Coyle suggests that engineers and technical people will be in greatest demand "because high-technology industry in general is seeking the sun as probably no other; computer programmers, because of the extraordinary growth of state and local government, banking and other information intense activities; and naturally, managers to administer it all."

If you decide to move from your home location to seek greener pastures, Coyle advises you to investigate specific metropolitan areas. In Texas, for example, Houston and Austin are "hot centers", whereas Galveston and Odessa are listed at the bottom of the job opportunity barrel by the National Planning Association . . . as low as Buffalo, New York or Newark, New Jersey.

While it is true the highest rate of growth appears to be in the sunbelt cities, the successful job seeker would be wise not to completely overlook any area of the country. Boise, Denver and Cheyenne are cities that rate poorly with regard to some industries, but are booming with others. Keep in mind that many young men who flee big cities because of urban problems will find that the smaller cities have the same problems, though perhaps on a smaller scale. And, as they grow, the sunbelt towns will face the same urban problems as the northeast. Climate preferences are a consideration: if Cleveland's snow is driving you away, Tucson's 100° in midsummer can be just as much of a problem.

Money lists these ten cities as the best job-growth areas:

BEAUMONT, TEXAS: ". . . A chemical town first and foremost, with oil refining, rice milling, steel making, and port activities rounding out a picture of very heavy, fairly dirty industry . . ."

FORT LAUDERDALE, FLORIDA: Attracting high-tech, "clean-air" industries. Attractive because Fort Lauderdale "epitomizes a prime attraction of the sunbelt — being able to work in a playground."

TAMPA/ST. PETERSBURG, FLORIDA: "Long line of corporate lodgers" are knocking at Tampa's door. Up and coming industries: chemicals; electronics; insurance, and food. Also tourism. According to the State of Florida, there will be a 75% rise in office management jobs in the next few years. Also in banking, computers, and related fields.

HOUSTON, TEXAS: Still the biggest U.S. boomtown, and will continue well into the '80s. City fathers are out to "rival New York" and be, according to a Houston spokesman, "the most ambitious city in the world . . ." Youth is no handicap in Houston.

ALBUQUERQUE: Heavy in electronics, research and development, and government-related jobs.

EL PASO, TEXAS: One of the places to watch in the electronics industry. Great opportunities for electrical engineers, managers, computer specialists and technicians.

AUSTIN, TEXAS: A city that turns up on many lists of "most livable" cities. Over 40 percent of its working population is in the government business. Austin is busy recruiting science-based industry and there promises to be jobs for accountants, attorneys, general business management. *Money* magazine says that Austin can recruit people from San Francisco. Try doing that if you're in Chicago.

COLUMBIA, SOUTH CAROLINA: South Carolina, generally, is in a business and population renaissance. Jobs available for bank executives, accountants, sales managers, doctors, restaurant managers. Great growth potential here.

TUCSON, ARIZONA: Manufacturing base beginning to broaden. IBM alone will bring almost 5,000 new jobs to the area by 1983.

GREENVILLE/SPARTANSBURG, SOUTH CAROLINA: One of the largest concentrations of foreign industries in the U.S.: Hoechst Fibers Industries from Germany and Michelin Tires, from France.

TEN WORST AREAS: Jersey City; Buffalo; Boston; Paterson, N.J.; New York; Utica, N.Y.; Newark; Binghamton, N.Y.; Philadelphia, and Youngstown, Ohio. Many economists predict a turnup in the northeast, but "not much before the turn of the century."

A GOOD BET: *Money* magazine discusses subjects like this in every issue. Consider reading such magazines as *Money* as often as possible.

WHAT IT COSTS TO LIVE IN THE TOP 10 JOB-GROWTH AREAS

	TOTAL EMPLOYMENT: ANNUAL COMPOUND GROWTH RATE 1977-85	HOUSING	TAXES (INCLUDING REAL ESTATE)	TRANSPORTATION	TOTAL	RANKED BY COSTS
Beaumont	6.0%	$5,841	$8,463	$3,603	$17,907	(6)
Fort Lauderdale	5.6	6,901	7,056	3,301	17,258	(9)
Tampa	5.0	6,345	7,511	3,278	17,134	(10)
Houston	4.7	9,798	7,978	3,603	21,379	(1)
Albuquerque	4.6	6,732	7,529	3,322	17,583	(8)
El Paso	4.6	7,928	7,641	,287	18,856	(2)
Austin	4.5	7,115	8,007	3,156	18,278	(4)
Columbia, S.C.	4.2	6,868	8,263	3,279	18,410	(3)
Tucson	4.1	6,462	7,840	3,524	17,826	(7)
Greenville/ Spartanburg, S.C.	3.9	6,617	8,327	3,169	18,113	(5)
... COMPARED WITH SOME OF THE BIGGEST METROPOLITAN AREAS						
Minneapolis	2.8%	$9,628	$10,591	$3,179	$23,398	—
Los Angeles	1.7	12,413	10,372	3,642	26,427	—
Chicago	1.6	9,633	9,223	3,260	22,116	—
New York	1.0	10,912	10,780	3,746	25,438	—

One charm of many sunbelt cities shines through in this table prepared for *Money* by Runzheimer & Co., a corporate cost-of-living consultant. Figured for a family with two children and a $30,000-a-year income, the list includes most basic cost items except food, clothing and health care. While a Tampa family would have more than 40% of its $30,000 income left over for these items and for recreation and savings, a similar family in Los Angeles would have less than $3,600, or 12%, left over.

The computations, based on composites of residential areas in or around each city, cover a 2,100-square-foot house with a conventional mortgage keyed to March 1978 money costs in each community; federal, state and local taxes; a '77 Impala still under a finance contract, driven 10,000 miles annually, and a '74 Nova fully paid for and driven 6,000 miles a year.

"Go to the places where they don't have so many young turks, and that's the place to show what you can do ..." **INTERVIEW**

DOUGLAS ISAACSON

Douglas Isaacson is not at all restrained about his desire for success. "I am ambitious," he says, "and it's a good thing if you want to succeed in the world of business." At 27 years of age, he is goal-oriented, articulate, intelligent, smiles a lot and, though his dress is conservative, he wears his suits with flair. He cares about his job. He wants to be a credit to his organization and to himself; he is pleased with his progress. At the moment, he is an executive with the Character Merchandising Division of Walt Disney Productions. This division licenses a variety of manufacturers to utilize many of the Walt Disney copyrighted properties as products, to decorate products, and/or to promote products. These licensed products run the gamut from toys to housewares.

"I love what I do," Isaacson says. "I'm probably so happy with my job because the product and philosophy of the company complements many aspects of my own personality and interests. Many people make the mistake of feeling that happiness relates to day-to-day living. It is a life thing, an overall theme. One day you might be depressed; that doesn't mean life is depressing. It's not, but you have to be able to deal with the pitfalls, as well as the success."

Do you believe in planning a career?

"I have a kind of amorphous five-year plan for myself, which I think is kind of useful. Everybody is in a continuous process of education. I think it is important to give commitments a certain time frame. Create a superficial point of reference. Keep looking at your career to see if it is going anyplace. But give yourself enough time. A person cannot learn a job discipline in one year."

Is this your first major job?

"No, I did some experimenting after college to see what I wanted. I had a job at another concern which, though I learned a lot, turned out to be a modicum less than pleasing. So I moved on to another job. I think it's important to remember you do have options. Many people needlessly self-impose their own limitations."

What did you get from your first big job?

"Unfortunately, the old 'Catch 22' is right; you need one job to get another. But doing well on one job, even if you outgrow it, or if it is wrong for you in some way, is a positive indication of success. Working for a company gives you a credential. It is through your credentials that other people view your achievements and potential."

Do you plan everything?

"I try. I would advise anyone to have a plan. Control is one of the most important aspects of business and life. If working with a plan you can maintain a steady growth, it means the plan can work. It is one of the distinguishing factors, I think, between those who succeed and those who fail."

How did you come to get this job at Disney?

"I had the opportunity to go with several Fortune 500 companies, good ones with interesting potential. But I happily chose my present position because I felt there was less competition. There weren't as many young turks in this division. Not that competition is bad, but it's reasonable to think that in a large company, where there are many bright and ambitious young people, your chances are better if, at your level and above, the vast majority of fellow workers are older."

Do you think dress is important for success?

"Definitely. I used to dress more loudly and trendier than I do now. But I learned to dress correctly. The image is important. If you can develop conservative taste, you will gain an important advantage in establishing initial relationships in the business world. People dress in costume. An ad agency artist can be a bit more flamboyant and gain acceptance with a conservative client. The costume kind of identifies the role. But in many jobs, if you dress conservatively you gain respect. And you show respect. There is also a practical aspect to dressing in a classic style. It won't go out of style. So you are building a business wardrobe you can wear for years."

What do you think are the keys to success?
"One, I would say is motivation. If you're not motivated, you can't really deliver. And the ability to deliver is what they pay your salary for. I would also say you should be consistent; managers worry about erratic employees, even talented ones. As a general rule, I'd say integrity was important in the long run."

A lot of success manuals advise young executives to get married. Do you agree?
"In my own case I do. I guess it is important, depending on the fulfillment you get from a relationship. A good relationship allows you freedom to work. My wife is an excellent sounding board for the things I think about during the day, and emotions which can't necessarily be discussed in the arena of business."

How about continuing education, especially in your formative years as an executive?
"Definite yes. You must force yourself to be continually educated. There are always new things to learn; to be successful you have to keep up. And education and reading offer a variety of sources from which to form your attitudes."

Do you think the 1980s will be a difficult period to achieve success?
"Everybody seems to forecast a time of turmoil and changing life-styles, changing priorities, changes of self-image, back to being a nation of individuals again. The economic power seems to have shifted to the energy producing countries. The national consciousness is being raised. Important issues, social, technological and philosophical are being focused on us. We might see a future in which we have fewer freedoms; unimportant freedoms, such as where to set your thermostat. We won't be able to drive unreasonable distances at unreasonable speeds, which just might be the metaphor for life in the next few years. If and how people deal with these changes will determine the future. Yours as well as mine."

"If at first you don't succeed, you're running about average . . ."
— M. H. Alderson

GETTING THAT JOB

"By working faithfully eight hours a day, you may eventually get to be a boss and work twelve hours a day."
— Robert Frost

"Always take a job that is too big for you."
— Harry Emerson Fosdick

"We are told that talent creates its own opportunities. But it sometimes seems that intense desire creates not only its own opportunities, but its own talents."
— Eric Hoffer

... AND FIGURING OUT WHICH JOB IS BEST FOR YOU

So many of us are trapped by our childhood notions. Henry Klepperer, a psychologist with the highly regarded Institute of American Career Development, told a *U.S. News and World Report* correspondent that "most of us have a totally misconceived idea of what our life's work should be. Very few people match their ambitions with their talent and the result causes a lot of work for psychoanalysts." There was a movie some years back called "Marvin Middleman, Fireman." Marvin, like so many boys, was desperate to grow up to be a fireman. Fortunately for fire departments, the majority of us change our minds somewhere along the line, but Marvin actually became a fireman. He found he not only disliked it; he wasn't even very good at it. Klepperer claims that every one of us has it in us to succeed at something—but "Americans really can't face the fact that we can't be good at *everything*. Nobody has to stay an accountant, if he learns within a year or two that it isn't the job he thought it would be. What a man has to do is find out how to take that accounting training, and use it in a discipline that serves his own personal needs."

Sterling Tucker, assistant secretary of the U.S. Department of Housing and Urban Development, warns young men "not to hitch their wagon to a single star." He says that there is "a whole galaxy out there." Of course, the wisest thing to do is to choose a career right at the start.

This should be done late in high school, or in college. But it doesn't often happen. The majority of students, even those who get good grades, get through college, without the slightest idea of what path to take. "Colleges fail people," notes Dr. Arthur Witkin, chief psychologist for Personnel Sciences Center in New York City and an associate professor of industrial psychology at Queens college. "Work is a threatening idea to most young people," he says. "Young people are in the throes of fun. They all feel that life is supposed to be totally enjoyed. They don't understand at all that you are supposed to suffer a bit to prepare for life. My technique as a teacher to make them suffer is very popular. My classes are filled, which means that more young people are interested in succeeding. I tell them that vast terrors await them out there. In a sense it is true. I insist that my students know that it is tough and hard out there and that they will have to work. We talk about failure; everybody fails once in a while, even the most successful."

INTERVIEW
"Few of us get as high as our imaginations take us ..."

DR. ARTHUR WITKIN

Is it getting harder to find the right job?

"The Eighties will be the same as always—harder than ever. There are still over 35,000 ways of making a living. But we fail young people by not telling them what is available. There isn't one right plan, of course, for what is to be done. If your college hasn't given you a vocational interest test, do it yourself. It is worth every cent—and it's not really too expensive—because of the results. Testing centers are available in all big cities. If you want to know about a center in your own city, write to the International Association of Counseling Services, 1607 New Hampshire Avenue, N.W., Washington, D.C. 20009."

Are careers changing in the 1980s?

"I think people are changing. Today, everybody wants more personal satisfaction. Despite what you read about young people getting greedy, I think they put *less* stress on cash pay and on long-term job security, and more on job satisfaction. Not that money isn't a motivation, though. But the problem is to find that right job which is both satisfying and lucrative. Life isn't long enough for trial and error. Many people come to me crying that they have wasted ten years. If they knew how to find the right job, they would have had better lives."

How do you find the right job?

"Okay. Say you either have a natural proclivity for a certain profession or you've been tested and the professional advice is that you should go out and investigate a particular profession. There is something to remember: *Looking for a job is a full-time job.* You have to plan your strategy. List the areas you want to explore; the cities you would be willing to move to. And you can't give up. You must be able to withstand rejection. Just because you are turned down at a job doesn't mean you won't succeed elsewhere. Everybody has been turned down for jobs. The president of every Fortune 500 company. Everybody. The thing is to bounce back with the same enthusiasm at the next interview, and sell yourself.

"You have to be able to let an employer know what distinguishes you from the crowd. You have to know what makes this job right for you. You have to investigate the job—when it is offered—to make sure that you will be able to devote your energies to the particular profession. You must know why you are good for the company."

You like the word "you."

"Yes. I'm talking about individuals. Did you know that some people go out and apply for jobs together! Let's all get a job at Proctor and Gamble. That kind of idiot philosophy. You cannot go through life hiding in a group. Most of life is alone. You are born alone and you die alone. The world is a very competitive place. There is still an emphasis on individual achievement in this country. No employer ever hires a gang. When he puts your name on the payroll, it isn't a joint check. The company perceives you as an individual. But that doesn't mean you don't have limitations. When you choose a career, be sure you are aware of your limitations. It will help you climb faster."

What kinds of limitations?

"Well, coming to grips with the kind of person you are. The best manager is a team captain. If you are not a team captain, forget management. Salesmen usually make more money—and the best salesmen often fail as sales managers. The best technician is not the best supervisor. Part of growing up is realizing that actually reaching your goals may not fully occur. Few of us get as high as our imaginations take us. That doesn't mean we can't keep trying to reach it. Without that trying, we won't get anywhere. And keep planning. Planning shouldn't be an event in a person's life. It should be a continuing process."

How about toughness?

"When looking for a career, be tough on yourself. Success is actually a state of mind. Tough people can generally accept who they are; and in that sense, they are very successful. But a *leader* has to make hard decisions, like firing your brother-in-law if he's ruining your business.

"And also in terms of toughness, discipline, don't indulge yourself; and you have to have excellent attendance. My advice to a young person starting out is to come to work every day unless you're dead or dying!"

Any last words about choosing a profession?
"There are any number of satisfying professions for any number of people. It doesn't really matter if you sell machine parts or pruning forks. It's not the company that personifies the man; it's not *what you do* that counts. It's what you are. People remember what you are. One bit of good advice: There probably will be a shrinking of jobs in the 1980s. If you can, look for a profession in which fewer people can compete with you."

INTERVIEW *"I lost six jobs in five years . . ."*

PETER LEVINSON

When asked to define a primary quality of success, Peter Levinson doesn't hesitate. "Tenacity," he says. "All successful men have it. It doesn't matter what their field of endeavor happens to be . . . whether C.P.A. or a civil engineer. Successful men don't quit. If you want to achieve in a very competitive and often unfair world, you *must* force yourself through those terrible times when you want to give up. I certainly have had my share of setbacks, of depression. But if you have faith in yourself, you manage to withstand adversity, and carry on."

In the early stages of his career, Levinson admits it was a constant struggle. "I was fired from my first six jobs within a five year period," he says, "for a variety of reasons—some that were my fault, and some that weren't. It was all part of the experience of learning and growing." Obviously, Levinson learned and grew. He is now president of Peter Levinson Communications and represents Lorimar Productions, perhaps the leading independent producer of series and features for television and motion pictures, and a roster of some of the most distinguished names in American music: among them Chick Corea, Maynard Ferguson, Billy Taylor, Bill Evans, Stan Getz, and Woody Herman.

You say that it is important to keep striving. Does this hold true once you are successful?
"I think it was Norman Mailer who said, "It's hard to get to the top in America, but it's even harder to stay there." The amazing thing once you achieve a bit of security is you realize that success only buys you time and that you must continue to strive even more. I have less free time now than when I worked for somebody else. I'm not out to make a million. I'm just too busy trying to keep up with the constant changes in the industry I work in. You have to keep at it all the time."

Some of the successful men we've interviewed feel a role model helps a young man establish his own way to the top. Do you have any heroes who have helped you?
"Well, I've always admired Frank Sinatra. I've written several pieces

78

on him and I've known him slightly almost twenty years. I'm not talking about his personal lifestyle, which is his own choice. I'm referring to his dedication and persistence. He gave everything to his career in the beginning — learning and then developing his talents. In his Paramount Theatre days in 1943 and '44 he performed five times a day, seven days a week, plus doing a five-times-a-week network radio show. And in between performances he would give interviews, listen to new material from song pluggers, rehearse, and at night go out to see other performers and evaluate their work. What phenomenal dedication! This has aided him immeasurably in prolonging the great breadth of his career. And when his career faltered in the early '50s, he didn't quit. His belief in himself in this difficult period and his subsequent rise back to the top showed extraordinary courage. In a peculiar way his slump helped to hone his musical gifts, providing his singing with increased depth and meaning. Preparation, hard work, improvement. Those are three keywords to any great career."

Everybody who knows Peter Levinson says he is a very well-dressed man. A conservatively dressed man. Obviously, you care about how you look. Do you consider this a necessity for a successful career?

"I'm not sure about the word 'conservative.' I'd prefer to call it a classic style. I'm a graduate of the University of Virginia, and it was a very traditional school. I got used to wearing coats and ties there. I have a dozen winter suits and seven summer suits and a number of sports jackets. But they weren't bought at the same place. My taste has evolved and changed with the times. I think that's an important point, not only about clothing, but about life, success, whatever you want to call it. You establish the basics, the core of what you believe in, and then you let it evolve. Nobody wants to be behind the times, but that doesn't mean you have to immediately take hold of every fad. Times change, and the man who doesn't change to some extent, even to just understanding those changes, isn't going to move ahead. It's a sense of personal style that helps make someone great. I deal with a lot of successful people. They all display a sense of style in some way or other."

How important to success is keeping fit?
"I would say very important. All of us could do more. I exercise twice a week at a nearby gym. It's vital to have good health, of course, and a workout is terrific . . . especially if you have a great many anxieties. And anxieties are very prevalent if you are working hard and making decisions. Exercise also helps greatly in providing much-needed energy."

Here we are in an inflationary period, and we are told to tighten our belts and that the future will be limited. Will this stop young men from achieving success?
"The successful man adapts himself to his time. Personally, I think the 1980s will be phenomenally prosperous times. Americans are marvelously adaptable. It will be a great time to be young and ambitious."

You mentioned that you deal with a lot of successful men. From your observation, is there anything which all successful men have in common?
"Probably. I hadn't thought about it in those terms. I've already stressed tenacity and a sense of personal style. And then there's dignity.

Everybody doesn't have it, of course, but it's a terribly significant asset to possess. Most of the successful men I know have a great depth of understanding and confidence. Much of this comes, I think, from knowing your craft. They all have tremendous drive. There's intelligence, of course. And you have to be able to handle success, which is terribly important. If you can't keep striving at a fervent pace, you can achieve a modicum of success, perhaps. But you won't go all the way. I have to do some work at home. So do most of the successful people I know."

Is there anything we've overlooked?
"Yes. Just ask anybody who has made it and they'll tell you. It's an unknown factor called luck. Someone once said, 'When luck meets preparation, success often results!' I believe this is often very true."

SELLING THE MOST IMPORTANT PRODUCT: YOURSELF

"Remember, negotiation is very important."   **INTERVIEW**

ROBERT J. GERBERG

As Dr. Witkin succinctly put it, job hunting is a serious, full-time business. But it also can be quite creative and stimulating. First-rate job hunting skills can compensate for lesser qualifications.

"Those who arrive at the *right time*, whose personalities mix," says expert Robert Jameson, "and who appear the best qualified are the ones who get the jobs." Jameson, author of a number of books on employment, says that there is absolutely no such thing as real job security. In fact, if you are "underemployed," then you may not be too far away from being "unemployed." It's a rare person who completes a career without ever having been fired, dehired, or otherwise asked to resign. So, job hunting is part and parcel to every man's life. And he should be prepared for it at every stage of his career. *Most of today's successful people have built their careers on strategic job changes*.

Probably no man is more qualified in the field of getting new jobs for executives than Robert J. Gerberg, president of Performance Dynamics, Inc. of Parsippany, New Jersey. Gerberg began his entrepreneurial career while an Air Force supply officer, shortly after his graduation from Colgate. "I really couldn't be challenged in that supply job," Gerberg recalls (though the Air Force commended him as one of the ten outstanding supply officers of 1961) "and I went into the mail order camera business to raise money for graduate school." The Air Force offered to send Gerberg to school, but he figured that having to serve any more years as a supply officer was more than his patience could bear. "If the Air Force was willing to pay my way," Gerberg says, "I figured someone else would, too." He convinced the University of Pittsburgh to give him a fellowship to complete his MBA. Diploma in hand, Gerberg ran a direct mail campaign for himself, bringing in a number of specific offers. "It was then that I got the idea people could advance themselves if they were smart and went about it the same way." He eventually parlayed a number of jobs into a highly placed executive position with Pepsico. "I liked the company, and stayed a long time," Gerberg said. "It was there that some friends and I developed the idea of a business to tutor executives into becoming experts in getting better jobs. Performance Dynamics, Inc. is now leader in the field of executive placement, training high-level execu-

81

tives to get jobs which not only have more challenge, but pay a lot more money. Starting from a small company with ten people, it now has two hundred employees in several cities, serving both the corporate and consumer markets. "I'm in the business of teaching people how to be more successful. I still believe in the Horatio Alger dream," he says. "Everybody still wants to own his own business, I guess," Gerberg adds. "But that's really unrealistic in the 1980s. It is very hard to get money. There is less venture capital, especially for starting-up money. But a bright man can make a terrific future for himself in industry and create terrific opportunities where there apparently aren't any. I've seen people, who didn't think they had it at first, grow into difficult and responsible managerial jobs. People *can* reach within themselves. They can achieve a modicum of greatness. They have to ask themselves, 'How do I get to be more successful?' And there are a number of answers. But it all starts with being a master at marketing yourself. Having this ability gives a man a lot of inner confidence. It enables him to get ahead."

Does a man now have to be able to change careers?

"I don't know why people are afraid to do that. Most men seem to have a frame of reference. They are interested in photography and work for a photography concern. They feel at home. They say, 'I am being paid $15,000 so that must be what I am worth. They rarely think in another field their particular ability could get them $40,000 or $50,000. What counts is what you can do for some organization. A man shouldn't be frightened of changing industries, because there are always newer, smaller industries that are popping up, where there is no experience available. I talked to a young man recently who was making a fair living. We turned him toward the cable TV industry. We told him to look for a new job there. The presidents of the cable companies know there's no one with cable experience. The field is too new. So you get in on the ground floor. There are over a thousand new industries which will flower in the 1980s. A world of tremendous opportunity. Search the executive want ads in the faster growing industries. It's tougher to work your way up in the steel business, for example, than in an industry which has fewer competitors."

You talk about sending "letters" to prospective employers. Aren't you in favor of the traditional resume?

"There's a certain dullness existing among most resumés. And very few resumés are effective in producing interviews for attractive jobs. The reason resumés usually miss the mark is because they fail to distinguish a person from all the other applicants. They tend to emphasize information having little to do with the facts on which an employment decision will be ultimately based. Of course, the biggest fault of most resumés is that they contain much information that is not needed (which only works against the individual) and too little of the information which is really germane to the employer's decision. Then, too, there is no simple form of resumé which is best for everyone. The type of resumé which is good for one person may be the worst thing in the world for another.

"Most important, and little understood, is the fact that a resumé is a totally improper medium for contacting many employers. Many situations call for various forms of letters. Since these should be tailored, as well as more personal and persuasive, they are often dramatically more effective. If a prospective employer is looking for a specific employee, he will read his biography. For most people, the bio-narrative style of re-sumé (your bio in narrative form) is unquestionably the most consistently effective form of communication.

"In general, the more your biography is projected as a series of potential benefits, substantiated by accomplishments, the easier your job search will become. This is no time to be modest. The prospective employer will be interested. It is the David Ogilvy "long copy" idea. If someone is looking to buy a new lawnmower, he will read every word of the long lawnmower ad in his magazine. If he isn't looking to buy one, he won't read it at all — even if it is brilliantly written and ten lines long. Of course, it is useful to get professional help in writing a career biography. But a beginner can write about himself and what he has done in a creative, interesting and truthful way. In fact, the person with less background in business can help himself immensely by sending a letter about himself instead of a resumé. The letter should reveal who the person is, and it helps the prospective employer to know whom he is hiring.

"Most people walk into an interview with only a ten percent chance of getting the job. If the prospective employee has sent an emissary to the employer in the form of a long biography, tailored to that specific company, it is an excellent pre-sell document. In fact, I would recommend first sending a letter about yourself. Then follow it with a long biographical resumé. And *then* the personal interview. When you get there the interviewer already knows you, and that puts you at a great advantage. You have already told him in your long biography that you feel the company needs you. That you can produce for the company. It puts the roles in reverse. You become the interviewer."

Should a person take the first job offered?

"I think you should run a large enough campaign so that you might get four or five offers. Remember, negotiation is very important. Some men, smart in other ways, are so happy to get a job they leave thousands of dollars on a negotiation table. Someone called me recently and told me of a job offer he had received. He said he wanted the job, but he really couldn't afford the move at the salary offered. I suggested he tell them that he needed two thousand more dollars a year. They wanted him. The sale had been made. He could have negotiated. To make a long story short, they split it. He got one thousand dollars more than he had in his own mind agreed to accept. Not only would it make his move easier; that thousand dollars also goes with the salary for the next several years. All the raises are over that thousand dollars extra. So if he stays at that job five years, that bit of negotiation has already earned him $5,000. Still, if you are young and just starting out, my recommendation is to always put future opportunity over starting salary."

What is outplacing?

"It is a word that is going to be in every 1980s business vocabulary. Outplacement guarantee will be as much a part of an executive contract as health insurance. Face it — executives, no matter how good they are, only last a certain number of years before they use the company up or vice versa. More and more intelligent executives are negotiating outplacement clauses in their contract. It means that your company will pay to help you find a new job. It means severance with a handshake, really no hard feelings. Many of our clients are top executives whom we are helping to find new jobs. Their old companies are paying. And people

83

want to leave jobs on their own after a number of years. People keep changing goals, remember that. We must be goal oriented to succeed, but the goals can — and should — change. Or we'd all be in terrible ruts."

Where are the really big money jobs?

"It's always the same. Sales. There is a terrible image of selling, by the way. Many young people avoid it. But that's where the money is."

SIX GUIDELINES FOR NEGOTIATING A SALARY

1. Set optimistic goals for yourself and always sell quality rather than low starting price. If you are looking to get a new job for financial reasons, you should be looking for at least a 20% increase in net annual take-home pay. If you allow yourself to be talked into a 10% or 15% increase, you may only be fooling yourself. This is particularly significant because there are people from $10,000 through $100,000 who have been getting increases of 25%, 50% and even 100%. We're not saying it's easy, but don't sell yourself short.

2. When people ask you how much you're looking for, don't give them any numbers unless they are on the high side. Better yet, avoid the question until the firm is completely sold on you. Once you have committed yourself, just remember that if the potential employer meets your financial request, he will be looking for immediate acceptance of the job.

3. Before you do any negotiating, you should always make sure that the employer is going to extend an offer. *Complete the sale before you try to close the deal.* Remember that your first objective is to have an employer make up his mind about hiring you. If he isn't sure, premature financial discussions may turn him off.

4. The fine art of negotiating requires some precise insight into the other person's alternatives, along with a knack for phrasing your needs so that they seem very reasonable. You will have to communicate your point of view or the background to your thinking, before you get to the stage where you are pinned down to a number. Make it easy for the employer to have some empathy with your situation.

5. During your discussions you should focus on *standard of living* and short term *take home pay*, as opposed to gross annual income. Also, depending on how much you are presently earning, it may be better to speak in terms of "percentage of increase" instead of "thousands of dollars."

6. When you receive an offer, and regardless of how excited you may be, you should never accept it on the spot. Always ask for time to think it over. Then, if you want the job you should try to negotiate a better financial package. An organization is not going to withdraw an offer just because you think you are worth more. The worst that could happen would be that they might hold firm to their original offer.

When you negotiate with a prospective employer, you should be absolutely enthused about everything but the financial part. Be completely *outgoing* in your excitement . . . about the job . . . about your future boss . . . about the firm . . . and about the future opportunity. In short, everything but the money. Make sure that they know you'd love to start immediately. Then, you might say that after carefully reviewing your situation, the intangible costs of the move and other alternatives, that you wish they could see their way clear to meeting your needs. If that doesn't work, then try to get them to meet you halfway.

If you do not meet with any success in your negotiations concerning the present, focus instead on the future. This can take the form of a review after six months, a better title, an automatic increase after twelve months, etc. These are reasonable things for an employer to consider.

One of the authors of this book has long advocated what he calls the "calling card" resumé. Simply arrange your calling cards on a clean sheet of paper and Xerox them. Several acquaintances have used this successfully. Of course, it means that a beginner can't do this —but it's something to remember. It is impressive, partly so because it's different.

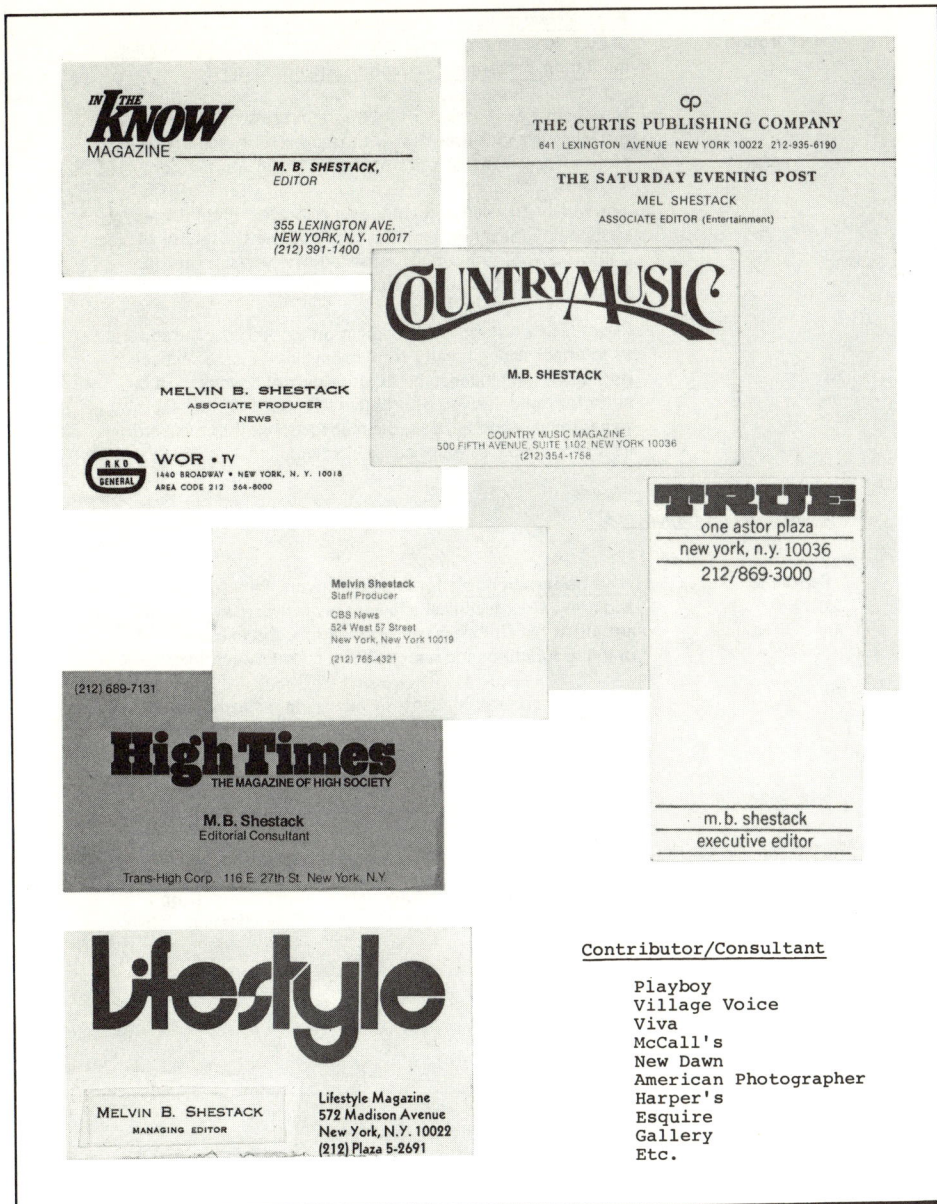

IN THE **KNOW**
MAGAZINE

M. B. SHESTACK,
EDITOR

355 LEXINGTON AVE.
NEW YORK, N.Y. 10017
(212) 391-1400

cp
THE CURTIS PUBLISHING COMPANY
641 LEXINGTON AVENUE NEW YORK 10022 212-935-6190

THE SATURDAY EVENING POST
MEL SHESTACK
ASSOCIATE EDITOR (Entertainment)

MELVIN B. SHESTACK
ASSOCIATE PRODUCER
NEWS

RKO GENERAL WOR • TV
1440 BROADWAY • NEW YORK, N.Y. 10018
AREA CODE 212 564-8000

COUNTRY MUSIC

M.B. SHESTACK

COUNTRY MUSIC MAGAZINE
500 FIFTH AVENUE, SUITE 1102, NEW YORK 10036
(212) 354-1758

Melvin Shestack
Staff Producer

CBS News
524 West 57 Street
New York, New York 10019

(212) 765-4321

TRUE
one astor plaza
new york, n.y. 10036
212/869-3000

m. b. shestack
executive editor

(212) 689-7131

High Times
THE MAGAZINE OF HIGH SOCIETY

M.B. Shestack
Editorial Consultant

Trans-High Corp. 116 E. 27th St. New York, N.Y.

Lifestyle

MELVIN B. SHESTACK
MANAGING EDITOR

Lifestyle Magazine
572 Madison Avenue
New York, N.Y. 10022
(212) Plaza 5-2691

Contributor/Consultant

Playboy
Village Voice
Viva
McCall's
New Dawn
American Photographer
Harper's
Esquire
Gallery
Etc.

General Manager / Functional Resume (2 Pg)

William Cross   168 East 60th Street, New York, NY 10022   212-726-3463

General Background

Experienced general management executive — with a record of over 20 years proven accomplishments in the areas of sales, marketing, personnel, production and purchasing.

Have held a wide variety of jobs and progressed from Foreman through Vice-President with responsibility for the complete management of sales/profits for a major division.

Am widely traveled and willing to relocate. Presently 46 years old. Education includes study at the University of California. Military service consisted of 4 years in the U.S. Army Infantry (discharged as Captain).

Personal attributes include dedication to a job . . . the ability to affect strong loyalty from subordinates . . . effectiveness in working independently or as part of a team . . . a facility for rapid analysis of problem situations . . . the capacity to get things done . . . also, the managerial skill to meet stringent production, sales, or cost objectives.

Areas of Major Experience

Personnel. . . . . Have been responsible for large scale work forces . . . union and non-union, technical and administrative. Have had full authority for all hiring and termination, the execution of union negotiations and responsibility for salary administration.

Numerous accomplishments in managing a staff skillfully. Proven ability for inspiring loyalty and minimizing absenteeism, turnover, and serious labor problems.

Sales/Marketing. . . . . .Have been responsible for a sales organization which generated a volume of $7,000,000. During a 5-year period, sales and profits were tripled.

Opened new markets for products through contacts on a direct basis with chains as well as through wholesalers, jobbers, etc.

132   Resume Example

Conducted continuous <u>market research</u> which was oriented toward expanding distribution on food products normally sold along ethnic lines.

Personally developed <u>sales promotions</u> and associated point-of-purchase materials. Directed various promotions under widely varying circumstances.

Have <u>strong personal contacts</u> with officers and owners of various chains including firms such as A&P, Bohack, Hills-Korvette, Jewel Tea, Finast, Safeway, Penn Fruit, Food Fair, etc.

Production . . . .<u>Widely experienced in managing production output and problems.</u> Previous positions held include Foreman — Production Supervisor — Assistant Plant Manager — and Plant Manager.

Have a record of accomplishments in all of the above positons. Some examples are the following:

(1)   Frequently overhauled production schedules and coordinated work between shifts to effect significant savings in time, direct labor, and overhead costs.

(2)   Initiated sweeping quality and product controls which led to superior performance.

(3)   Introduced systems of cost and price controls and insured their useful implementation.

Purchasing. . . . .<u>Have been completely responsible for the entire purchasing function.</u>

Assisted in the design of new plants in major cities. These included facilities for production, warehousing, and shipping.

Introduced quality control reports for raw products which permitted guides to be established prior to bulk purchasing.

Provided guidance to Plant Managers on problems involving pricing and inventory control.

Instituted procedures and controls which guaranteed the availability of diverse materials to meet critically timed production schedules.

Resume Example   133

MARTIN WETHERSBEE
74 Sycamore Drive, Louisville, Kentucky 24101
(415) 621-8336

Summary:

A Financial Executive with an extensive background in cost controls, budgeting, profit planning, competitive price analysis, forecasting and financial analysis.

Also author of a leading textbook on Corporate Finance; active as a fund raiser for major universities; and as a counselor on contracts to recent graduates who enter professional athletics.

**MAJOR CONGLOMERATE
(1971 - Present)**

AS VICE PRESIDENT — FINANCE

- Monitored and negotiated the final closing on a $25 million cash acquisition.
- Renegotiated loans totaling $20 million with financial institutions.
- Extended credit lines with vendors to effectively double accounts payable level without serious adverse reaction.
- Initiated control programs resulting in 18% reduction in inventory levels.
- Directed the evaluation of facility realignments and proposed mergers.
- Directed all financial activities of our division.
- Assisted divisional managers in numerous management problems.

**PENN CORPORATION
(1968 - 1971)**

AS DIVISION CONTROLLER

- Directed the evaluation of profitability for a number of consumer and industrial products on both variable and accounted contribution bases.
- Recommended plant closing which reduced assets employed by $2,500,000 and improved profits by $500,000 a year.
- Installed a budgetary program and reporting system to provide effective control of product line profits and manufacturing costs.
- Directed the financial evaluation of proposed acquisitions.
- Exercised functional supervision over the Controllers in five operating plants.
- Assisted general manager on a major turn-around program.
- Counseled on possible effects of various union contract proposals.

134   Resume Example

GENERAL FOODS
(1964 - 1968)

AS DIVISION CONTROLLER

- Directed all financial activities at G.F.'s largest manufacturing facility which had sales of $200 million and 4900 employees.
- Counseled management on the development of operating plans, performance reports, variance analyses and evaluations of operating alternatives.
- Directed the transition from mechanized to computerized data processing.

AS MANAGER — PRICING ANALYSIS

- Exercised functional supervision over all cost accounting, cost estimating and manufacturing expense budgeting activities in the Corporation.
- Installed a program for competitive price analysis and directed the development of end product prices.
- Developed and installed budgetary controls for all manufacturing operations.

COCA—COLA
COMPANY
(1958 - 1964)

AS SUPERVISOR — COST ACCOUNTING

- Exercised functional supervision over cost accounting activities in forty-three manufacturing plants (seven divisions) of the Corporation. Also developed and installed direct and indirect labor control programs.

AS STAFF ASSISTANT/MANUFACTURING

- Evaluated the financial implications of varied operating problems.
- Participated in the development of budgeting and profit planning programs; guided operating divisions in the implementation of these programs.

CORN
PRODUCTS
(1953 - 1958)

AS COST ANALYST

- Worked at the plant level and at the division staff level in financial control activities, including budget development, performance analysis and reporting, forecasting, facilities studies and operational analyses; also developed and installed a standard cost accounting system.

Education: Emporia University   Bus. Adm. - Acctg. Major
                                                3.6 Average - 4.0 Basis

Personal: Age - 48   Height - 6'1   Weight - 180
                  Health - Excellent   Married - 1 Child

Resume Example   135

WHERE THE JOBS ARE IN THE 1980s

The word is that salaries are getting higher, growing even faster than the inflation rate. Job openings in the 1980s are predicted to be up about 15 to 20% according to estimates from the more than 700 employers polled by the College Placement Council, a non-profit organization. This compares with an 11% jump in 1978. Salary predictions state that engineers and business majors will be the highest paid. Bachelor engineers will average about $20,000 a year, chemical engineers a thousand more than that. Most general business graduates can look forward to starting salaries of $13,000 and over; accountants $15,000-plus, and computer science majors (still a growing field) about $16,000. At the bottom of the class will be the liberal arts majors who will find salaries offered beginning at $10,000 and topping at $12,000. Teachers will likely maintain a starting salary of about $10,000.

The MBA is going to be the status degree throughout the early 1980s. Graduates from any of the top ten schools can expect a minimum start of $20,000, with big companies offering as much as $30,000 to students who are in the top five percent of their class, or who have had some previous business experience.

Lawyers are still in oversupply, although the really top students will do all right. Department of Commerce estimates put the yearly surplus of new lawyers at 10,000 graduates a year—through 1985. If you are a new lawyer, and you can connect with a major firm, expect at least $25,000 a year. Corporations are starting lawyers at $16,000 and, if inflation continues, starting salaries in 1983 will be $23,000. Many young lawyers are now settling for $8,500 jobs.

The government is cutting down, which is bad news for liberal arts grads. For the first five years of the 1980s, government agencies predict a 15% drop in hiring. Declining school enrollments dictate that 10,000 fewer teachers will be needed each year, during the first half of the 1980s. Fortunately for them, the number of education majors is declining, too, and supply and demand could equalize by the early part of the decade. College recruiters say that the students who aggressively pursue jobs are the ones who get them.

(Michigan State University Statistics for US Dept of Labor)

Best Bets for Jobs: 1980-1984

Accounting	Metals
Auto Industries	Nursing
Chemical Industries	Paper
Electrical Equipment Industries	Packaging
Electronics	Petroleum (super bet)
Finance	Public Utilities (super bet)
Banking	Research and Development
Insurance	Engineering
Food Processing	Retail Merchandising
Hotel Industry	(super bet, but moderate pay);

Average Bets: Jobs available, but nothing great.

Aerospace
Agribusiness
Construction
Hospitals and Health
Pharmacy
Printing

Publishing
Social Work
Tires
Rubber Products
Entertainment

Faltering: Good jobs, but fields overcrowded, competitive.

Communications (TV and journalism)
Law
Military

No Bet

Education
Government

THE CORPORATE VALUE SYSTEM

This little section might stick in your throat, but it is true. Despite claims to the contrary, most big companies choose their future managers according to carefully proscribed criteria designed to perpetuate the system. The preference is for what William H. Whyte, Jr., noted economist and socialist, has described as group virtues: *conformity; savoir faire; tolerance; willingness to compromise*, and *moderation*. Top management buys these virtues, in order to maintain a status quo within the establishment. And an effective manager is sensitive to this "way of life, way of thinking."

Management consultant John Wareham says that "genuine top level executives can usually juggle effortlessly with counterbalancing ideas," but what management really wants to know is whether a man on the go has any strong commitment to prevailing corporate values. "While independence of spirit may be admirable," writes Wareham in *The New York Times*, "it's not going to draw him any closer to the senior people. The most effective executive in a corporate environment will usually share the values and standards of the people that he is leading." The top exec might live in a bigger house and drive a fancier car, but his colleagues and co-workers, even subordinates, should still view him as "one of us."

If you don't share these virtues (or liabilities, depending on your viewpoint) it doesn't mean you won't do well in a huge company, especially if you have technical expertise. But don't expect to be a manager.

If you are interested in management, and have a spirit that is a modicum more independent than big corporations seem to want, aim at smaller companies where executive life style is often left to the whim of the manager. Remember: You sacrifice something when you get into a big company. It is a way of life. To those who agree with it, there's no trouble. But if you can't accept it, it can cause you a lot of grief.

STERLING TUCKER

Sterling Tucker has been serving his community in a variety of responsible decision-making positions ever since he graduated from college—from serving as chairman of the City Council of Washington, D.C. to his recent appointment by President Carter as assistant secretary of H.U.D. in charge of Fair Housing and Equal Opportunity. He is a great believer in preparing for a job. "The nature of our society is that you have to be qualified. It isn't necessary to be born with a great skill, it can be acquired," Tucker says. "But it takes alot of hard work and concentration. The upcoming decade will be even more highly competitive than it is now. Women are competing for the same good jobs. And the machine is still cutting down the need for humans. Competition will be greater and it will just be a little harder to achieve real success. But that doesn't mean they won't make room for you if you really work for it."

What do you feel young men do wrong in preparing for the future?
"They fritter away a great deal of time. The future achiever begins early. I'm not saying you shouldn't have fun. But I can't stress enough how competitive the world is and the fellow who works harder, concentrates and studies more, is really preparing himself."

What advice do you usually give to young men?
"Well, I tell them to have faith in the basic fabric of democracy; to realize that life isn't totally just, that there are many kinds of intolerances and discriminations in society. I tell them to let that 'I' emerge. The personality must develop strength to penetrate that veil. If society offers any opportunity, then go after it. You don't always win. But that doesn't mean you shouldn't compete. I wanted to be Mayor of Washington. I ran a pretty good campaign and lost by only 1,500 votes. I was pretty blue, spent time licking my wounds, thinking that I'd get out of public life. Then I got a call from the White House and an entire new exciting life began; new problems, new people. You have to stay in there; don't give up."

Is your advice particularly for black people?
"We all have the same desires. It's sometimes harder for black men, for those who have not known security. They tend to grab the first brass ring and hang on for life. One of my teachers recognized my desire to succeed. He told me to do a number of things in life, to seek adventure and not security. It's worked for me, and I pass it on to all young people, black and white."

Do you think dressing correctly is important to success?
"Of course. If you want to know how to dress, just take a peek at the most successful men you know, and they'll undoubtedly be more or less conservative. You're dealing with enough problems already. Why have any more that will be drawbacks to success? Don't be Don Quixote and fight windmills. Deal with reality. It will pay off. Another thing: when you are working toward the top, you do nothing but make decisions. Any decision that you can allow to be made for you, like how to dress, will save you time and energy. The fewer minor decisions you have to make, the better. It leaves your mind free for more important things."

93

You mention "cluttering the mind" throughout the conversation.

"Yes. I'm opposed to cluttering the mind with useless things. Why remember telephone numbers when you can write them down? You can make a thousand decisions in a week, so why do you have to remember a lunch date? Write it down. In fact, that's a good bit of advice. Successful men always keep lists of things they must do. Don't trust your memory. It isn't worth making the mistake. The mind should be in as good shape as your body."

Are you an advocate of physical fitness?

"Absolutely. I don't mean you have to be a fanatic. I play a little tennis, for example, and I jump rope. Eight minutes. About 500 revolutions. I started at fifteen and worked it up. But whatever exercise program you decide upon, do it. Keep fit. Responsible jobs take up a lot of energy. A few extra pounds around your middle will cut down on that energy."

In your wide experience, what have you discovered about successful men? What do they all have in common?

"Superior energy. All of them. They might be quiet types, but they get things done. They can solve problems. I would say all successful men have deeply competitive spirits and can cope with a great deal; a multitrack operation. Concentrate on a number of things at one time. Confidence is another quality I've noticed. They all have a healthy dose of confidence and talent. And integrity. Without integrity they won't last very long. And one last thing. It takes a large ego. No, there's one other: The ability to dream."

Dream?

"Most successful men have to have some kind of vision. They are dreamers who have the ability to translate that dream into reality. I always daydreamed as a child, imagined myself as all kinds of things. The successful man works to make those dreams come true. A bit romantic, maybe. But I'll stand by it. Out of dreams come the ideas, the standards, the goals. I should talk about goals. Successful men set goals, it's true, but when you're young, don't set your goals too soon. Don't miss the other rainbows. There are many opportunities. Some might not be as right for you as you imagined, but you don't know until you try. You shouldn't hitch yourself to a single star. There's a big galaxy out there."

EXPLODING A MYTH: THE EXECUTIVE DESK THE CORNER OFFICE

During the 1960s and 1970s a great amount of column space was devoted to the power potential of desks and offices. Windows were *de rigeur*, especially in New York and Chicago. It meant you had power. The wise writers who proclaimed the virtues of the specially designed office undoubtedly knew what they were talking about. But times change. We made a quick examination of more than twenty top-executive offices.

If there is any word that describes the big-money executive's office, it is "busy." Not unkempt nor sloppy— but busy. Of the twenty-two offices, three had mahogany desks, two had old tables, a dozen were nondescript modern office furniture company specials; one was specially designed to surround its occupant. One was starkly modern. Another baroque. They all seemed to complement the personality of the executive.

All were correct. That is, they gave off "important vibes" (if we may hang on to an archaic 1960s term). You walk in and you learn about the person: his tastes; the kind of pictures he likes around him. Some companies have very strict policies about how an office should look. Most don't. In one place, a young man at his desk was correctly attired and offered the sweetest smile—we think. It was hard to tell from behind the jungle of plants which made his office into a botanical garden. We are not derogating plants, but it would be a difficult place in which to close a deal.

Another, the office of a young advertising executive, was obviously designed by himself; he beamed with pride at one wall. "I did it myself," he confided. The wall was a montage of centerfolds from men's magazines. Very sexy, but also very embarrassing to anybody but his contemporaries. It would be fine behind his apartment bar. Not for an office. Individuality, yes. Bad taste, no!

Back to the desks. "If a man's desk is too clean, too antiseptic, too empty," says industrial psychologist Dr. Arthur Witkin, "it could mean that he has nothing to do." A company president can get away with that. A young employee with a shiny desk top devoid of papers will be in real trouble. Even if he's done with the day's work, he should generate additional work on his own. Initiative.

Anybody on his way up in a company wants to be noticed, but not noticed that much. He can't afford to be too offensive. We know a young marketing executive who was given a very small office—without a window. His two rivals in the company, both contemporaries of his, had similar offices. Neither did anything to it to speak of. One hung an art-shop poster picked up at a discount book store. Another put a map of the United States. Both correct decorations, if unimaginative. Our friend spent more time in thinking about the office. Given permission to hang framed photographs, he covered the walls with tastefully framed portraits of acknowledged heroes—from John F. Kennedy to John Wayne—-as well as two men who had distinguished themselves in the early days of the business. Anyone entering his small office would be immediately struck by the gallery of twenty distinguished men. There, in the midst of them, seated behind his desk covered with important looking papers, was our young marketing executive. To everybody who saw him, the twenty-first hero.

There are lots of do's for decorating an office—all dealing with acknowledged good taste and simplicity. You cannot go wrong with being simple and tasteful. If you feel you have no expertise in decorating, solicit the help of your immediate supervisor. He will be pleased you asked. He will also remember.

As for the don'ts, they are simple, too.

1. Don't put too many huge pictures of your mother, wife, sweetheart, children. A drawing by your five-year-old nephew is alright, if it's pinned to your bulletin board.
2. No cheesecake. Under any circumstances. It is perfectly alright contained in a magazine. But not on the wall.
3. Use subdued, business-like colors. Remember, your office is a place of business. It is not a circus. In the 1960s, offices became movie sets to backdrop the costumes that were popular for a short time. The costume party is over. If any words symbolize the 1980s, they are "conservative" and "classic." Elegance is fine, so long as you can carry it off. But how many of us are Oscar Wilde? And what would Oscar be doing in a Fortune 500 company, anyway?

INGREDIENTS FOR MOVING AHEAD

You already know, if you've come this far, that the secrets of success include working hard and having some degree of talent. But that combination doesn't necessarily spell total progress up the corporate ladder. "To reach the executive ranks," says Dr. Witkin, "understand the structure of the corporation. Keep your goal firmly in mind, and follow the success route of your company."

To find the right map to corporate success, to achieve a top-management position — a goal to which every ambitious fellow who doesn't want to start his own business seems to aspire — it is vital to view the career map from a proper perspective.

1. Where you are on the corporate chart at any given time.
2. Where that job leads in the company's structural crazy-quilt.
3. Remember the goals of your company. Whatever else it may write about itself in the annual report as a producer of fine products for a better America, its sole objective is to make money. If a company fails to do that for any length of time, it is in trouble.

If you work for a publicly held company, always watch the quarterly and annual financial reports. You are one cog in the money-producing wheel, so the nearer you can situate yourself to the company's profit centers , the more rapidly you will route yourself toward management.

There are two types of jobs.
1. **Line jobs** — those which have a direct connection with a company's profits.
2. **Staff jobs** — those which do not have a direct line with a company's profits.

Look at it this way: If a company has to cut employees, will they cut someone who is helping make money? Your devoted efforts aren't worth a hoot if they are viewed as largely non-essential by senior officers. A very personable executive we know allowed himself to be maneuvered into a job where he was in charge of employees' complaints, office parties (it was a big company), vacations, company picnic, internal public relations. He loved the job. He did a spectacular piece of work. He was beloved. During a bad year, when the company had to "trim fat", out went the personable P.R. man.

Important: Study the backgrounds of the men whose jobs you eventually want. Find out what they have in common. If, for example, all the top executives in the firm have had experience in finance and money managment, you know you can't progress in the company without some experience in that area. If you don't qualify, you'd better start looking (quietly) for another company in your particular industry where the executives don't need to have been accountants. If all your contemporaries have MBAs, and you have no intention of getting one at night, look elsewhere — where the degree isn't necessary for promotion.

Betty Lehan Harragan, who has written widely on corporate gamesmanship, says that hierarchy in a company is "amazingly simple." Ms. Harragan notes that every person reports to one other person, his or her superior. That tends to make your association with your immediate supervisor a very important one. Do not treat the relationship as one that is unique, a special one-to-one relationship. Do not assume that your superior can do his or her job well. "These are romantic notions," Ms. Harragan claims. "A boss commands respect, exerts authority and controls your future mobility purely by virtue of his or her position's superior rank in the chain of command — and for no other reason." When you are applying for a job, you should *interview your boss with a great deal of care*. Make sure you can work with that person or you are in for a difficult time.

Dr. Arthur Witkin believes in conducting business-like interviews when evaluating job applicants. He feels that you should use good business judgement, and avoid these six mistakes in interviewing:

1. THE TELEGRAPHER: This interviewer "telegraphs" the expected answer to each question. The applicant simply says "yes" or "no". A favorite question of the Telegrapher: "Do you really think you can do this job?" No applicant has yet said "no."

2. THE OGRE: When he interviews, he tries to scare the applicant to death. He sets up traps, purposely keeps the man waiting, browbeats. If the applicant survives this assault, he's "in." But nothing is known about his real self. He's been too busy defending himself to reveal anything.

3. THE BLABBERMOUTH: First, his interviewer tells about the company, then he tells about the job, then he tells about his own work, his family. He has yet to learn the basic truth that he can't find out anything about the applicant while he himself is doing all the talking.

4. THE STENO: This interviewer is so busy writing down every word the applicant utters that he forgets to listen, to look, to give himself a chance to react to the applicant. When he later comes to read the voluminous notes, he can't make head or tail out of them. He still doesn't know what kind of a person the applicant was.

5. THE CENSUS TAKER: During the interview, he fills out what is really the application blank for the applicant. He gets the social security number, five past residences, and wife's maiden name. His application blank may even be labeled, "Interview Form," He is very well liked by illiterate men who are unable to write out their own applications.

6. THE STAR GAZER: He is able to see qualities in the applicant of which even the applicant's own mother is unaware. He perceives honesty, loyalty, hard work capacity and great organizing ability. Six months later, he fires the man for lack of these same qualities. This interviewer doesn't know what to look for, what can and what cannot be accomplished in an interview.

You should like the work you do. That's an optimum. but all jobs have their boring parts and that's where discipline comes in. To be able to discipline yourself is primary. You will go nowhere without it.

When you are head over heels in love, you knock yourself out to make that relationship work. Why not apply the same principle to building a career? Dr. Erika Freeman, a New York psychoanalyst, has criticized the "instant success" syndrome of the past two decades. "The problem with expecting instant success is that when you don't achieve it, you may lose confidence and give up too easily."

Dr. Freeman also cites a common phenomenon, one that cripples many otherwise ambitious young executives: *procrastination*. A quick way to get bounced is to be known as someone who constantly puts off doing assignments and instead lets them pile up. When he does finally succeed in doing them, they are hurriedly completed in a slipshod manner. "It can strike in the beginning of a career," Dr. Freeman says, "or in the midst of it. You want to excel, but fear you might not, and therefore you put off starting the process which would allow you to succeed."

The remedy is to start out with a plan. The absolute key to reaching your goal is steady, consistent, never-fail, disciplined organization. Very successful executives seem to be compulsive list makers. They create priority lists every day. Every week. Every month. They are always ahead of their schedules. They keep a calendar of deadlines. They keep follow-up files. They always set aside time to examine progress and time to re-evaluate aims.

INTERVIEW *"The time plan frees me ..."*

KLAREN ALEXANDER

Klaren Alexander is thirty-five years old and in charge of the New York office of Elmer Fox, Westheimer, one of the largest accounting firms in the country. Alexander is an organized man and admittedly ambitious. He is married to his job and manages this devotion without sacrificing family life. "There is nothing haphazard about my existence," he says. "Except when I am comfortable with what I am doing, I need something new."

Alexander was brought to New York from the Minneapolis office. He was born on a farm in Minnesota. "I've always been ambitious," he admits. "I went to a University of Minnesota experimental high school. From the time I was fifteen years old I haven't lived at home. At school we had a rigorous schedule. I was very good at track as a boy, and I had to sacrifice athletics to go to this school. My local community high school didn't have math and languages. I started out in sciences but I began sometime about then to explore the financial field. I had an awareness of money. Very much intrigued by it, I worked for a CPA during the summer. By the time I was a junior, I had made a decision to work in the public accounting field. I enjoyed it, and liked the firm I worked for: Peat, Marwick. It was very comfortable.

"But too many people stop looking for a job when they find one. I think it is important to keep an ear open to new opportunities. To always listen. So I joined this firm in Minneapolis. I had only four days to move to New York when they gave me the order. We worked it into our schedule. You have to schedule in order to do quality work. And you have to sacrifice. Nobody I know who is worth anything punches a clock. They all work hours over and above nine to five. You have to take risks. Don't be afraid to take on new jobs—have confidence in your basic talent.

"Integrity is another important requirement for success. Also, keeping in shape. I run four miles about three times a week. I live in the suburbs, so there is commuting time for me. I am not usually home for dinner. I work six days a week. I enjoy the responsibility of the job. I stay in the office late, because I have to. I work in heavy time commitments. Fifty to fifty-five days at a time, committed. *You don't just manage time. You manage time in respect to yourself.* I keep a very detailed notebook.

"I've designed a plan sheet, a time sheet for myself. It might have some imperfections, but it works for me. I tend to overcommit my time, and when I look at my commitment sheet, I can evaluate and decide what I have to cut out. When you have a tight schedule like this, and can look at it in a minute, you don't have to be married to a schedule. The time plan frees me. I block out major time commitments. I have to travel three days to Omaha. Four days in Wichita. I have to cut fifteen minutes here, fifteen minutes there. When you are committed and dedicated, it is hard to accept other people's not being as intense as you are in a job. But I always act with restraint. I specifically recall losing my temper twice. Restraint in interpersonal relationships is important. Your colleagues respect you for it. I am extremely candid. If I can't gradually nudge a person into doing something correctly, I tell him right out. It's good advice for the budding executive. If one of your colleagues — subordinate or superior — is doing something that bothers you, just tell him right out. Nicely. But tell him. I find it works. It's all part of being committed to doing the job well.

"I probably have an inordinate amount of drive. For as long as I can remember, whenever there is some kind of problem, I charge in. I think that's excellent advice. Some years ago, while doing the books of a utility, I found that I was forced to write a law brief as part of the work. I hadn't any idea how to do that, so I had to spend about seventy-six hours researching what writing a brief is all about. I learned an awful lot that I was able to use time and again, one way or another. I tell young people in the firm not to back off, not to run away.

"I would also like to say something in defense of marriage. A good wife is supportive to success. I don't think a man can go it alone; even with a facility for scheduling, as I have." *(See plan pages 100-101)*

Andy Warhol has said that this is the age of the celebrity. "Everybody can be famous for at least fifteen minutes." And that fifteen minutes can get you promoted. Being capable, but *invisible*, won't help you one whit.

Learn to take credit for your work. A nice way to do that is with the subtle use of the memo. Let's assume that you have just successfully completed some kind of minor financial deal. It will eventually pay off for the company. Now deals are made every day; that's what most executives do. Very simple. Write a memo and send it around to all the management people you think are important to your career. Don't say that you have really done a major act. You are being paid to complete transactions successfully. What you do is outline the deal in a very businesslike manner, and make suggestions on how the deal may affect other departments, how it might be publicized by the P.R. department to help make the company better known. To your immediate superior, add a pencil note asking for help. "I had trouble with the second paragraph in the contract," you say, "and I'd like your advice on how to handle it next time."

Don't be a pest, of course. But the Public Relations people (if you are with a big firm) are always on the lookout for company items to publicize. If your name just happens to appear in the papers with the story, it means that managment will know you are on the scene. The problem of being known, however, is that you can't take it as easy as those who stay in the corner. But getting there isn't supposed to be easy.

LEARN TO GET CREDIT FOR THE WORK YOU DO

| KLAREN ALEXANDER | *Week Beginning Monday* |

P R I O R I T I E S

Personnel	*Finance*	*Office Services*	*Other*

S C H E D U L E	A C T I O N I T E M S
MONDAY	
TUESDAY	
WEDNESDAY	
THURSDAY	
FRIDAY	
SA	
SU	

TASK CONTROL	COMMUNICATION CONTROL
PHONING	**NATIONAL**
	PIC
WRITING	**PERSONNEL COORDINATOR**
	FINANCE COORDINATOR
MEETINGS	**OFFICE SERVICES SUPERVISOR**
PROJECT & OTHER	**SECRETARY**
LUNCHES	**CLIENTS & CONTACTS**

IMPROVE YOUR WRITING SKILLS

If you can write so other people can understand it — in clear, concise, and forceful English — you are way ahead at the start. You read the papers. We hope you do. All the successful people we know keep up with events. And you know that our schools are failing. Even the freshman classes at Yale and Penn State aren't up to snuff. Both those august institutions have refresher courses on how to write English sentences, for incoming freshmen whose high schools have failed them. There is a phenomenal amount of paperwork required in all businesses. Communication is of vital importance. *If you can't write well, you won't become a manager.* It is that simple. You must sell all the time, in most businesses. Most of the selling is done on paper — reports, proposals, memos, letters, speeches. The executive who is articulate and literate is the man with the best chance to move on. If you do have trouble, for your own sake don't wait one more minute. Go to your local university's extension division. Take one of the business communication courses. Many urban schools have them, and most of the classes are packed. Other people on their way up know this importance of being able to communicate, even if you don't. A word to the wise, right?

WHEN SHOULD YOU SAY GOODBYE AND SEEK OTHER EMPLOYMENT?

1. Boredom is getting you down. You can't concentrate. You are looking at that statement, that proposal, that brief and you can't get from line fourteen to line fifteen without your eyes closing. Make sure it *is* the job thats boring — and not the way your life in general is at the moment. Don't ever quit rashly. Always talk it over first with someone in the company whom you can genuinely trust.

2. You have been passed over for a raise and promotion for the third time. If the less tangible rewards — praise, a pat on the back — are missing, then it might be an early warning signal that you are at odds with the organization. It is time to do some heavy self-analysis. But talk to someone. You could be all wet. There might be something else in the same company you could do better. Investigate all avenues before packing your bags.

3. You are having a personality conflict. Well, remember that it isn't totally necessary to *love* your colleagues. You don't have to socialize with them, you don't have to go to lunch. You just have to work with them without too much friction. Many excellent business partnerships are between people who never see each other after five o'clock and whose lifestyles and perceptions are very different. You just have to have a shared vision about the company. It takes all kinds of psyches to people an organization. If the conflict is with your immediate superior, and there seems to be no way to alleviate the situation, you might leave. But do it nicely. On the other hand, if it is just that you can't get along with co-workers Charlie and Evans, eroding your own self-confidence is too high a price to pay for security.

4. You are ready for heavier responsibility. The best way to change jobs is to take what you've learned at one and capitalize on it in a new place.

5. If you wake up in the morning with a big smile, realize that in exactly ninety-three minutes you'll be at your desk at Acme Bolt and Screw, and then become nauseous, start looking no matter what the problem may be!

We are going to be very conservative about this. So many romances start in offices. When men and women get together in a working situation, several are bound to be attracted to one another. It won't stop. But it shouldn't be encouraged. And you ought not to encourage it yourself.

As an example, let's say that you are a very ambitious guy on your way up. You are nearly perfect and you've made no mistakes. You are certain for promotion. Then you start talking to the big boss' secretary. She is, to use the vernacular, "stacked", and sweet. And with big brown eyes that meet your glance with true love. The two of you become an item. You are the office sweethearts. Only the marriage isn't made in heaven. You do something foolish, and she hates you. You aren't too crazy about her anymore, either. The result is tension in the office. Finally, she can't stand it anymore; you made her sad. You are a reminder of awful things. There is no way to be friends. She resigns. Is the big boss mad at *her*? No sir! He is terribly upset about losing a secretary it took three years to train. He gives her a party. Who doesn't come? You guessed right. The relationship between you and your former mentor has sprung a leak. You are up the famous creek without the proverbial paddle. Bye bye career in that company.

Now, this incident may be a trifle overstated. Nonetheless, everybody, including the authors of this book, advise against playing around with office staff. At the very least, if you must have an affair, then be *discreet*. And that means, don't tell *anyone*. Make sure she doesn't, either.

There was a small story in the *Wall Street Journal* about a meeting of the expense account committee of the National Association of Manufacturers. To a man, they decided that it was time for all employees to hold back on expenses. Take fewer cabs, don't buy lunch for friends who are customers just for *auld lang syne*.

The 1980s are going to witness a massive holding back of expenses. CBS just announced to its executives that, if they want to travel first class on planes, they have to pay the difference themselves. The best rule of thumb on how to handle expenses is to do it honestly. Keep a tiny expense notebook. Get in the habit of really writing down your expenses. We mean all of them. Even if you can't get receipts for everything, the notation is enough to remind you of what you are spending. No worthwhile company expects you to take someone to lunch at Burger King. But you don't have to stay at the Ritz, either. Again: Live decently when traveling for your firm, but live reasonably. Life will be very pleasant that way. and you will never be faulted. You might be able to get away with hustling your expense account for a while, but when you are caught — and you will get caught — the consequences won't be worth that extra bottle of champagne.

Nobody says you have to join professional trade organizations, but many organizations will pay your way. It's a good idea. It's another credit to add to your biography in Who's Who, and it affords an opportunity to meet the cream of your profession. You never know whom you are going to impress; and besides, it's an excellent way to keep up with progress in your field.

Even if you are a minor supervisor, chances are you're going to have to fire someone at one or more points in your career. Successful people always have to face this unpleasant responsibility. Nobody likes it, but it's a fact of business life. When that happens, remember that the man failed under your supervision. Bernard Weiss, a management consultant in Stamford, Connecticut, offers this advice in conducting a terminating interview:

1. Keep it short and snappy. Get right to the point. Neither one of you wants to stretch it out. Keep it five to seven minutes.
2. Forget the criticism. It's too late now, anyway. Most vital: don't criticize anything about the person himself. It's likely that he can't change.
3. Don't review the past. Simply state the facts.
4. Don't allow yourself to be sidetracked. Don't give him a chance to plead for a second chance. Make sure your mind is made up.
5. Don't say, "You're not happy here." He can say that he is happy and he likes his work, a response for which you have no argument.
6. Give emotional support, if you can. "Under different circumstances, at another company, you might do real well."
7. Offer severance pay. If you can, be generous. Giving more than the required minimum alleviates both your pain and his. Offer to write letters of reference. Make a phone call to help him, especially if the man has some ability. Ask him to stay in touch. (He won't.)
8. Do it in the morning, early in the week. Firing people on Friday afternoon is barbaric because it gives them the whole weekend to feel rotten and grow more depressed. Early in the week, there remains time to get down to the business of getting a new job.
9. Don't allow him to stay until the end of the week. There is little to be gained. Walk out together with him when he leaves. It gives you a chance to be supportive and reassuring. Selfishly, from *your* standpoint, this also makes it more difficult for him to "bad-mouth" you and the company to other employees.
10. Be introspective. Dismissing somebody is difficult. It should be difficult. If firing someone becomes easy for you, if you actually enjoy it — then something is wrong. Actually, the best you can hope for is a cold, clean break.

"Almost anyone can be creative given enough time, budget and space, but the ones who succeed today have the common denominator of being 'poets of the possible.' "

INTERVIEW

The *New Yorker* calls him a "restauranteur of grand repute." The *London Sunday Telegraph* cites him as "a world expert on culinary affairs." Gael Greene's panegyric to George Lang includes the words, "linguist, litterateur, alligrapher, bibliophile, scholar, showman. The experts' expert."

GEORGE LANG

He gave lectures at the Hotel School in Cuba and was the first restauranteur to visit Red China. (He reported that the food had lost an awful lot on the way to the revolution). "I have seen the future, and it needs seasoning." His company, the George Lang Corporation, which he founded in 1970, has been described as "the only think tank in the food and beverage industry," and is involved in developing myriad projects circling the globe — from a resort complex in Thessalonika, Greece to the charming Café Des Artistes in New York.

The Hungarian-born Lang is quite willing to discuss success. "There are three distinct periods in a man's life. The first is the *collecting* period. You collect knowledge, information — and you develop your skills. You should have a number of skills in addition to your profession, relating to your available talent, and develop them to a high and unusual level.

"The second is a period of *organization of what you have collected.* Understand it. Digest it. You must organize what you have learned. The third, of course, is the period when you *put into actual use the fruits of the first two,* when you can choreograph your accumulated knowledge. Your muscles are in perfect tone. You know all the steps. You also know your own limitations. You have to be a "poet of the possible". You are now able to create something that wasn't there before. Most fields are applied arts fields — variations on an existing theme, or playing the game of mosaic, putting the same basics into different shapes, patterns. Too many young people overestimate the importance of being original at all cost at all times. Sometimes, you can become constipated that way. And you have to be aware of the parameters of the subject at hand.

"Personally, I am able to see problems like a simple-minded Hungarian peasant: in the simplest of terms. When I look at a chair for instance, I look at it like a child. Why does it have legs? Why does it have a certain number of legs? Why is it sitting on the floor, couldn't it hang from the ceiling? I don't take anything for granted. On the other hand, there are the facts that have to be taken into consideration in any project, in any business. *Concept, budget,* and *schedule.*

"Anybody can be successful given enough time, money and very few obstacles. Unfortunately, a real professional — in other words, a successful man — must do his job when he might not feel like doing it. The Muse might not be knocking at your door at a given time, but people have paid their money and you must deliver. I developed eight or nine specific skills to a fairly high level. My original field is cooking. I think I am inventive in cooking, but first I've done my homework. I've read most available books and I learned that everything has already been done. There isn't much that is really new. My second skill is my ability to deal with people. To sell what I have. Like any man hopeful of success, I had to become knowledgeable and skilled in many areas. In my case it was design, dishes, kitchen planning, systems design, merchandising, marketing, packaging, public relations and connected parts. What makes people feel good at a given time and place. The successful artist, lawyer or businessman knows what will succeed. I am able to dream on other people's behalf. But my dream is always contained within built-in limitations; that is one of the facts of life.

"The trouble I find with young people is that they didn't learn the basic techniques. How do you collect information and always be on the lookout for ways to use this information? The most important word to go with success is discipline. You must keep discipline while not losing the ability to dream."

HOW TO GET A VERY GOOD LUNCH: EAT AND WORK AT THE SAME TIME. IT'S CALLED "THE BUSINESS LUNCH," AND IT IS AN AMERICAN INSTITUTION.

There's no doubt that President Carter lost points with the business community last year, when he attempted to introduce legislation demanding that businessmen no longer be allowed to write off "three-martini lunches" as a business expense. Congressman Elkan Muhler (D. Wisc.) is an opponent of the President's plan (which didn't go through, though at this writing it is still in committee and can be presented again). Muhler defended the business lunch as the place where "the deals are made, people are hired, and new board chairmen are chosen." To not consider the business lunch as part and parcel of the routine of American industry, Muhler claimed, was terribly "un-American." We are confident that even President Carter has concluded a peanut sale at an Americus, Georgia restaurant. It is widely recognized in the corporate world that a business lunch can provide a rewarding opportunity for two or more executives to discuss plans in a relaxed atmosphere, away from ringing phones and interruptions. "Half the people who come here for lunch," says Michael Carey, manager of Claret's, New York's fashionable east side wine bar and restaurant, "are here to sell something and the other half are here to buy. It's a nice system and it works."

John R. Wareham, who heads an international executive search firm, feels that the business lunch is "an opportunity to go beyond the facts and figures of a candidate's life." The latter can be easily checked by a personnel officer. At lunch, however, a candidate's values, opinions and tastes can be probed—"those imprecise but vital qualities that constitute a total person."

Wareham feels that the office is a bad place to ask questions of a personal nature. Chairmen and presidents want to be sure, Wareham says, that a candidate for a top-level job is "one of us." That's why interviewers often select a restaurant that they know. (Salesman do this, too. It puts them on their own turf; they can more easily control the situation when they know the headwaiter, the menu, etc.) If you are reading this book, it's unlikely that you are a board chairman. But it might be wise to know what board chairmen are looking for in candidates for top-level positions, and how they use the business lunch to find out. Often, a regular in a restaurant doesn't have to ask for a drink; the waiter or bartender will know in advance. It is always wise to have your lunch drink a little light—no use getting even the slightest bit tipsy. Most corporate leaders drink socially, not heavily.

A manager's effectiveness, says Wareham, derives "in large measure from his own sharing of group ideals and aspirations; he is adroit at holding his group together, because he more than anyone values its continuing stability." What if you don't order a drink? Most authorities agree:

"Don't be harsh about it. Say, 'I'll have a Perrier and lime.' Just don't be preachy." But Wareham disagrees. "A candidate's refusal may indicate deficiencies — possibly a certain lack of savoir-faire, or an inability to adapt and conform to the conventional practice of moderate drinking at social gatherings."

Wareham advises the candidate for a job to order "unadventurous food." Appetizers should be avoided at a business lunch, because "the arrival and removal of dishes can frequently disrupt a train of thought. Wareham writes in *The New York Times*, "All anyone at a business lunch expects to do is enjoy the food."

When you take somebody to lunch, be sure you know the restaurant. If you have an important problem to discuss, don't select an unfamiliar restaurant. Wareham cautions that business lunches are no place to be adventurous. The business is what is important; a pleasant surrounding with good food and service make it easier to have that business work out.

"A man's appearance is his personal packaging.
To your eye, he is at that moment what he's wearing
and how he wears it "

INTERVIEW

THOMAS McWHIRTER

Thomas McWhirter is senior vice-president in charge of marketing for Cricketeer, one of the leading manufacturers of conservative but fashionably designed men's clothing. He has been with the company for twenty-nine years, and within the men's clothing industry he is considered one of the experts on grooming and appearance. McWhirter believes the essence of good taste is dressing well enough to be appreciated, but not so as to be noticed fifty feet away. "People should look at you instead of the clothing," he says.

Why is good grooming and appearance important?

"Somebody once said that you don't get a second chance to make a good first impression. If you don't think this is so, just think about your own eye-reaction to people you are meeting for the first time. With a man, you see face and hands and the clothes that he is wearing. About ninety percent of what you see is his personal packaging. To your eye, he is — at that moment — what he's wearing and how he wears it. And there's proof about what I'm saying. Actual statistics."

What kind of statistics?"

"The survey isn't new, but it holds true today just as it did a couple of years ago. I believe it was run by the Research Institute of America. Conducted among executives in decision-making positions, I think. And the idea was to find out what makes the *worst* impression when they meet a salesman or prospective employee for the first time. The results offer some excellent indicators of the things you must be aware of when you prepare for an important call, interview, conference, or other occasion when your first impression must be a good one. The survey showed that 100 percent of the executives noticed that a man needed a haircut;

107

97 percent noticed a soiled shirt collar and cuffs; 79 percent a shoe shine needed; 76 percent a badly fitted shirt collar; 76 percent that trousers needed pressing; 59 percent if a suit didn't fit properly; 59 percent observed run down heels; 46 percent caught a wrong suit color or style; and 41 percent cited the gap between the top of the sock and the trouser cuff.

"I believe that dressing for the occasion helps one's performance. At the very least, if you dress for the occasion, it allows you to perform more easily. Obviously, the food at a dinner is more important than the table setting and the friends you spend your evening with are more important than the way a room is appointed, and a product's performance is more important than how it is packaged. But the setting, appointments and packaging are important because they are the things that establish the mood, the attitude, and the eye-reaction I mentioned previously."

Do successful American men really think about fashion?
It seems so. There is a new breed of men's wear consumer. He's better informed and he knows what he wants. He's surprisingly particular about the way he looks in clothes, far more so than were his father and grandfather. He's adamant about authenticity, eager for what's new, especially in sportswear. Although the young man on the way up isn't in the big financial bracket, it's only because he hasn't had the time to get there. But he spends a larger share of his income on clothing than do his elders because he understands that the clothing will help him get there. Yes, the American male is more aware of himself. Take the barbershop, for example. The old-fashioned barbershop hardly exists. The new hairstylist is creative, and throughout the country men are willing to spend upwards of ten dollars for a haircut. That couldn't happen if men weren't interested in themselves, and in good taste."

We are always hearing about the words "good taste."
What exactly is good taste in clothing?
"Good taste is hard to define, and has different meanings in different part of the country. I always say that the essence of good taste is to dress so you are appreciated, so people know you are well dressed but the clothes don't overshadow you. If a person dresses simply, and according to his personality, it probably will be in good taste."

Can you give an example of good taste?
"Well, say you are with a big corporation, close to the top level of management, and you go to a meeting. Everyone is dressed in a subdued manner but you decided to wear a very high-style European cut suit—a suit which calls immediate attention to you. It might be a very expensive, custom-tailored suit, but at the moment it wouldn't be in good taste. It would stand as a barrier between you and the men you were doing business with. You would be considered foppish. It seems to me foolish to build obstacles between you and your goals; it is so easy to dress properly for your job in clothing that both looks and feels good."

Besides dressing correctly, from your long experience what
qualities do successful men all seem to have?
"A strong sense of responsibility attached to determination and persistence. I honestly believe that the majority of corporate heads have

a strong sense of ethics. They are able to perform in all circumstances. They come through; they perform."

Is good taste in dressing part of performance?
"Absolutely."

LOOKING THE PART

It's Really No Secret That Looking the Part Is a Big Key

LORD CHESTERFIELD (the topcoat with a velvet collar was named after this august fellow) once advised his son, "Take great care always to be dressed like the reasonable people of your own age, in the place where you are; whose dress is never spoken of one way or another, as either too negligent or too much studied."

It might be put into modern language this way: *take care that the care you take is not obvious*. What is obvious, according to Stanley Hyman, president of the Identity Research Institute is that, "between five and forty-five seconds after you meet someone, he has decided if he likes or doesn't like you." And that's why it is important—in business, as in life—to look right. Mr. Hyman, like a number of other experts in the "dress for success" field has been touring the country, advising young men on how to look. He feels that suits with vests look authoritative and symbolize sincerity. He strongly advises against fancy watches; especially the new kind—with push buttons to light up the new digital face. Try to do that with one arm loaded with packages, or when you are giving a speech and want to glance at your watch to see how much time you have. "Wear a white-faced watch with Roman numerals," Mr. Hyman advises. "And a leather strap. Stretch metal bands are out except on a Rolex." Rick Hinden, president of Britches of Georgetown, a group of men's stores, suggests that jewelry be kept to a minimum. Cuff links, Mr. Hinden says, are a sign of insecurity. And hairpieces? Well, if you are on the success route, just forget them. Ninety percent of hairpieces look like hairpieces. Hinden feels that businessmen should always wear white shirts, while on the job.

Moise Bloch, one of the "grand old men" of the men's wear industry, is vice president of marketing for Gordon of New Orleans, a manufacturer of men's shirts and ties sold in specialty men's stores from coast to coast. He warns against buying fads. "A young man who is serious about his career," Bloch says, "should buy tasteful merchandise. Man is a package, skin and bones. Clothing tells his story. A man dresses, or should dress, the way he feels will reflect his own particular life style. It should be traditional, but with an updated approach. With clothing as expensive as it is, it should feel comfortable and should last. It ought to look as good tomorrow as it does today. The wise man will buy clothes that use only natural fibers.

"A man should buy his own clothing; today's young man does, more and more. He knows what he wants. He doesn't want his girl friend's taste,

Moise Bloch

110

nor his mother's taste. He should dress for authority, because a classic good suit can make any man look and feel better, no matter what his shape. Clothes reflect exactly what the man wants to project."

Moise Bloch is probably one of the world's leading authorities on neckwear. After twenty-five years in the business he knows more about ties than any other person in the neckwear industry. "Of all items of apparel," Bloch insists, "a man uses his tie for image projection more than any other item of apparel. The tie says everything. It is the key to the individual. From his tie, you know how daring he is, or how solid; what sort of taste he has. The best suit can be ruined by a poor tie."

There is some difference of opinion about the acceptance of a bow-tie as part of business dress. John J. Malloy, author of "Dress For Success," says a bow-tie is a no-no; that no managers really wear bow-ties. Bloch feels that the bow-tie is a real sign of an individualist. "If a man can tie a bow-tie," he says, "he has to be a dedicated dresser."

Egon Von Furstenberg, the internationally known designer, feels that standards vary from man to man. In his best seller, "The Power Look," he advises men to adhere closely to classic standards. But he warns, "Also keep in mind this corallary: Avoid die-stamp uniformity . . . to be a carbon copy of the next man, no matter how impeccable that man's taste, is unsuitable, not only because you could not feel at home in someone else's clothes, but also because an original always has more authority than an imitation."

In the color pages immediately following this section, we are going to demonstrate how to build an "investment wardrobe", and how to outfit yourself for business in a way that is fail-proof. You might not have all the talent in the world; talent is a kind of accident. Few of us have genius. But all of us can learn to dress for success. It isn't easy, but we guarantee that you will look one hundred percent better by following our set of guidelines—an established code of dress which will allow you to be successfully dressed all of your business life, because the rules have never really changed.

"To be a really successful human being you must have faith – in what you do and what you are." **INTERVIEW**

CLIFFORD GRODD

Clifford Grodd is president of Paul Stuart, Inc., one of the most respected and successful men's clothing operations in New York City. While at the University of Connecticut, Grodd met his wife on a blind date. She was the daughter of the owner of a men's clothing store on Madison and 45th street. Against his wife's advice and wishes, Grodd accepted his father-in-law's offer to participate in the business. Under Grodd, the company has grown from a small store to the large-scale facility it now enjoys. "It has never been my philosophy to expand for the sake of being large," Grodd says. "There are very potent advantages to controlling your own operation."

Grodd feels that the person who is best at something is the one who usually enjoys it most. "It's the same with wearing clothes; the man who cares very little about it won't look as good in the same suit as someone who takes great pride in the clothing he buys. It's all a matter of personal involvement."

Grodd doesn't believe that a man should consciously be a fashion plate. "No man carries clothes well when the clothes carry him. A man should feel comfortable in his clothing. There is nothing more uncomfortable than watching a man struggle with his own discomfort in a suit, no matter how stylish the suit may be."

The young achiever, according to Grodd, should think of fashion and style within his own time frame. "Classic styles are always acceptable in whatever circles you may move, but if they are slightly modified to contemporary taste, it shows that the wearer is in step with his times — which is a must to be successful in any business."

Basically, Grodd feels that clothes should make the viewer look to the man instead of the clothing. "Don't say 'I'm gonna knock 'em over,' " Grodd warns. "Don't let the suit take you over. But dressing properly is vital. Looking eccentric can offend people."

Asked about success in general, Grodd advises that the bright man should always strive in areas where he needs improvement. "We cannot mark only one area of ourselves and consider that we are completely successful. You're not only successful because you earn a certain amount of money, or lead what you consider a good life. We all have some weaknesses, and we should work to eliminate these weaknesses. Insecurity is avoiding real problems. You have to face up to problems and be willing to improve. Confrontation with a problem is half the battle in overcoming the problem."

Grodd feels that there is a slight change in men's clothing coming in the 1980s. "As the pressures build up, we're going to loosen our clothing," he predicts. "During the 1960s, it was more a 'hey look at me' world. Notice my physique. Look at those tight pants. Miniskirts for the women. In the 1980s, we are going to be more reserved, less obvious. We're already looking toward old values. Nostalgia for a quieter time. Clothing is going to reflect this; it will be less fitted, and more subdued. There is a minor desperate element in the air. We're all concerned about where we are going financially, and when we have this concern we tend to molt our feathers somewhat, mute our colors. Yet, with all this, we seem to be less self-conscious and are able to express ourselves.

"That's a real success point, being able to express yourself. I think the more one believes in himself, the easier it is to develop a personality. To have integrity. But of course, no one can be successful consistently. A young person should be aware of this. We all make mistakes and even when we do things right, it doesn't always work out. The thing to do is to keep going."

Grodd says that most successful people have a number of things in common. "They all have a sense of being alert, enthusiastic and interested. They know how to look right, and understand how to change with the times. I think most achievers suffer from workaholism; but I don't believe that's a minus. It means you must constantly be challenged. Without challenge, life loses its force. I also find that leaders generally are able to set an example. That's a primary attitude to run a good business; be neat, tuned in and set an example. And long ago, I came to the conclusion that to succeed you really have to organize yourself. Without organization, without leadership, things can degenerate into an arrested state. *Leaders and managers should be able to allocate responsibility, but allocation doesn't mean abdication.* Supervisors must motivate. **They must make life exciting for the people who work for them. It makes the job into a quality job. And quality is so essential in life."**

Turning back to his specialty, clothing, Grodd concludes, "When you see a man who is well dressed and well groomed, you know immediately that he appreciates good quality. It's a kind of instant respect. It works. It helps his performance."

Talk to any group of successful men and you will find at least one area of complete agreement: IT IS IMPORTANT, EVEN IMPERATIVE, TO KNOW HOW TO DRESS TO GET AHEAD.

In this area, especially for young men starting up the ladder, there are rules which can each be condensed into a sentence or two.

Wear a suit and tie every day—the suit usually navy blue or grey. The shirt should be white, or a subdued solid color, the tie simple and one that complements the suit. Sport jackets and blazers are acceptable, *sometimes*, depending on the unwritten procedures and rules of your company. But suits are always acceptable. A single attitude governs these rules: Think *conservative*.

For the most part, successful men dress conservatively. As Jim McWhirter and Clifford Grodd explain in their interviews, dressing correctly gets you *in the game*. And if you're not in the game, how can you win?

We decided to work out a little experiment. In the course of two days we dropped in on twelve successful businessmen we know. Their ages ranged from twenty-nine years old (an executive of a computer-repair company) to sixty-four (president of a leather findings company).

• Of the twelve, the two youngest had neatly trimmed moustaches.

• None had long hair; most had fashionably "styled" hair, neither too long, nor too short.

• All but one wore white shirts. The exception was the advertising copy chief who said he always wore "blue shirts," which is alright.

• Seven wore some variety of blue suit (plain, striped, etc.). Two wore vests.

• Five wore some variety of grey suit (flannel, worsted, striped), one of these with a vest.

• Nine wore black shoes (four slip-ons, five laced).

• Three wore dark brown shoes (one-slip on, three laced). (*Nobody wore a blue suit with brown shoes.*)

• All wore ties of subdued colors—either foulard, repp stripe or challis. Most had a touch of red in the tie.

• Nobody wore brown. Nobody wore green.

It is our opinion that, if we had visited twenty or thirty or a hundred more top executives in as many businesses, our results would have been the same. Call it a uniform, if you like; or just accepted business taste. But it is a *fact of life*: most successful businessmen tend to wear conservative clothing—mostly grey and blue, with white shirts and quiet ties. There is a reason: *most men look very handsome in this type of dress*. It suits all occasions—and there are infinite choices within the acceptable formula. If there weren't, Brooks Brothers, Fenn & Feinstein, Paul Stuart and similar clothing stores across the country catering to successful businessmen would have gone out of business long ago.

To those who complain that wearing this uniform undercuts their originality, consider instead that *originality* is something which dwells in

IF YOU'RE GOING TO SERVE IN THE ARMY OF SUCCESS, BE PREPARED TO WEAR THE UNIFORM.

your mind. You don't have to wear flamboyant clothes to have spectacular ideas. In fact, in most companies—whether it is fair or not—people are judged by the way they look. So if you look and dress as much as possible like the top executives, even your "way out" ideas have a much better chance of being accepted than if—heaven forbid—you came to work in a John Travolta disco suit. *We are not discussing here the morality of the situation.* Dressing for the part may be a compromise, but it's a compromise that will pay off with a future as handsome as the suit you have been wearing.

Think of your "business uniform" as an investment. It is part of the equipment you need to be successful. If you are a graduating dentist, you have to invest in an office, in a dentist chair, in electronic drills. You certainly wouldn't buy faulty equipment; you would want the best equipment you could use for a long time. That's why it is wise to invest in a wardrobe that will last a long time. The thing about a correct business wardrobe is that it *rarely goes out of style*. One of the people we visited during our little experiment was a fifty-year-old bank executive. When we complimented him on his dark-blue pinstripe suit, he replied, "I bought this suit twelve years ago. It will be in fashion twelve years from now, too. The only change in my costume is the tie. They are a bit thinner now. No use looking old fashioned."

The Investment Wardrobe

If you are starting out in the business world, here is the minimum wardrobe you should have.

1. *A blue suit.* It should be single-breasted, with a tendency toward Ivy-League cut, but one which fits *your* figure. It can be two-button or three-button. The lapels should be neither too wide not too narrow. The pants can have pleats (latest style) but most businessmen we spoke with preferred no pleats. Cuffs are currently back in style, but most men divided on this score. Both cuffs and cuffless trousers are alright, but if you want to lean toward the "stylish", wear cuffs. Vests are always correct. They don't help a portly figure; yet there is something "important" about a vest. The suit can be very dark blue, or have a pinstripe or chalk stripe. These don't always look well on a very young-looking man. They tend to make one look even younger. The blue suit is favored by most board chairmen. It is very solid, very affirmative.

2. *A gray suit.* Now this suit, like the blue one, can be of flannel or worsted, have a herringbone weave or a stripe. Gray is always correct. Younger men look important and successful in gray; that's why such suits are so popular. Again, single breasted is better. There is nothing wrong with a double-breasted suit, but most men don't carry it off very well.

3. *A blue blazer.* This is the all-around correct garment. You can even wear it in the board room (especially if you are under thirty or over fifty). Two-or three-button, single breasted. It can be worn with a variety of trousers, informally (even with jeans to a garden party or some such occasion.) But nobody will think you are out of sorts if you wear your blue blazer and gray slacks in the office—especially with a white shirt and conservative tie. The blue blazer is an indispensable addition to your wardrobe.

4. Some gray trousers.

5. Plain colored (non-patterned) socks; very dark—blue, dark gray or black. Make sure they stay up. Make sure that, when you sit down and your pants rise, only the sock is seen—no leg. Wear garters, if you have to—or get socks that stay up.

6. The best shoes for business are conservative black or dark brown leather shoes which lace up and have very little decoration. The slip-on shoe is correct, and in wide use. The Gucci-type shoe, with the tell-tale buckle, is very much in fashion. Here again, stick to the most conservative. Even way-out people will respect you. Remember—take risks with your mind, but play it safe with your clothing. Never, never, never wear sneakers, running shoes, or any kind of funny shoes to work. Black shoes are the only color to wear with blue. Either black or brown is okay with gray.

7. If you can only buy a few shirts, and have to wash them each night, they should be WHITE. A white shirt is always correct. Button-down, pin-collars—prevailing collar styles are all suitable. But white shirts work. Light blue is acceptable, as are very unobtrusive striped shirts.

8. Ties: the most conservative. Repp silk, foulards, solid colors, polka dot, little diamond shape. Not too thin, not too wide. This is the area where you can express your individuality, as Moise Bloch says elsewhere in this book. *But not too individual.*

9. Hats: Most young men don't wear them. Of the men we polled, not one wears a hat regularly—not even the man in his sixties. The fashion industry says that hats will be back in the 1980s. We're not so sure. But if you do wear a hat, pick a conservative one. A plain fedora type.

10. Overcoat: We are recommending the classic Burberry as the coat to buy (or if necessary, one of its imitators). It is both conservative (worn by British army officers and gentlemen) and dashing at the same time. It can be worn year round. The lining, which is removable, keeps you warm in the winter. Without the lining it is the perfect spring or fall topcoat. And it becomes more correct as it grows older.

There you have it. Nothing too fancy. You can build up a wardrobe slowly. Grey suits come in dozens of subtle shade differences. There are summer suits not in the same shades as winter wear, and classic tan cotton suits and cord suits are always correct. (We discuss this in more detail in the color section.) How about brown, green, and colors in between? We suggest you read John J. Malloy's "Dress for Success," which is available wherever paperbacks are sold. Malloy is the world's greatest expert on why people wear clothing, and he goes into intricate detail about why businessmen should never wear brown nor green. It's worth the few dollars it costs to buy the book. You may not agree with everything Malloy has to say, but he gets his message across—and we've banished green from our own wardrobe after reading his book!

A P.S. About Formal Clothing

"... if you are told only the classic black-and-white uniform will do, you are in good hands ..."

—John Berendt,
WRITER & EDITOR

One of the authors of this book landed one of his best jobs because he owned a tuxedo. "My boss did not want to attend a fund-raising dinner. The company had bought a table, and suggested that all top executives go. My boss asked his three subordinates if they owned tuxedos. I was the only one who did, so I was dispatched to the dinner as his stand-in. It was one of the most fortuitous evenings of my life. At the dinner, I became involved in conversation with a man who owned a company I admired. Two days later he called me, offered me a job. At better pay and more responsibility. I never would have met him had I not owned a tuxedo."

This won't happen at every formal banquet, of course, but if you are serious about making it, in a big company particularly, then we'd advise that you invest in a tuxedo. The 1980s promise to be a more elegant time; at least more formal. Every company has at least one or two affairs at which the men and women are required to wear formal dress. You can rent a tuxedo, but they always look rented. And the prices are quite high—and add up, year after year. So, get yourself a tuxedo. Make sure it is black. It's probably better if it is single-breasted. The style should be as conservative as possible. You are not an M.C. at a hip nightclub, nor a musician. Don't buy a ruffled shirt. The pre-tied tie is all right, as long as it is not a clip on. The one you tie yourself is preferred, but unless you are an expert, or have someone close to you who can tie it for you, don't attempt it.

A BRIEF GLOSSARY OF MEN'S FASHION TERMS

*Things to know about 20th Century Men's Fashion

A

acrylic, Pertaining to fiber made from acrylonitrile.

Acrylonitrile, Polymer resulting from the reaction of ethylene oxide and dyrocyanic acid. Brand names: Acrilan, Creslan, Orlon.

American-Egyptian cotton, Type of cotton developed in Arizona and California as a result of an exchange of seeds by cotton growers in the United States and Egypt.

B

basic, Forming a starting point or base. In apparel, the noun "basic" refers to a simple classic.

bespoke, Custom made; term applied in England to articles made to individual order.

bias, Diagonal line of fabric, at a 45 degree angle to the selvage.

blazer, Single-or double breasted sports jacket with metal buttons, in dark blue or another solid color or in stripes. It is sometimes edged with a solid color braid.

Various regiments in England have regimental blazers, always in blue and double-breasted but distinguished by the number of metal buttons on the cuff. The Grenadier Guards have one button; the Coldstream Guards, two; the Scotch Guards, three; the Irish Guards, four; and the Welsh Guards, five.

Bradford spinning, English process of spinning wool into worsted yarn. Before the wool is combed, oil is applied so that the yarn will be smooth.

British warm, Double breasted outercoat of military origin, in knee or above-the-knee length, with shaped body lines and a flare toward the bottom and often with epaulets. It is usually of fleece or melton cloth.

Broadcloth, Closely woven fabric with the tip running weftwise, made of lustrus all cotton, polyester and cotton, all polyester, or other fibers. It is used for shirts, undershorts, and sportswear.

C

cambric, Tightly woven cotton material calendered on one side to resemble linen; also a linen fabric with a sheen, used for shirts, underwear, pajamas, handkerchiefs, and other accessories.

camel's hair, Fiber from a camel, ranging in color from natural tan to brown. Used alone or blended with wool, it is made into woven or knitted material for outercoats, suits, sweaters, hose, and sportswear.

cashmere, (kashmir) Fine wool from the undercoat of the long-haired Kashmir goat, which is woven or knitted into soft fabrics that are luxurious to the touch. The fabrics are used for coats, suits, sweaters, and many other articles of apparel.

cavalry twill (tricotine), Sturdy diagonal-cord fabric made of wool, worsted, cotton, rayon, or blends of fibers; used for suits, jackets, slacks, outercoats, and riding apparel.

chambray, Woven cotton, ppluester, or rayon material with a colored warp and white filling; used for shirts, sportswear, and other apparel.

chino cloth, All-cotton twill used in military uniforms; also a blend of polyester and cotton used for slacks and sportswear.

classic, Something of enduring value and interest, as in literature or apparel. In apparel a classic is characterized by simple lines or design maintained year after year.

cord, Fabric with a raised rib effect, produced by twisting two or more yarns together.

corduroy, Plain or twill weave fabric of cotton, rayon, polyester, or blends with a cut-pile surface of wide or narrow wales; used for sportswear, jackets, slacks, overcoats, and boy's apparel.

D

denim, Sturdy twill-weave fabric, in cotton or a blend of fibers, with a solid colored warp and a white filling. It may be blue, brown, red or another color with white. The surface is smooth or brushed to achieve a suedelike finish. Denim was first made about 200 years ago in Nimes, France and its name is a corruption of "de Nimes", of Nimes.

E

end-to-end, (end-and-end) Term applied to a weave of alternating white and colored warp yarns that form a miniscule check effect; used in chambray, broadcloth, and oxfords for shirts, pajamas, underwear, and sportswear.

F

Fair Isle sweater, Sweater of allover colorful design, originally hand-knitted on Fair Isle, off the coast of Scotland. Crofters on the island knitted scarfs, socks, and sweaters in multicolor allover and cross patterns.

fedora, Men's soft felt hat with a center crease and a rolled brim. It takes its name from the drama *Fedora* (1882), by Victorien Sardou.

four-in-hand, Neckwear knot, tied by wrapping the spron, or wider end, of a tie around the other end, drawing it under and then through the loop formed, and tightening and sliding it into place. The name is derived indirectly from the four-in-hand coach. The driver of a coach drawn by four horses, in two teams in tandem, held by lines of all four horses in one hand. Such a driver wore a slipknot tie, which became known as the four-in-hand.

G

gabardine, Steep twill fabric of wool, polyester, rayon, cotton, or blends of fibers, closely woven of single or two-ply yarn. It is made in solid or irridescent colors for suits, jackets, slacks, outercoats, and sportswear.

gingham, Plain-weave cotton material in checked or striped patterns or plain colors. Blends of cotton and polyester or other fibers may also be used. The word is derived from the Malayan *genggang,* which became the French *guingan.*

glenurguhart, (glen plaid) Scottish tartan of predominantly gray, blue, brown, or greenish casts with multiple colors, in which a group of stripes run vertically and horizontally to form a boxlike pattern plus an overplaid. Made of various fabrics, including wool, worsted, cotton, polyester, linen, silk and blends, it is used for apparel and accessories.

H

hard finish, Finish of worsted, woolen, or cotton fabric the surface of which is without nap.

Harris Tweed, Trademark of woolen material spun, dyed and woven by hand by the crofters of Harris and Lewis and other islands of the Outer Hebrides.

herringbone, Ribbed twill fabric in which equal numbers of threads slant right and left to form a pattern similar to that of a fish skeleton; also a chevron design for clothing and accessories.

I

Ivy League, Term applied to a suit in which the jacket has natural-width shoulders, is straight-hanging, and has a center bent and the trousers are made without pleats at the waistband and are straight-hanging. The name is registered by Botany Industries.

J

jean, Twill fabric of cotton or blended fibers for all types of work clothing. Pants made of this fabric are called jeans. The name is derived from "jene fustian," as the English called a coarse fabric first made in Genoa.

K

khaki, Neutral color the name of which is derived from a Hindi word meaning "dust"; also the term applied to military uniforms or sportswear made in twill or other fabrics of this color.

L

lisle, Fine quality of tightly twisted long-staple cotton yarn that is passed near a gas flame to remove fuzz and give it a sleek surface; used mainly for men's socks and underwear. It is so called because it was first made in Lisle (now Lille), France.

M

madras, Plain-weave cotton or blended material in stripes or checks; used for shirts, underwear, and sportswear. It is named for Madras, an early source of textiles.

mercerized cotton, Smooth, lustrous fabric resulting from the treatment of cotton yarn or fabric under tension with a solution of caustic soda; named after John Mercer, an English calico printer, who originated the process in 1844. Mercerizing strengthens yarns, adds to absorptive qualities and improves dye penetration. The fabric is used for underwear, pajamas, shirts and sportswear.

mohair. Sleek, lustrous material made of angora goat fibers; used for suits, coats, evening clothes, and linings.

N

nap. Fuzzy fibers on the surface of a material such as flannel or doeskin.

O

oxford. (1) Low shoe with two or more sets of eyelets for laces, made in bal, blucher, and fillie styles; (2) a very dark shade of gray for fabrics; (3) a plain or basket-weave shirting of cotton or cotton and polyester, used also for summer clothing and sportswear.

P

paisley. Intricate allover pattern, woven or printed, resembling the patterns of woolen shawls made in Paisley, Scotland. These in turn were adaptations of cashmere shawls originally made of Kashmir. Paisley patterns are used in neckwear, mufflers, other accessories, sportswear and linings.

pajamas. Suit consisting of a button-front or pullover top and trousers with a drawstring or an elastic waistband, made of cotton, cotton and polyester, silk, or other fabrics; used primarily for sleepwear but also for lounging and beachwear. The word is of Hindi origin, and the garment was brought back from India by the British.

percale. Plain-weave, medium-weight cotton or cotton-and-polyester fabric, made in a solid color or a print for shirts, sportswear, and pajamas.

R

regimental stripes. Colors identified in England with various regiments and used in ties worn by their officers in civilian dress. Not only are authentic regimental stripes worn, but similar colors and arrangements are used in neckwear in England and the United States.

S

sack suit. Business suit of worsted, flannel, cheviot, tweed, or other fabrics with a loose-fitting single or double breasted jacket.

saxony. Coating fabric made originally from the wool of merino sheep grown in Saxony; also a lighter-weight fabric with a slightly napped surface similar to flannel, used for suits, jackets and slacks.

serge. Smooth-surfaced material in a twill weave with the diagonal rib on both sides. Originally an all-worsted fabric, it is now woven as well in polyester, cotton, rayon, and other fibers or blends; used for suits, slacks and sportswear.

sharkskin. Smooth finished twill-weave material in two tones of yarn, made in worsted for suits and coats and in polyester, rayon, or silk for neckwear and sportswear.

stain removal. Stains should be removed from garments as early as possible. Plain cold water or carbonated water, if applied early, can minimize a stain, and a spot remover can clean most soilage. Dry cleaning is the final answer.

synthetic. Term applied to fibers such as nylon, acrylic, and polyester created by scientists from nonfibrous materials to resemble natural fibers. It does not refer to acetate, rayon, or other cellulosic products and therefore are known as man-made. However, the two terms are used interchangeably in the apparel field.

T

tick (as in tick-weave), A small spot or mark; especially one used to direct attention to something.

trench coat, Double-breasted outercoat patterned after the gabardine coat worn in the trenches by British army officers in World War I. The original had a gun flap, a removable processed lining, an all-around belt, and brass trimming. Most of these details are present in the authentic adaptation for civilians.

trousers (pants), Garment covering the lower torso and the two legs separately. Among the early uses of trousers was the covering of silk breeches while riding, much as cowboys employ chaps. The Duke of Wellington exerted some influence in the adoption of trousers by wearing them on ceremonial occasions. After the war of 1812 trousers were widely worn in the United States instead of silk breeches and stockings, which seemed too British.

tweed, Rough textured woolen fabric appearing in many different patterns in plain and twill weaves; used for sportswear and other apparel. First woven by crofters near the Tweed River in Scotland, it derives its name from *tweel* or *tweed,* the Scotish word for "twill."

U

ulster, Double-breasted long overcoat with a big convertible collar, wide lapels, and a half or all-around belt; originally worn in Ireland.

V

viyella, Registered name of a blend of wool and cotton in woven or knitted fabrics.

W

whipcord, Twill-weave material made of highly twisted worsted yarn; used for suits, topcoats, and sportswear. When used for military uniforms, it is known as elastigue.

Windsor, Duke of, Member of British royal family, who as Prince of Wales, King Edward VIII, and Duke of Windsor exerted a fashion influence from the 1920s to the 1940s. He was credited with popularizing the tab collar, Grenadier Guards tie, snap-brim hat, Windsor knot tie, brown buckskin shoes, and Fair Isle sweaters.

worsted, Yarn spun from combed long-staple wool fibers; also the closely woven, smooth-surfaced fabric made from this yarn. The name is derived from the village of Worsted (now Worstead), in Norfolk, England, where the fabric was first woven.

*ESQUIRE'S ENCYCLOPEDIA OF 20TH CENTURY MEN'S FASHIONS by O. E. Shoeffler & William Gale, used with permission from McGraw Hill Book Company, © 1973

PART III:

LIFESTYLE SUCCESS

*"Be it ever so humble,
there's no place like home . . ."*
—John Howard Payne

That's the refrain we'll all be singing in the 1980s, according to the predictions of Dr. Lael Mardion of the Foundation for Future Research. In a report before a meeting of the Western Association of University Professors, at Pepperdine College in the spring of 1979, Dr. Mardion said that we are all spending more time in our homes than we did in the 1960s and early '70s. He claimed that in the 1980s, "We will all spend at least fifteen hours a week more in our houses or apartments than we've done previously." Dr. Mardion cites as reasons the energy shortage ("We'll undoubtedly have energy, but it will cost us a lot more and we'll become energy misers . . . ") and inflation, as well as such new products as Home Entertainment Centers, where king-size screens will be used to project new movies that will be either bought like record albums (and will look just like them, too) or rented. "Entertainment will be centered around the home. It is all a matter of economics."

Now we all agree that the *way* one lives at home is often an accepted mirror of one's achievement. With time, we manage to collect items — art, furniture, books, souvenirs of journeys — and synthesize them into a home which portrays to even the most casual visitor the kind of person you are. But if you're more or less at the beginning of your career, you have to use a little ingenuity to project a lifestyle that immediately says: This man is on his way. He's someone to watch.

Again, you have to follow the same rules:

Projecting a successful lifestyle is possible *only if you are beginning to believe that you are successful*. It is a matter of attitudes, and those attitudes will translate themselves into success symbols, without your having to try too hard.

There is no set way to live; there are as many choices of successful lifestyles as there are successful people. But there are some similarities in the taste and outside activities of successful men which we will try to explore.

But first, let us explore *ourselves* once more, with another section of Gail North's success inventory. This one is keyed to how you think of yourself in regard to the way you look and live.

LIFESTYLE QUIZ

Taking a good, solid assessment of your own mirror image is a tough task, especially if early in life someone sold you an image that you never relinquished. What you wear, how you comb your hair, your weight, your personal accountrements all may fit the original image you had in mind — but, do they fit your image of success?

Take a look in the mirror. Be a harsh critic. Assess yourself each morning as if someone else was commenting on your image and perhaps even being a bit snotty. Keep track of the adjustments you'd like to make.

1. What image do you want to present? Is it clear in your mind?

2. What image do you actually see? Is it a bit askew? What parts?

3. Do you stand tall? Do you slump?

4. What about your weight?
   a. Do you habitually pull in your stomach to hide the growing bulge?
   b. Do your pockets lay flat or do they pull at the sides?
   c. Does your jacket or vest button easily?
   d. How many holes are left on your belt?

5. How about facial hair?
   a. Are you wearing a beard? Is it appropriate?
   b. Have you grown a moustache?

6. When you get dressed, are your clothes ready for you?
   a. Are your pants pressed?
   b. Are your ties clean?
   c. Have you had the heels and soles of your shoes fixed?
   d. Are they shined?
   e. Any missing buttons? Frayed collars? Shiny pant seats?
   f. Are your socks matched? Any holes in the heels?

7. Does your wardrobe lend itself to many occasions?
   a. Could you run out for a last-minute invitation to a weekend at the beach or mountains?
   b. Attend a black-tie affair?
   c. Easily join dinner with three top executives in your field?
   d. Meet an important client for lunch?

8. Do you panic when you receive last-minute invitations?
   a. What do you feel you need to 'race out and buy'?
   b. What do you wear that you feel you 'can get by' with?

9. How about accessories?
   a. Sunglasses?
   b. Wristwatch?
   c. Umbrella?
   d. Hats?
   e. Wallet?
   f. Attache Case?
   g. Are your accessories in good shape? Are they appropriate to your position?

10. When was the last time you did a complete inventory of your wardrobe?

11. If you don't know what to wear, do you know how to find out? Whom to ask?

12. Do you spot fashion trends? Do you defer to them or shape your own?

13. What clothes do you feel most comfortable wearing?

14. Can you define your own personal power outfit?
    a. Power suit?
    b. Power shoes?

15. Are you superstitious about your clothes? Do you feel a certain 'old' tie will secure a successful meeting?

16. Are you willing to sacrifice a flashy, racy look for the more conservative image?

17. Do your clothes fit you well? Do you have them let out and taken in?

18. Have your clothes ever triggered insecurity about yourself in the middle of an important occasion?

19. Is your haircut becoming to the contours of your face and body?
    a. Are you willing to cut it short?
    b. Are you willing to change the style?

20. Do you keep you nails trimmed and clean?

21. How do you feel about 'dressing the part'?

22. With your personal appearance in check, are you aware of the freedom to pursue success? What about your home?

23. Do you feel the way your apartment looks projects your personality?

24. Do you always apologize for the way it looks?

25. Do you have things in your home because you care about them, or do you worry what others will think of them?

26. Are you always looking for new things to buy for your home?

27. Do you pay any attention at all to decor?

28. Do you feel you could throw a last minute dinner party in your home and know your guests would be comfortable there?

29. Is your place generally clean and neat?

30. Do you practice the same kind of hygiene with your home as you do with your wardrobe?

31. Do you worry your place will look too masculine, or too feminine, if you have it decorated professionally?

32. How about appliances? Do you have them all?

33. Do you use them?

34. Are you as at home and as good a host there as you are in your office?

"The way you package yourself and the way you live is what's written on your membership card to the success country club . . ." **INTERVIEW**

RAY POELVOORDE

Ray Poelvoorde is president of Lippincott & Margulies, one of the world's most interesting companies. Although it works on many levels, its objective usually is to design a new corporate identity program for companies like Eastern Airlines, N.Y. Life, RCA and Uniroyal. One out of every ten Fortune 500 companies is a client of, or has been a client of, Lippincott & Margulies.

"I started out as a practicing architect," says Poelvoorde. "My interest grew in the control of space; the control of environment. Although I'm not sure where my influences come from, on a conscious level I have an extreme desire to change the environment." Poelvoorde attended Princeton, the University of Florida, and Cranbrook Institute in Bloomfield Hills, Michigan. Poelvoorde works in a stark, white office, almost without accoutrement. He sits behind a simple, functional desk. There is nothing on the walls. "I have to sell," he explains. "I always focus on new business. When someone comes in this office, it is very important that I become the center of interest. The paintings, the bookcases, the posters, the bulletin board—nothing should distract a client from listening to me."

What do you think personifies a very successful lifestyle?
"We are all different. It depends on how you present yourself. You have to represent your own character. I think you could safely say that anyone who cares about himself is packaging himself. It means being your own guru. Some people buy Colonial design houses and that's absolutely right for them. Others would be wrong in such a house; the visitors would sense that it is wrong, and that the house was bought perhaps because Colonial is very acceptable in that neighborhood among a certain set of people. But most of us aren't fooled for long. The man who buys a Colonial house and doesn't fit in there does not really have any image of himself. He is obviously not in touch with his feelings."

You feel it is important to be in touch with your feelings?
"I think it is extremely important. Nobody can be truly successful without it. I've dealt with my feelings in depth."

You mention 'strengths' quite often.
"It's another word for knowing yourself; what shall we call them? Limitations? People so often run on other people's programs. The real membership of life is to find that program where you fit, your program, and then there's no stopping you. You need to know those strengths so you can know how to live, where to work. Go to a psychological testing consultant service if you have trouble figuring them out yourself. There are many people around who can help you."

What do you say to young men who come to you for help in becoming successful?
"I tell them to go small at first. I use medicine as a metaphor. Don't start out as a neurologist. Become a general practitioner. Learn every facet. And above all, set goals. I admire people who set goals. Have a progress chart in your mind—or on the wall, if you aren't that abstract. And then chart your interests, energies and ambitions. Another thing: *be an excellent listener.* It's a way to learn a great deal.
"I'm a kind of workaholic. It doesn't hurt. It certainly will get you ahead. Back to goals—I don't think you should set monetary goals. If you set a goal for a certain place in an organization, the money will come. Do the work. The money will come. Doing work means you have to be committed. You'd be surprised what you can do if you're committed.
"When I first came to work in New York, I actually lived in Birmingham, Michigan. For a variety of personal reasons, it was the best place for me to live at the time. So for ten years I commuted—every Friday afternoon—to Bloomfield Hills and I was in my office in New York on Monday morning. People would say to me that I was out of my mind. But it worked for me because it was a necessity for my particular lifestyle at the moment; and I was committed to the job, so I worked my schedule around it."

If you wanted to live in Birmingham, wouldn't it have been better and easier to get a job, say, in Detroit?"

"The job I wanted was in New York. I can honestly say I wouldn't have progressed as well as I have, if I had settled for a job I didn't want in Detroit. You program yourself to your needs. It takes an enormous commitment, but without the commitment you won't reach your goal."

What do you do to keep in shape?

"I do about an hour of exercises every day. But what I recommend for loosening up and feeling good is dance. There is absolutely nothing better for people than to dance. Why waste time sitting in a cocktail lounge? When you dance you perform, you use a number of muscles, every part of the body, and your mind is involved. It makes you loose. Just take a look at the tense people you know, the uptight men. How much better they would perform if they could loosen up. Being loose is all part of the package. It helps your popularity, too."

Is being popular important?

"It is extremely important to be more or less liked by the people you work with. Part of creating an image for yourself is to be liked. It's much easier to do business with someone who likes you and respects you. Being liked is a very serious approach to business. When you are working toward a goal, toward being a success, you always have to be on stage. It means that you are a kind of actor; you wear some kind of costume. Where you work, and to a lesser extent where you live, is a set. It should give you pleasure. If you derive satisfaction from your office and your apartment, visitors will sense this satisfaction and will pick up on it. Again, *it's a matter of being in touch with yourself. Your feelings.* I can't emplasize that too strongly."

"Real estate is a tricky business with different types of practitioners ... some more honest than others ..." **INTERVIEW:**

IRA WEISSMAN

It used to be that neighborhoods were very well defined; you knew immediately which were "okay", which were marginal, and which were absolute "no no's". One of the authors of this book once worked for a major corporation in a medium-size city. On a city map you could point out where top management lived, where middle-management lived and where the lower level of workers lived.

"It doesn't work that way anymore," says Ira Weissman, president of his own building and construction firm. Weissman has been involved with some aspect of the real estate business "ever since I started working." A civil engineer, Weissman has built every kind of structure except giant high rises, and "I've rented apartments in those." He has been an executive for Levitt, builder of suburban tracts, and has built homes in Florida; Rochester, N.Y.; and Puerto Rico. Weissman, once again an extremely successful man, knows what it is to be at the bottom. "There are times in my career when I have been penniless, and have worked as a paint-stripper. It's better to be at the top. You can still get there. And I'm personally excited about real estate."

127

What sort of neighborhood should a young man look for?

"That's up to the young man. If someone starting out goes to an acknowledged status neighborhood, it's going to be very expensive. If there is anything as sure as death and taxes, it's that rents in the 1980s will be higher than they were in the 1970s. And if the young man isn't the son of rich parents who are willing to help him, anyone who comes to visit him in a status neighborhood won't really be impressed that someone with a limited income is living in a fancy apartment way out of his range. In fact, they might think him a fool, and anybody who's thought of as a fool isn't going to go up that ladder very fast."

What, then, do you suggest?

"Take several weeks to educate yourself when you are looking. Don't think it a waste of time. But if you want to learn about anything, and this includes looking for the right apartment or learning about office management or building cabinets, *you look and look hard*. Just look at a lot of stuff. Information. Apartments. See what is available. You'll soon see where the best investment dollar is; where you can get the most for the money you have to spend."

How much of your salary should you put in rent?

"It used to be twenty-five percent of the gross income. But that's changing. Lots of people are spending more, because they have to. That won't change in the next few years, anyway. And since you are not going to get exactly what you want, try to look at it as an investment in your own future. But for God's sake, look around.

"Don't take what some agent tells you is good. Use your own common sense. Is it near your job? Is the neightborhood relatively safe? Is it convenient to transportation? All these things count. A great, huge apartment in a section of town a long way from your job isn't going to help you if it takes two buses to get you to work, and you have to leave at 7:00 a.m. to get to a 9:30 job. It would be better to have a smaller, more accessible place. Many young men like to live in places where there are people like themselves, but this isn't always necessary. It's what you do with the place you have that counts, anyway. Especially in bigger cities, and I think most big jobs are in big cities. Right? One other thing: Listen."

Listen?

"Real estate is a tricky business with different types of practitioners, some more honest than others. If you keep you mouth shut, and let them do most of the talking, you will learn much about the situation as far as getting apartments is concerned. You'll be able to read between the lines. What I mean is, be as silent as possible. 'What's available?' is a far better approach than, 'I want a six-room apartment with air conditioning.' You're going to have to settle, anyway. So you'd better get the best settling you can."

What do you mean, 'settle'?

"In today's apartment market you almost never get your money's worth. Maybe you can get a great place in West Kokomo, way out by the turnpike. But most apartments in today's market are less than adequate. We are going to have to live within limits, you know. It's up to you to make gold out of straw. The 1980s are going to be chaotic. I don't think we'll see as much moving around from apartment to apartment as we've seen in the past. There is a faction among buyers — that is, people looking to rent — who feel it's worth 'investing' in an apartment. If a guy really has faith in his future, he just might get a bigger apartment than he can afford at the moment; not extravagant, mind you but just a modicum bigger. One that he can grow into as his salary increases. It's taking a chance, of course, but successful operators take chances. It might be better to have an apartment you can expand into, since the prices are going to rise. And it should be one that you plan to live in for a while. Don't really worry about the neighborhood. If people like yourself are moving into it, it's moving up — just like you are."

"People aren't easily impressed as you think. I believe they'll think better of someone who is just starting out who lives in an unpretentious place than someone who is obviously living beyond his means. If a place projects honesty, it's pretty impressive to anybody. Nobody expects somebody 28 years old to have Limoges china or fancy silver. If he does he's either an heir, which puts him out of most classes, anyhow, or a crook, and we don't want to know him, or a spendthrift, and you can bet your bottom dollar you won't know him long after the process servers come to let him know the furniture is about to be taken away . . ."

— Lucius Beebe
"The New Class."

THE STATUS APARTMENT

Deciding Where To Live

Here is a super quickie quiz:

I am going to use my apartment for business (entertaining, cocktail parties, client meetings.)

Yes( ) No( )

If you say "*no*" and mean it, then you can live anywhere, anyplace that suits the inner you. However, if your place of living is in any way connected with your career, you have less of a choice. If your boss is coming for dinner or if your associates are coming over for a drink before an evening meeting, then you should know that where you live reflects your professional personality much the same way your clothes do.

In one of our instant experiment surveys, we visited the apartments of six young executives. All are in their thirties, and in these particular cases all the men are single (two are divorced). All the men are extremely successful; none *runs* a company, but the odds are that at least half of them will occupy leaders' chairs within the next five to ten years.

Of the six, two lived in large one-room "studio" apartments. Three had one-bedroom flats, and one had an elegant affair — a bit out of his reach, but as he said, "I work harder, knowing I have to pay the rent for this."

Every apartment was decorated differently. One was a kind of hodge-podge. Another was what is now called "hi-tech," (furniture made for institutions — like hospital carts that now serve as tables). Most of them were, in a sense, *conventional*; but they had the aura of IMPORTANCE. The apartments exuded success. They were all immaculate, yet they had a lived-in feeling; you knew the books were there to be read, the furniture to be used. One particularly interesting sidenote: All six featured a kind of monochromatic color scheme — the walls were all off-white, the furniture was of matching, solid colors.

In her excellent book, *"Good Taste, How To Have It, How To Buy It"*, (David McKay, $9.95), Elaine Cannel advises one to choose furnishings with great care. "Be sure you love everything in it. If you are at a point where you realize that the room just happened and you don't like it, start weeding out the bad. You probably know very specifically what you don't like. Do something about it. Don't say 'I'll do it next month or next year.' Your house should be a comfort and a haven. It should make you happy. Don't live your life with things you don't like."

Don't be afraid to hire an interior decorator. Most of the time, you don't have to pay them — they make their commission from the furniture they help you buy. And don't feel guilty about it. The reason the interior decoration business is so successful is that most of us welcome help in the same way that we need a lawyer to draw up contracts and a travel agent to book hotels and planes. You are probably some kind of expert yourself, and we live in a world in which expertise should be utilized. An interior decorator, when he or she becomes aware of your budget, will be able to take you to places you'd never find yourself; and a good decorator will help you to pick things *you* like.

If you are going to entertain a lot, spend the most money on your living room. The bedroom is very personal, and most guests never see their host's bedroom, anyway. A word more about decorators. Look at pictures of his (or her) work; see whether or not it suits your taste — i.e., masculine, distinguished, and *conservative*.

There are ways to give a distinguished room warmth and originality: with the art on your walls; the things you collect on your travels; your books. Don't let the place look trashy or trendy. A trendy apartment gives off the feeling that its occupants have no stability, that they are about as tenacious as a leaf in the wind. Remember, with today's rents and inflation, most of us stay in an apartment or house much longer than our parents might have; moving is not a pleasant experience. So in choosing things you have to live with, make sure you *can* live with them for a long time, and consider that they ought not to be offensive to your guests.

Roger Milkowski, now an attorney in Buffalo, New York, but for many years an executive with Epwroth-Carlsen, a leading midwestern executive research firm, tells the story of a "perfect young executive."

"His resumé was really something," Milkowski recalls. "Nobody could fit the needs of this client better. The client came to town one day, read the resumé and decided he'd like to see the kid. Wouldn't you know, the boy had a cold. It was snowing. This doesn't happen very often, but I suggested the client got to the kid's apartment, which was within walking distance, in a good neighborhood. I didn't want to lose the commission. I thought it was in the bag. This boy was sharp. Ivy league. Good looking. So the client went to his apartment which turned out to be a hippie-like thing with pillows on the floor, a water bed in the middle of the room, nude women's photos on the walls. Naturally, the kid didn't get the job. The client was put off by the apartment. The prospective employee had the credentials and bearing, but the apartment was a bummer. When I talked to the boy later, I learned that he'd lived in that apartment in college with two other fellows, and in six years hadn't redecorated it. He had planned to, but there was always something else to do with his money. He lost out on a spectacular position in a growing company in his field. Just because he didn't think that his pad did matter."

The Success Uniform ...

There is a "success uniform" and yes, it is very conservative. The costume party of the 60s is long gone, and the sartorial ambivalence of the 70s has returned to the closet. The "success uniform" has always been worn by an overwhelming majority of the top ranking officers in the business "army." The "success uniform" makes you look both good and important.

Blue and gray are the most powerful business colors. Whether the suit has two or three buttons depends on your physical stature. Forget what the fashion magazines tell you: the lapels should be moderate; neither too wide or too narrow. A single vent is less flashy than the double vent. The vest is a strong symbol of authority. Never wear brown or green suits to the office.

Ties for summer wear can be lighter and plaid ties are not only acceptable, but look good. Gordon's noted tie authority, Moise Bloch says ties in summer "should convey the notion of being cool and efficient."

Your personal style is communicated by your tie. All of these (from Gordon of New Orleans) are both fashionable and absolutely correct, and combine good taste, tradition, and excellent quality. *Never* wear ties with "big pictures" or flashy colors, or patterns which make your eyes dizzy.

The tie is your symbol of both authority and respectability. Many psychologists believe that the tie with very small polka dots or a small repeated pattern (especially in subdued shades) connotes "importance and confidence." There are acceptable substitutes: rep stripes; solid colors; thin stripes; club ties. Never wear a bow-tie to the office. Wear white shirts to the office, because white shirts *work*! They command respect. The collar style is up to you, but it shouldn't be any kind of extreme. Button cuffs are preferable.

Although cuffed trousers are making a fashion comeback, this is an area of choice. Our personal survey resulted in almost 50% of executives polled preferring cuffs; 50% did not. It is not the controversy of the ages. More important are the style and color of shoes you wear. *Only* black shoes are correct with a blue suit. You *can* wear brown shoes with gray, but our investigation proves that black shoes convey a sense of responsibility and seriousness. Traditional, plain, lace-up shoes are more businesslike. If you do wear slip-ons, no buckles or tassles, please!

Suits by Cricketeer
Shoes courtesy Paul Stuart, Inc.
Shirts and ties by Gordon of New Orleans

Is Great . . . Because It Works . . .

Make no mistake, the road to success is highly competitive, so don't jeopardize your career by dressing for failure. "Successful dress," says expert John J. Molloy, "cannot put a boob in the board room, but incorrect dress can definitely keep an intelligent, able man out." The dark suit (left) is always correct, even at non-business functions. If you are at a cocktail party and every man is wearing a sports jacket but you are wearing a suit, you are not out of place. However, if everybody is wearing a suit and you are wearing a sports jacket, you will stand out like the proverbial sore thumb. *Think "suit" and you'll always be okay.*

Of one hundred executives asked if they would hold up the promotion of a man who didn't wear proper suits in the office, seventy-two said yes. Success is an *attitude*; one that says I am a contender, I am going to do my damndest to win. The achiever *knows* that suits are synonymous with position and power. And, no suit has more authority than the classic gray (right), whether flannel or worsted.

With black shoes wear dark blue, dark gray or black hose. Anklets which reveal bare leg are absolutely forbidden. Should you wear garters to hold socks up? Droopy socks are a particular turn-off to the viewer, so make your choice.

There is one exception to the rule that it is generally inappropriate to wear a sports jacket to the office. The traditional blue blazer (left) is immediately recognizable as an "aristocratic" garment; as elegant as one can get in sports clothing. With gray slacks and a white shirt, it is formal enough for an ordinary work day. (Don't wear it at a meeting where your ideas have to count.) The two or three-button blue blazer must be part of your wardrobe; if you own only one sports jacket, this is the one. With white or khaki pants it's the perfect summer informal coat. Especially with the blazer, brown shoes (below) may be worn with gray slacks, but again, black shoes will add a touch of respectability to the outfit.

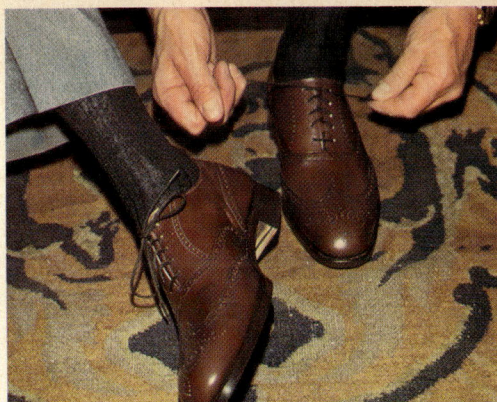

James Bond (007) wears a Burberry trench coat for the same reason we recommend it as a kind of symbol of success. What other outercoat is not only correct, traditional, conservative, but also fairly radiates with the spirit of adventure at the same time? It is versatile: the removable wool lining, keeps you warm in the winter. It is water-repellent. The Burberry is as proper over a tuxedo as it is over a sweater and corduroys. It's moderately expensive but it is an excellent investment because it lasts, and fits into the *zeitgeist* of any era. There are several excellent substitutes for the Burberry that look *almost* the same. We all can't own Rolls Royces. We *can* own the Rolls Royce of trench coats. It is a dashing classic, as is the dark brown kidskin Mark Cross attaché case with solid brass fittings.

In the summer we adjust our uniform to conform to the climate. Authority is still a keyword, despite the heat. The idea is to look cool, crisp and business-like. With or without the vest, the glen-plaid summer suit has received "business uniform" status. The collar pin holds a no-wilt look. Remember, one of the buzzwords of the 1980s will be "serious." If you are *serious*, you will look *serious*, and you will be taken *seriously*.

Although the time-honored seersucker or cord suit still holds first place in the hearts of businessmen for traditional summer dress, we recommend the British tan dacron/worsted tropical suit as the garment with the most authority for hot weather. It is always correct, looks good with an open-collared knit shirt at garden parties, and the suit holds its crease much more than seersucker. Don't ever wear one of those see-through white shirts so popular with Europeans. It just doesn't do anything for you or your image this side of the Atlantic.

In the summer, and in some warmer sections of the country, the slip-on shoe has become acceptable. It certainly is in wide use. But again we stress, no buckles, no metal at all. It only diminishes the distinction leather has. With shoes, as in every area of success dressing, it is worthwhile to pay attention to the advice of Thomas McWhirter. "Nothing is more fashionable than good taste; nothing is more stylish than quality."

BEN LLOYD supervises the creation of the dynamic rooms which appear each month in *Apartment Life* Magazine.

A Success Apartment Works, Too ... But It's Less Uniform ...

A man has much more latitude in the way his living quarters look than he does in wearing the right clothes to conduct business. Everybody expects an apartment to be personal; a room too "uniform" would be suspect — but like the business suit, a man's apartment should exude the qualities of taste, comfort, and correct use of space. "An apartment tells me so much about a person," Ben Lloyd says. "It reflects his habits, taste. There is no one correct way to decorate an apartment. But there are ways to make a visitor say 'this apartment belongs to a somebody.' The successful man, I think, knows what he wants his rooms to do. Like any other area of his life, the apartment is the result of planning. If a man isn't dedicated to an idea, the room will reflect that ambivalence."

"The living room is the main room in your life. It should be a classic room, one which functions in an 1980s way. Like a zipper, rather than Victorian buttons. There are many kinds of good taste and a good way to exhibit your personal good taste is to decorate with a leaning toward your special interests. For example, the terrific light fixtures in this room are photographic reflectors used over a clamp-on bulb holder. The gray and silvery fabric gives a unique look to the lighting and is probably a sign of the photo hobbyist. The colors are neutral; good colors for a man. He isn't overshadowed by a barrage of color, and neutral colors blend so well. The idea of a successful apartment is just like the personality of a successful man: to make every facet of it do something for you and work hard, and do double duty, like the sturdy chairs which can double at the dinner table. If you examine this room you can see a mixture of canvas, chrome and pine, but they all work. And that's the secret, blending things that work together."

...And Should Reflect Your Personality...

"Space being what it is these days, many of us use bedrooms as work spaces. You must make it reflect you and not a decorator. In this room, a closet was removed to make room for a settee and the items in the room are all very 1980s. Stuff bought in the 'livingstores' that are popping up all over. The architect's lamp, for example, is what we at *Apartment Life* call one of the "new classics." More than a product, it is an emblem of successful living. The chair is a new, affordable version of Marcel Breuer's classic chrome and cane chair..."

"Another working bedroom with a sense of both comfort and efficiency; a combination that fairly announces 'success.' The things in this room aren't especially expensive, but they have quality and design; very much the kind of room which synthesizes the 1980s with the past. The crane lamp, for example, echoes the old turn-of-the-century apothecary lamp, but it's lightweight molded plastic. The successful bedroom is a retreat, a place to do exercises, or entertain. Remember: don't buy things you don't like. Forget what you think you should have and do want you want to do. People who expect you to conform in the office are usually delighted to discover your originality at home — as long as it is efficient, neat and works. Like a salad. All the ingredients keep their own identity. The tomato remains a tomato. But they all work together. Toss ice cream in a vegetable salad, and it doesn't work. What doesn't work, no matter how much it pleases you, has to go."

"... This is a simple, almost monochromatic apartment with very few pieces. It shows that you don't need many things to create a successful living space. The plants add contrast to the starkness. And polished wood floors are good looking enough to get by without a carpet. The 1980s kitchen is a place to entertain *from*. Your guests will enjoy seeing you cooking. Everybody now understands that less space means more informality."

We polled several young businessmen, asking
them to tell us, in as few words as possible, what
qualities best describe the living quarters of a
successful man. Not one used the word
"expensive." They all agreed that the apartment
should have a "contemporary look," and function
well. "Unity," is what one suggested. "A place
which is cluttered and disoriented makes guests
feel very uncomfortable." Another said to avoid
sterility. "Don't be afraid to make a statement.
Your apartment is *your* corporate headquarters.
If racing cars grab you, have pictures of racing
cars on the wall—but hang them with class,
style. That's the secret. Do it well." We
photographed the rooms of three successful
young men who "do it well." Advertising
executive Jay Schreick, II (top) consulted a
decorator, but the basic ideas were his. The wing
chair in which he's sitting is covered with a piece
of leather he found on a business trip to
Germany. The cut glass goblets he collects not
only add elegance to his apartment; he uses
them at dinner parties. Charles Gifford (center)
keeps a "current projects" drawing board in his
working bedroom. A simple basket, an Indian
bedspread accent a room of otherwise Shaker
simplicity. The ubiquitous architect's lamp, in
this case, is used in its original incarnation.
Gifford is an architect. John Berendt's living
room reflects both his keen, highly-organized
mind and his finely-honed sense of the dramatic.
Mixing both contemporary (abstract painting)
and traditional (silver serving set) he uses the
natural bright colors of fresh fruit to accent the
distinguished neutrality of the color scene; a
perfect setting for author-editor Berendt to both
successfully work and entertain.

For some more specific suggestions, see the four pages devoted to decorating a status apartment in the color section of this book.

Having a man for a roommate makes life cheaper. But it's like having a kind of male wife. There is a great rule of thumb in choosing a roommate: *Know him and know him well!* Remember, if you snore, it's okay with you. But if *he* snores, it's a colossal pain-in-the-middle-of-the-night. Most experts would advise you to live alone if you can, until you find the woman you want to live with. It may be more expensive, but the apartment will project *your personality*, not a mixed bag.

The trend, the pundits seem to think, is moving toward *group* living: several men sharing one house. This is all well and good and is probably very lively. It's also easier to find someone to go to the movies with. And it's all very nouveau fraternity house. But our advice is, *live alone if you can manage it*. As an executive with a great deal of responsibility, you're often going to be called upon to make strong decisions, where you are going to have to *stand alone*. You might as well get used to making decisions on your own and standing—alone—on your own two feet. The man who stands alone, who believes he is right, earns a lot of respect. That's the kind of role the late John Wayne always played, and you know how most of us felt about John Wayne.

It's the "John Wayne" in us that motivates success.

Advice: *Live alone. Make your own decisions. Manage to do it on your income.* The rising executive needs privacy at night, in order to think. Try to think when roommates are arguing or watching TV. Consider living alone as a success investment. It'll pay off, Duke.

SHOULD YOU HAVE A ROOMMATE?

It's hard. Most of us demand company. It's a fact that single men living alone *smoke* more than men living with someone else. They also pace the floor a lot, and often spend more time in outside social activity (bars, discos) than do people living together.

Almost no one we queried had a panacea for living alone. But the fact remains that executives who spend so much time socializing spend less of their time thinking about the job. People who live alone tend to socialize a lot more than people who live in tandem (men and women).

The answer is *discipline*.

And it takes character to move ahead.

And it is almost impossible.

But you don't have any choice.

So you do your best to *plan* your evenings. Leave very little to chance. If you're busy you're going to have a full calendar, anyway. Make sure it isn't too much disco, not enough work at home. There wasn't one successful executive with whom we talked who didn't take work home at least two nights a week.

Advice: *Plan.* Leave very little to chance. Leave three nights open, if possible, for being alone. To think. To fill out reports. It's important. The higher you get in your career, the more work nights you are likely to have. You had better get used to it. The story of the grasshopper and the ant works, where success is concerned. Ants get ahead. And if you are too lonely, plan to find someone to live with and possibly marry. According to most executives, that's the best solution.

LEARNING TO LIVE ALONE

INTERVIEW

"Most ambitious and talented men want to leave a mark; they have a deep-seated compulsion to do some good things with their lives ..."

JEFFREY F. KRIENDLER

Jeffrey F. Kriendler terms himself a "dedicated airline executive" and is currently System Director, Dining Services for Pan American World Airways. He has been with the company for several years in a number of responsible positions in finance and government relations. Before he accepted his present job, he was director of public relations for the airlines.

Kriendler, who is a member of a family whose restaurant is a New York institution, graduated from Cornell's highly-rated hotel school. He has also been on the school's faculty, teaching a course in tourism. Probably one of the most well-traveled men in the United States, Kriendler flies for both pleasure and business. During the twenty-five weeks previous to this interview, he spent all but five weekends in the air, visiting such exotic places as Hong Kong, Rio de Janeiro, London, Tahiti, Tokyo and Lake Tahoe. "Even when I fly just for my own sake," Kriendler insists, "I'm always checking on the service, the food, the flight itself. Or, if I'm on another carrier, I check out how it compares to Pan Am. It's a full-time job with me, and I'm crazy about it.

"I don't think of myself as ambitious," Kriendler says. "But I'm competitive, which is probably the same thing, and that's necessary to forge ahead in today's world. I probably got my competitiveness from sports. I was a good athlete. I played on the squash team at Cornell, and I like football, baseball and golf, though I don't have as much time these days to participate. So I run to keep in shape. I'd advise any young man who wants a competitive career to keep in shape, no matter how hard it is. The ability to be able to force yourself to do something is vital in any responsible position. I think it's generally called discipline, and a budding executive better develop it, or he isn't going to last.

"Somebody once said there's an A-B-C to defining success — Ability, Breaks and Courage. You need ability, otherwise you'll fall out early in the game. And courage explains itself. One of the facets of courage is having the strength to make decisions which might make you unpopular, but which you know are right. It separates the men from the boys.

"I happen to be a bug on punctuality and I would advise anybody to be on time, all the time. The early bird catches the worm, you know. Get in *before* your boss. It's not as important to stay late at a job as it is to get in *early* and organize your day. You save yourself a lot of agony by being organized.

"It goes without saying that a neat appearance is necessary if you are to conduct business. Dress conservatively, but with some style. It's always amazing to me to meet young men who are otherwise capable, who think they can get somewhere without any awareness of the world around them. Be *au courant*. Take an interest in world events; at least, listen to the radio on your way to work. I can't think of one top executive I know who isn't completely up on international affairs; who doesn't know what's going on.

"Social graces are important and can be mastered. Know about good food and wines. If you are going to live among executives, you will be respected if you have knowledge about food and wine. You will also notice how relaxed top executives are both at work and at play. It's important not to be uptight all the time. Find some kind of activity to loosen up. Personally, I happen to like disco dancing, not because it's the current 'in' thing, though that's fun, too, but wanting to dance shows you are loose, coordinated and not embarrassed.

"Now, I don't smoke, and I think that by now every smoker wants to quit. There is absolutely no pressure on a man to smoke. But I don't drink either, and there is some pressure that way. Don't feel that you *have to drink* just to be sociable. Frankly, no one cares. What you shouldn't do is what so many non-drinkers do, and that's make the drinker feel uncomfortable. Just say, 'club soda,' or whatever, and let it go at that.

"Of course, I'm not talking about heavy drinking when I say the work drink. Successful men are generally moderate in their behavior. Absolutely no one respects a man, especially one in a position of responsibility, who is constantly loaded.

"Let me get back to organization. I want to stress that again. Be organized, or forget it. Write down what you want to remember. Take notes, even on little pieces of paper. Don't trust important things, even little things, to memory. Nobody can remember everything. If possible, try to make your handwriting neat. Your office should be neat. Your files should be well kept. There is a reason we are taught 'neatness counts' in grade school. Because it does. It makes life a lot easier for the executive; neatness is part of organization. It is a kind of visual honesty. And *honesty is a real keyword of success*. Don't be a yes man, for example. Nobody appreciates a yes man. Every manager who is worth his salt wants to know how his subordinates really feel. But you also have to take orders and respect authority.

"Writing is so important. I happen to like to write, and had a lot of opportunity to improve my skills when I was involved in public relations. But writing is a major tool of all managers. If you have trouble, take a course. Every extension division of every university has excellent courses in writing. You'd be surprised how many executives fail because they can't make their views known, simply and clearly on paper. And for God's sake, answer calls. I don't like to deal with people who don't return my phone calls, and nobody else does either. But it's prevalent. And having a good secretary is mandatory. She shouldn't be too sexy, but she should be neat, business-like, and good on the phone. Train her to work for *you*. Tell her what is important for you. She is there to make your job easier.

"Develop good rapport with low echelon people. Don't be sour with them or anyone else. If you sound sour, people will think you are sour. And don't be aloof. Those below you will just love it when you get fired. In fact, they can spur your departure by lack of cooperation. It's so easy getting support from the lower echelons by just being honest, friendly, and interested in what they do. Just follow the good, old, hackneyed golden rule. It works."

Kriendler believes that people will travel less by car in the 1980s, but train and plane travel will increase by leaps and bounds. He offers the following suggestions for the executive traveling in the 1980s.

TRAVEL TIPS FROM ONE OF THE WORLD'S EXPERTS

Jeff Kriendler believes that many people take plane travel for granted—that they don't think about it as a part of business behavior. "It takes planning," he says, "because you have so many unknown factors—weather, mechanical failures. So planning helps expedite your trip even if there are some delays. It makes it much easier." Here are Kreindler's suggestions which he maintains will reduce the rigors of air travel:

Pre-departure

1. Develop a working knowledge of airline terminology (lexicons can be quickly expanded by dating flight attendants.)
2. Learn about different aircraft types (seating configurations, operational capabilities, etc.)
3. Know your rights — carry a CAB listing of consumer protection rights in case of overbooking.
4. Use indestructible luggage . . . Name brands are nice but handlers exert no extra care when they see a Gucci emblem.
5. Be sure to check on visa and shot requirements. More than one business traveller has been turned back at the border for want of visa or cholera inoculation.
6. Do not overpack. Overstuffed or extra suitcases are a burden. Remember, you usually never see the same people on consecutive days during a trip so you can be less self-conscious about carrying a limited wardrobe.
7. Try to carry a pocket airline guide (OAG). This can be very helpful when connections are missed or you cannot get through to airline reservations.
8. Invest in Airline V.I.P. Clubs. Determine what routes you most frequently fly, then select the carrier which best serves those sectors and join their private courtesy club for frequent travellers.
9. Always carry an extra pair of glasses with you in case you break or lose yours. And it is also prudent to carry your prescription for glasses and medications.
10. Be sure to have confirmation of hotels/car rentals etc. in hand before leaving. You can still be turned away, but the chances diminish greatly with written proof of reservation.

Enroute

1. Call to confirm departure time of your flight before leaving for the airport.
2. Never arrive too early before your flight. This can fatigue you and make for an unpleasant trip.
3. Conversely, never show up too late. Airlines must overbook to protect against "no-shows" and the early bird catches the worm and seat.
4. Never drink to excess in flight. This alienates crew members and fellow passengers and is often a sign of latent anxiety.
5. Refrain from overeating. A bloated stomach can preclude good rest.
6. Board as late as possible and try to stretch out over empty seats if you can find any.
7. Try to take a nonstop flight whenever possible. Multi-stops have a great probablity of being delayed.
8. Bring plenty of reading materials. Interesting reading can make even the longest of flights seem short.

9. Try to disembark early and carry on your bag, if it is small enough. Literally hours per week can be wasted in line or at baggage belts.

10. Research good buys at duty free stores. Sometimes you'll pay more for liquor in European airport tax-free stores than you would at the corner liquor store.

Downline

1. Try to exchange money at airport banks. Currency rates abroad are usually more favorable than in the U.S. Never exchange currencies at hotels—you will be bilked.

2. Exercise judgement in what you eat. A queasy stomach can ruin a business or vacation trip.

3. If possible, travel to arrive in the afternoon. Often rooms have not been made up for early arrivals, and late arrivals, can spell over-bookings.

4. Do not make overseas calls from your hotel. They will exact a large surcharge. Go instead to the central Post Office or train station. The inconvenience is worth the savings.

5. Always watch your valuables and check them with the hotel's safety deposit box if one exists. Hotel rooms are security risks.

6. Often one can visit hotels and use the property's facilities without being a registered guest. Say you're considering staying there next time and ask for permission to use the pool, etc.

7. Be cautious about black marketeering in currencies or goods. Punishment can be brutal.

8. On the same track, never deal in drugs. Perhaps the best testimony to this is the film *Midnight Express*.

9. Try not to send laundry out the day before you leave. It frequently gets delayed.

10. Carry a menu translator with you and pocket dictionary. A little homework before the trip, on language, culture and customs, can come in very handy.

MR. CONSUMER, U.S.A.

For a new apartment you will buy things. When you do, remember—you are climbing a ladder. Men who are aiming for the executive suite should act like men who live among executives. Don't buy things just for the sake of buying them, but rather with the future in mind. This doesn't mean of course, that you can't sometimes be frivolous. But instead of buying a junk ashtray, or stealing one from a bar, you'd do better to buy an ashtray that costs a little bit more and that you'll be able to *keep* when you buy a house someday for you and your wife and children. If you buy an "art" ashtray, for example, from a craftsman, its value may increase. More than that, in a "success" apartment, even a tiny one-room affair, something that is obviously tasteful and worthwhile will stand out. It will reflect your discriminating taste.

The things you buy should be in good taste, and you should like them. Never buy anything you don't like, just because someone tells you it's "important" or "worthwhile" or that it is "art". (More on decorating your apartment will be found in the color pages immediately following this section). There are enough good-taste things that you *will* like, and it's just impossible to live for any length of time with things you don't like. Often, it's those little accessories around your apartment that reflect the inner you, and that give you individuality. People are not going to judge you by whether the picture on your wall is the work of an abstract painter or a Currier & Ives sporting print. Instead, they will be influenced by good taste and honesty. A pretentious place means that you are pretentious; if it is too effeminate, then people will assume you to be the same, even though you may regularly have sex with three different women a week.

THE SPORTY YOU

The clothes you wear at home aren't as important to "success" as the clothes you need to conduct business; you have more latitude in selecting the former. A general rule of thumb would be to *wear the kinds of leisure clothes sold in the stores where conservative business suits are featured*. You can't go wrong there. But jeans are okay. And tee-shirts. Again, get to know the prevailing standards of good taste in your section of the country. White patent-leather loafers *in the summer* are absolutely acceptable in Georgia and Texas, but might be frowned upon in Connecticut and eastern Long Island, New York. Even loud colors (at home) may be correct, as long as the cut of the clothing is quite conservative. The classic clothes, of course, are sneakers and jeans or chino pants with a sport shirt cut as nearly as possible like a dress shirt, or a knit shirt of the Izod (alligator) variety.

Suggestion: Be sporty, but never be sloppy. At least when anyone is around; and since a thinking executive is *always* doing business, it might be well to shave on Saturday and Sunday even though you don't feel like it. You never know who will drop over.

It might be somebody you are dealing with professionally, somebody who can help your career. You are always at an advantage in a deal if you look good. Neat. Crisp. It adds up to image, and image is power. It's worth the extra effort.

And if people tell you that top executive so-and-so never shaves on Sunday when he goes boating, and wears old jeans to boot, remember— he's earned that luxury. His image has been formed and is recognized by his peers. You're not there yet, and so you are going to be judged by your actions every day until you do make it.

INTERVIEW
"Set Out To Be The Very Best"

LOUIS MEISEL

Louis Meisel is the 36-year-old director of the Louis Meisel galleries, one of the pioneer showcases for photo-realist paintings in New York. Although only in business for a relatively short period of time, Meisel has prospered. He now exhibits several styles of art and is expanding his exhibit space to about twenty thousand square feet, which he proudly claims will make his gallery one of the largest *private exhibit spaces* in the world. Among the celebrated artists he represents are Mel Ramos, Theodoros Stamos, and Audrey Flack.

Meisel has long been an award winning competitor in speedboat racing. Though often seen on a motorcycle, Meisel's attitude toward achievement is personified by the car he drives—a Ferrari "Dino" 246GTS. It isn't just an automobile you hop into and turn the key. In order to get it to function, the driver has to know the mechanism of the machine, and has to put something of himself into the operation to gain its rewards. "Anybody who has the money," Meisel says, "can buy a Rolls Royce or a Mercedes but you need a special personality and spirit to own and drive a Ferrari."

The genial Meisel doesn't permit his projection of informality to obscure the seriousness of his purpose. He has very pronounced conceptions of success and achievement, and doesn't feel one is worth

136

much without the other. "If you set out to be the very best," he insists, "and you have the drive and the talent, you will not only make money, but chances are you will end up the very best."

"On the other hand, if your only goal is making money, you might succeed, but you will never be the very best. And your life will lack quality because of it, no matter what you can buy.

"Quality is a big, important word. We have to think about what success is. Is it money? Is it fame? Is it happiness? I think we all want a little bit of all of them. But without quality in your work—setting out to be the best—you lose pieces of all the results. These days, you can't make a lot of money without being a little 'famous', especially in your own field.

"Andy Warhol says that everybody is famous once in his life, but that such fame only lasts fifteen minutes. A really success-oriented person will make it last longer than that. Being well known means you've created something special and that means people will have confidence in you. Business life is easier when people trust you.

"*Most successful people I know are aggressive both intellectually and physically. And basically honest.* I've known some men who've made money through cheating but, as I've said, making money alone is not the mark of success. My own basic instincts are to be straight and honest with people, and I've found it works. *You also have to be tough. Tenacious.* I call it 'character.' It means you are able to withstand set-backs. You can't be successful if you run away every time something bad happens.

"And you have to know when to make the right decision. The first really right decision I made was in the choice of a wife. And it was a careful, well-thought-out decision. I'm not denigrating love, not at all. That's a big part of it. But part of my being a success is having a lifelong satisfying mate. And my wife Susan is just that. She's my partner in more than the business and racing. I can give this advice to everybody. *Success without someone to share it with wouldn't be success at all.*

"I also think it's important to let young people know that success brings enormous problems. At some point everybody's hand is in your pocket. You have to develop the strength to know when to say no. When not to let people hit on you. It's the truth that when you achieve success you have to face the jealousy of less successful friends. There are times when I want to say the hell with it all. Toss it all away. But I don't. Only people who can't handle success do that, and then that's a kind of failure. You have to be able to break out of a syndrome. I am an art dealer and a kind of status for me would be to own one of those big purple and black Rothko paintings. There are very few of them up for sale. Most are in museums. I could have bought one for $12,000 in 1967. Now they cost $200,000. If I had $200,000 to spend on a painting, though, I probably wouldn't buy the Rothko, as much as I want it. I could buy twenty masterpieces for $200,000. I could buy gambles for $200,000 and maybe some of them would pay off in twenty years. That's the excitement, that's the thing that keeps you going. Anyone with $200,000 can buy a Rothko. *You learn to stop chasing the other guy's status symbol.*"

CULTURE AND THE MAN CLIMBING THE EXECUTIVE LADDER

"If you want to know a person without ever speaking to him, examine the books in his library; look at his record collection, and examine the pictures on his wall. Of course, if he doesn't have any, that tells you a hell of a lot, too . . ."

— Lucius Beebe
"The New Class."

VERY FEW MEN sitting in board rooms are philistines anymore. Take any executive board; chances are one man will be intensely involved with a civic orchestra; another will be a trustee of the art museum; yet another will be a collector of rare books. U.S. Senator Bill Bradley, who was no slouch as a professional basketball star with the New York Knicks, can frequently be seen at art galleries. He's a collector. Today's successful man is a renaissance man. He can disco to rock-and-roll one moment, then sit down and contemplate a Brandenburg concerto. His eyes will be glued to the TV set on Super Bowl Sunday, but he's spent the morning reading the book review section of the New York Times. A recent study by the American Booksellers Association pointed out that the men who buy the most hard-cover books are management level executives.

What we're trying to say is that if you have a resistance to culture, break it. Open up. Loosen up. There is a reason why Beethoven has lasted all these years; people love to listen to his music. If you think it is sissified to go to art museums, disenfranchise yourself of the idea. Knowledge is never effete. And by learning to look, you learn, you improve your thinking.

Men who are interested in success can never stop improving their thinking. A blade becomes dull when it isn't honed, and minds are the same way. Take a course in art, take a course in classical music. You don't have to become an expert, but you will find that the men at the top executive level often talk about things other than sports and making deals. They are well-rounded men, with myriad interests. They focus on their business, of course, but as many of the successful men we've interviewed have said, *successful minds operate on many levels*. Nobody said it was simple to get there; but taste can be developed.

One of the best ways to improve yourself is to buy fine records and listen to them; buy good books and read them; buy real art, instead of cheap prints. It just might help to set you off from the boys.

Louis Meisel says that art can be two things: decoration, or something that pleases your eye. It can be inexpensive depending on your financial situation at the moment, or it can be costly, if you can afford it. Or it can be

138

an intellectual pursuit.

"Having original art on your walls," Meisel says, "can be a kind of status. It is impressive. People are impressed if you have real paintings. There are artists in every city. Endeavor to know and meet them. It's easy. They are always looking to sell their work and are delighted if you call them. They'll invite you over to see the work in a minute. Or your local gallery dealer will send you to see his or her local artists or sculptors. Start buying what you like. Remember, even acknowledged great art may just not please your eye. Of course, if superstatus is what you are eventually after, you will have to buy big names, and that is expensive. You buy popular names with popular imagery. That goes along with Cadillacs. You can't fake that. Anyway, *find an artist whose work appeals to you. Start collecting him*. Hang three or four original paintings by one artist in your apartment, and you become a collector. Your friends may not see big names, but they will see the personality and taste of the owner: you. If you have a sense of good taste, you will be considered an individual immediately; the very fact that you are investing in one artist will make people think you know something they don't."

If you don't own any books other than your old college texts, a dictionary and a Bible, you should start a library, slowly. *Read two books a month. Make this a habit*. That is twenty-four books a year. In four years, you will have a bookshelf with one hundred books, the titles of which will reflect your taste and personality. This is a better way than buying one hundred books at one time, which can be expensive. And we do mean, read them. Few things are more foolish than having a bookcase filled with volumes that look good, but which have never enriched your mind and your life. You will feel better about yourself if you can refer to them in conversation—perhaps lend one to a friend from time to time—and know you're not being dishonest by merely displaying them for "show."

If any complaint seemed endemic among all the people we talked to, it was that the pressures of business eliminated time from their schedules for reading. Most top executives read extensively in their own field, read books on current events, and tried to read at least "two or three good novels." We asked everybody to share with us the books they felt were indispensable. Here are the results:

EXECUTIVE BOOK LIST

1. Any good dictionary. We recommend the *Webster's New Collegiate*, but there are any number of excellent dictionaries. Anybody who writes memos or proposals or letters cannot do without a dictionary at his side—at home or in the office.
2. *Elements of Style*, by Wilfred Strunk and E.B. White. This venerated book on how to write clearly and concisely is written in a clear and concise manner and is now available in paperback.
3. *Roget's Thesaurus* or any of a half dozen word finders. Helps you look up a synonym when you need one.
4. An *Almanac*. Several companies put out yearly Almanacs: the New York Times; Hammond, others. All of them are good, and come in inexpensive paperback editions. The word almanac, by the way, comes from the Arabic. "Al" means "the" and "manakh" means weather.

5. Some kind of encyclopedia. Even the one-volume variety, such as the *Columbia Desk Encyclopedia* or the new *Random House Encyclopedia* (expensive but worth every cent).
6. A foreign language dictionary in whatever language you are most proficient: Spanish, French, German, etc.
7. *The Pan Am Travel Guide* — indispensable, for the world traveler. Gives everything you need to know about where you travel, customs; weather; what to wear; buy; where to stay, etc.
8. The Bible.
9. A good world *Atlas* (for maps).

ACQUIRING GOOD TASTE

"Tell me what you like, and I'll tell you what you are . . ."
—John Ruskin

Nobody is "born" with good taste. But without it, you will have a harder time making it in the world. Although every successful man isn't necessarily the epitome of what may be considered good taste, it's safe to say that the majority are. The offices and homes of the successful men and women represented in this book reflect a wide variety of different styles; in fact, each pretty much mirrors the personality of the person who lives or works there. But *all* are in good taste.

What we call good taste cannot be acquired, as the late humorist W.S. Gilbert said, like "trousers, ready made." It is learned through experience and experiment — and of course, a desire to improve. Then, too, we tend to change our tastes as we get older, or move a step up the ladder.

Taste, of course, is a terrifying word. Just pick up an issue of any of the home decoration magazines. There's an excellent chance that one of the headlines will exhort you to decorate to express *your own taste*.

If that thought sends shivers up and down your spine, just relax. Most of us don't spend a great deal of time thinking about our taste. But we do take it seriously, as Russell Lynes, former managing editor of Harper's magazine, stated in his best selling book, *The Tastemakers*. The fact is, says Lynes, that we do take taste seriously, "not only as an ornament of life but as one of its almost inescapable problems. Taste is our personal delight, our private dilemma, and our public facade."

Actually, the moment you select something in a store and place it in your home, whatever it is — a print for the wall, a tie, or a piece of furniture — you cannot escape expressing your personal taste. No two people pick all of the same things.

Fortunately, we live in an age of choice. Some of us would walk into a room of French provincial furniture and 19th Century genre paintings and think, "This is in good taste." On the other hand, a room full of Danish modern with a Motherwell drawing on the wall is in equally good taste — though it might not suit your own. Rooms which mix modern, early American and French provincial *can* be in good taste. A suit cut in the European style by Brioni of Rome is in excellent taste, if you have the bearing to go with it; but the same suit might be too rich for the typical American business office. Every man has a different definition of good taste, depending upon what is *au courant* in the circle in which he moves. *Is there a rule of thumb about what good taste is? Some people think it is the taste of the people with whom they hope to associate.*

140

Generally, the so-called "socially recognized good taste" is conservative, expensive (but not always), and— we hate to say this, but it is very true—*conventional*. Way-out things can become good taste, by use and acceptance. The Alexander Calder mobiles, for example, are prized free-hanging sculptures now worth a fortune and hung in the best contemporary homes. But when Calder first created them, only the avant-garde accepted them. Over the years, as abstract art became the *accepted*, *middle-of-the-road*, establishment art (just look at the art on the wall of your bank, for example), abstract art such as Calder's *became* "good taste."

If you have particular expertise about a subject—say, your father was in the rug business, and you know everything about Turkish rugs, even the most unusual ones—you can get away with decorating your apartment with exceptional flair. People can often readily sense the difference between *honest taste* or an affected put-on. That's why, until you develop a specialty, it's better to opt for the handsome, accepted conventional in art, music and books. Things you *like*, of course. Under *no* circumstances would we recommend that you live with a painting you had no feeling for—or listen all day to music you couldn't stand—just because you assumed it to be socially accepted "good taste." We point out the general rules of thumb only in the context of helping you to understand, and control to an extent, the impressions that other people have of you.

If your friends say, "Be yourself. If you want your apartment to look like a Salvation Army junk shop, that's how it should look," . . . well, ignore such nonsense. Taste is one of the subtle pressures of life. "Pressures that even the most reluctant among us can scarcely ignore," is how Russell Lynes describes it. "The making of taste in America is, in fact, a major industry. Is there any other place that you can think of where there are so many professionals telling so many non-professionals what their taste should be?" Lynes cites all the magazines and newspaper columns that do nothing but give advice on taste. "If the taste industry were to go out of business," Lynes jokes, "we would have a major depression and there would be breadlines of tastemakers as far as the eye could see."

This is How You Do It!

There are no rules for taste (except in business dress, and we cover those in another section). You know somebody who has good taste in clothes, furniture, deportment and speech. Emulate him . . . or her.

If there is an area of good taste that you want to learn more about, then do just that. Set a goal, work hard, and eventually it will take hold—if you *like* the subject, that is. Nobody knows *everything* about *every* subject. Most of us have a smattering of knowledge about many things, and that is enough to take us through life. But we should, and do, develop greater interest in certain areas . Say, for example, you decide to become serious about art. There are courses at every school. And galleries and museums to visit. You can go slowly, rather then try to rush into it. The idea is to *enjoy* cultivating your new interest; it should not become a chore.

A knowledge of art can be very helpful in establishing your credentials within a group of quality, successful people. Here is an easy learning process. Get the names of ten artists you should be familiar with from someone who knows about art—for example, your local gallery dealer. Then devote a week to learning something about each artist. Go to the library. Go to the art museum, and ask a curator. In ten weeks you will know *a great deal* about ten artists. In fact, enough to start you on an art appreciation career — if it should suit your fancy. You can do the same with musicians, or scientists, or any subject. We should never stop learning. Those people you admire who have good taste, who know about things like art and music and furniture — they didn't always know it, they learned it just the way you once learned the statistics about your favorite ballplayers. By being interested.

Let's try a practice session. Here are the names of *ten important contemporary artists*. (There are many other lists of artists who are equally important; this is merely a start.)

The leading American artists of the 1950s (when the great "New York school" was forming) were pioneers in what they considered to be a cultural wilderness. They were mostly abstract artists — that is, they painted symbolically, and from within, using huge forms of color rather than concerning themselves primarily with the image. Out of this group came a number of "household names," at least among art collectors and museum curators. We'll learn about ten of them, all names to add to your mind's computer. Then get a book from the library, and look at their paintings.

WILLEM DE KOONING (1904-   ) One of the most successful of the New York School. In his 1950s work, you can make out the figures of women, but the work is abstract. He is considered one of the giants of abstract expressionist painting and is a proponent of what is called, "action painting." Just look at one of his paintings, and you should get the idea.

MARK ROTHKO(1914-1970) He committed suicide and became the center of a major art scandal. The estate's executors sold his paintings to the Marlborough gallery for very little money. His children sued Marlborough, and won. The case has been the subject of a best-selling book and was a landmark court decision. Rothko's paintings were generally symetrically placed, rough-edged rectangles. He was included in every international exhibition of his time. One of the tourist attractions of Houston is the Rothko Chapel.

JACKSON POLLACK (1912-1956) Probably the most influential painter of his time, he was responsible more than any other artist for the abandonment of conventional pictorial composition. He changed the method of paint application, using sticks and dripping paint from large cans on a raw canvas. He was killed in an automobile accident in eastern Long Island, along with one of the women passengers. The other, his mistress, survived to write a book about Pollock, which was considered scandalous even among New York's art community. His wife, painter Lee Krasner, has been a careful executor of the Pollack estate, and has kept the value of the paintings at an astronomical level.

HELEN FRANKENTHALER (1928-   ) Developed her own technique, the "soak stain" which eliminates brush work and paint texture. Her work is planned during the actual painting process, not in prior sketches. She was married at one time to Robert Motherwell, another abstract expressionist pioneer.

LOUISE NEVELSON (1900-   ) Is one of America's foremost contemporary sculptors. In 1955, her natural affinity for myth and legend coalesced into a theatrical ensemble of symbolic forms, as in her best-known works:

"walls" of boxed wooden monochrome forms. A spectacular looking woman, she waited a long time for success. Now makes the news columns and moves with the 400. Wears very dramatic clothing, often with a classic riding hat.

ANDY WARHOL (1930-   ) Using contemporary advertising and promotion techniques to build his reputation as well as his painter's imagery, Warhol made headlines by turning Brillo boxes and Campbell soup cans into art. He produces outrageous films, and moves with the jet set. He has a workshop called "the factory," which employs myriad assistants. When the phrase "pop art" comes to mind, Warhol is generally the first name you think of. In 1979, the *Wall Street Journal* reported that the value of the Warhol soup cans had diminished and were no longer a good investment. He remains a celebrity.

CLAES OLDENBURG (1929-   ) Another major figure in "pop art," Oldenburg is best known for his odd "soft sculpture," such as giant hamburgers with french fries three feet long, or a huge "Soft Giant Drum Set." Our own favorite is a rug-like sculpture of a fried egg, sunny-side up. "Claes" is pronounced "Klowse" and his earliest home in the United States (Oldenburg was born in Scandinavia) was in the Chicago house eventually purchased by Hugh Hefner.

ANDREW WYETH (1917-   ) Son of the well-known illustrator, N.C. Wyeth, his pictures are highly subjective and sentimental; he may well be the most popular painter in America today. His last show at the Metropolitan Museum in New York drew crowds unprecendented in the gallery's history for a living artist. He commands the highest prices paid for the work of an American artist. He picks sitters for his paintings from among his friends and neighbors. His son, Jamie Wyeth, paints in the same genre, and is more social than his father (who lives in Chadds Ford, Pa.), making the gossip columns every once in a while.

If you want to know more, here are some names to look up: Robert Rauschenberg; Jasper Johns; George Segal, and Jim Dine.

A Few Words About Classical Music

The fact that you like rock music, or country or jazz dooesn't mean you can't enjoy classical music as well. Give it a chance; listen to it carefully, openly. There is a reason why so many top executives are on the boards of symphony orchestras; why so many companies support orchestras; indeed, keep them in business. It is not only for the benefit of the community. It is because the executive involved gets so much from the music.

Here is a list of selected recordings with which you can start your classical music collection. It is an investment of a bit over $100, if you allow yourself to become involved, it will pay off in countless hours of pleasure and relaxation.

1. Ludwig Von Beethoven: "Nine Symphonies." There are a number of excellent renditions of the symphonies in boxed sets at various prices. If you decide to buy them one at a time, you might start with "The Pastoral" (The Sixth Symphony) or the Fifth Symphony. Both of these are extremely popular.

2. Wolfgang Amadeus Mozart: "Symphony No. 40 in G Minor, K 550
3. G.F. Handel: "The Water Music"
4. Maurice Ravel: "Bolero" and "La Valse"
5. Frédéric Chopin: "Concerto for Piano and Orchestra in F Minor, No. 2 Opus 21"
6. Johann Sebastin Bach: "Brandenburg Concertos — No. 4 in G Major and No. 6 in B Flat Major"

Also recommended: Any recording of classical guitar music by Andres Segovia; Brahms; Schubert; Debussy; Liszt; Verdi. Don't overlook opera, or Stravinsky, Tchaikovsky, Rachmanioff, Rimsky-Korsakov, Shostakovich, Berlioz; and any among the following will provide hours of more quiet listening: Corelli; Torelli; Gabrielli; Teleman; Purcell.

SUCCESSFUL HOSTMANSHIP

A genuine warm spirit of hospitality is the key to successful hostmanship. Without it, all the trappings and formalities and good food and fine drinks degenerate into a cold chill.

The main ingredients for a successful host are self-confidence, self-respect, and a pretty good idea of what his responsibilities are to his guests.

If you don't enjoy entertaining, it will be more difficult to become successful in other areas of your life. Most successful men are mildly extroverted, gregarious, and enjoy social communication.

Here are some simple rules for all-around hosting:

1. Each guest should be greeted individually, even if two or more come in together. You should try to open the door personally for each guest. The important thing is to be warm and friendly, and to make everyone feel truly welcome.
2. If you have invited several people, introduce each new guest into the group. If there is a small group and the newly arrived guest knows somebody in that group, that's where you lead him, or her.
3. The good host takes it as his responsibility to protect guests from boredom, loneliness and a feeling of being left out.
4. Spend a little time with each guest. The host who says nothing but "hello" and "goodbye" won't be remembered. You give parties to be remembered. You should be remembered, not the canapes or whiskey sours. You want people, especially when you are doing business with them, to remember "what a great party you ran, Norman."
5. It may be necessary to have phenomenal energy. Someone once wrote, "Etiquette throws you to the mercy of the overstaying guest."
6. Say goodnight individually to each guest. Keep the closing conversation to a minimum.
7. When the party's over, the host must not repeat anything that may have happened to the discredit of any of his guests.

There are two parties which an on-the-rise executive should learn to host: the cocktail party and dinner party.

The Cocktail Party

The usual times for cocktail parties are between five and seven p.m., or from six to eight. A cocktail party is usually fairly large. It is a sensible way to pay back many other invitations all at once, get to know a special someone a little better, or introduce a number of your friends to one another. The crowd is generally large enough so that most everyone stands. As a result, it is easier for people to move freely from one group to another; but it also tends to make cocktail parties uncomfortable. Most people claim they dislike such get-togethers, but almost all will come anyway. It is the kind of affair where at least one guest will bring a friend. When that happens, be gracious. Avoid embarassing anyone.

There was a time when cocktail parties meant just that. But hard liquor for a large group is very expensive, and its popularity is on the decline, especially among the under-46 set. Jug wines are absolutely correct. People are happy with wine. Beer is okay, and so is punch. And disposable plastic glasses. It's up to you. People are not at the party to sample English gin; they are there to chat, to mingle, to participate in the event. Potato chips, peanuts, and simple packaged snack foods are sufficient. Keep it simple and unpretentious and everybody will be satisfied. Remember — it's the people you invite who will make or break the party, not the food.

Only the very first guests and the last to leave will be able to see what your apartment looks like. If it is a new apartment, *don't* call your cocktail party a "house warming" because some guests may think they have to bring presents for your new quarters. Afterwards, the place will look a mess. A good investment would be a maid to clean up the next day. It might cost a bit extra, but it will make you feel better not to have to sweep up those broken potato chip crumbs.

The Dinner Party

Most young men find it difficult to throw dinner parties without female help. That doesn't have to be the case. Forget your worries. Just don't ever make the parties too big. It's a really good way to do business, and if you "owe" your boss a dinner it's a lot cheaper and a lot less formal than taking him and his wife out to dinner. Moreover, you have a real advantage if the dinner is held on your turf. We would suggest that, until you have lots of practice, confine your dinner parties to informal, friendly affairs for no more than six.

First of all, nobody will expect you to prepare a really great dinner. People are very funny about accepting dinner invitations from single men. Even in today's "liberated" times, men aren't considered capable of working all day and then coming home and preparing dinner. Prove them wrong. You will really impress everybody with the *two* dinners we are going to discuss. Two *great* dinners. They have been tested by the authors on myriad occasions. They have never failed. Wives of guests always ask for the recipes, and nobody is disappointed. One of the meals is centered around hamburger, the other around chicken; these are foods almost everyone eats. You might check with your guests beforehand to find out if any happens to be a vegetarian, and act accordingly. Remember — you aren't expected to have help, and you aren't necessarily expected to serve sizzling steak. If you have your boss over, for example, he'll know how much money you make and you'll look rather foolish spending unwisely. Your motivation may be questioned.

Our "success dinners" are terribly unpretentious. One recipe comes from a variation on an old family dish, and the other was given to one of the authors by late President Lyndon B. Johnson. It was the dish *he* made as a *young* senator in Washington, when he entertained a few other lawmakers in his kitchen for fast dinner meetings. This dish was a favorite of John Wayne's (who got it from the same source) and of Prince Charles of England. It is a winner.

Each of these meals takes *less than an hour* to prepare. In fact, either can be prepared before you go to work and, as a one-dish meal, can be refrigerated right in the skillet, and heated just before the guests arrive. It's even better the next day.

These unpretentious dishes will help to reflect the fact that you are organized, versatile and creative. They will show your employer and other guests that you are very resourceful and it's just possible that your employer's wife will remember you. ("How is that nice young man who invited us for dinner? I hope he's doing well.")

Cooking a success dinner is also good practice for the future. Men *have* to cook nowadays. When your working wife is out closing that big deal with one of *her* clients, and you are home, you might as well know how to prepare a dinner or two so you don't have to wait until the little lady comes home.

Finally, though this may be the most important thing, it's a lot of fun once you know how. And the successful man must know how to do *lots* of things besides fill out report sheets and write memos.

We'll start first with the chicken dish. For want of a better name, let's call this one:

CHICKEN A LA SUCCESS

First, let's plan a menu.

Cocktails
Chicken a la Success
on a bed of rice.

Bread & Butter   **Peas**
Lettuce & Tomato with Success Dressing
Cherries Jubilee
Coffee

Chicken a la Success

This is what you need:

Boned chicken breasts	(one for each guest — it will come in a package at the supermarket, already boned. Two pieces make one breast.)
A kilbasi sausage	(Polish sausage. If none available, get package of "hot links")
A large onion	
1 cup raisins	
1 can garbanzos	(chick peas. Every supermarket has a can.)

146

1 can peanuts	(optional — but if you do this, it certainly adds something to the taste.)
Salt	
Garlic	
Pepper	(If you can, get a container of Lawry's Seasoned Pepper but plain salt and pepper is enough)
¼ pound margarine	
Two cans Franco-American chicken gravy	(yes — canned chicken gravy. We told you this was a simple, earthy recipe)

The pot you will need is a large skillet (more about pots later)

1. Take the stick of margarine and put it in the skillet. Turn the light on under the skillet, very low.
2. Slice the onion into small pieces. If you don't know how to do this any good cook book will show you. You should buy at least one. The paperback edition of the *Joy of Cooking*, available in every bookstore, has just about everything in the world you'll ever need, (except these two recipes, which are found only in *Secrets of Success*.) If slicing an onion confounds you, next time you are shopping go to the frozen food counter of your supermarket and get a package of frozen chopped onions. Open the package, while it is frozen, and dump it into the frying pan, on the melting stick of margarine. Turn the flame up a bit so the onions can thaw.
3. Slice the chicken breasts into bite-sized pieces with a sharp knife.
4. Take your sausage. Slice it into half-inch pieces. Make sure you get a "long" sausage, about the length of three hot dogs.
5. The onions should be melted and "browning" by now. Sprinkle some seasoned pepper on the onions, to taste. Also, salt and garlic. The easiest thing is to buy a small jar of minced garlic in the supermarket. Sprinkle to taste on onions.
6. As it simmers (you can smell it now), add the pieces of chicken. With a large fork, or spatula, keep mixing the chicken about until all the pieces turn white. Open the cans of gravy, and dump two of the cans into the skillet. It will look like a congealed mess for a moment, but the heat will melt it. Keep mixing.
7. Add the sliced kilbasi.
8. Add the can of garbanzos.
9. Add the raisins.
10. Add the peanuts. Now, if you have a food processor, chop the peanuts into little pieces. Or you can buy a hand food chopper, which is a jar with a chopper on it; this costs a couple of dollars. But the whole peanuts also work.

11. Stir. But let the whole thing simmer for about 20 to 25 minutes. Keep tasting the gravy. If you think it needs it, add some more salt and pepper.

12. That's it. If you are cooking this in the morning, just put the whole thing in the refrigerator until you come home. Start warming it about fifteen minutes before you serve it. Or, you can make it while people watch you; its surprisingly impressive.

The secret of Chicken a la Success is the *sausage*. The spicy kilbasi gives the gravy its flavor — indeed, it overwhelms the entire meal, but not enough to make it harsh. The result should be a subtle taste. If you can't get kilbasi, use another sausage. It is the sausage which changes the taste. If you want an Italian taste to this dish, use sliced pepperoni instead of kilbasi. Different sausages lend different flavors to this dish. So, in actuality, you come up with a dozen variations of Chicken a la Success depending on the sausage you use.

RICE —

We don't advocate minute rice. It's also easy to make the rice.
Buy Uncle Ben's converted rice. This is how you make it.
Use a pot that has a cover. Pour two cups of water into the pot, and bring to a boil. Take *one* cup of rice and pour it neatly into the boiled water. Bring it *back* to a boil, add some salt, then let it boil for one minute. Turn down the heat to the smallest flame your oven will allow. Cover and let it cook for just about 20 minutes.

PEAS —

Of all the frozen vegetables, peas taste closest to the fresh variety. Follow the directions on the box. Then, when you are just about to take them out of the pan, add about an ounce and a half of sherry, let it heat for a moment, and add butter. They are then ready to serve.

BREAD AND BUTTER —

If there is a real bakery in your town, get the best and most interesting bread you can buy. Don't ruin the meal by serving slices of poor bread. If you can't get bakery bread, get the parker house rolls offered in your supermarket. But not unless it is a last resort. A fresh baked bread — Italian or French variety — adds class. Many people like the spreadability of whipped butter. So, you might serve that.

SERVING:

Since there are few involved, you should do the serving to make the evening most relaxing for your guests. Set the table simply. The serving dishes don't have to be fancy, but it would be nice if all the dishes matched. Also the silverware. While your guests are seated, bring out the peas. The bread and butter is on the table. You dole out a pile of rice on each plate. While you do this *keep talking.*

It is your show. You are the master of ceremonies. Talk about the cooking you've just done; how you enjoyed preparing it for them. Tell them a story about it. How your grandmother learned about this recipe from a Polish boy friend; how it has been in the family for generations; how each child has been taught to make the dish. People, even your starchy boss, like stories. It is part of the ambience of the event.
When the rice is on the plate, dollop out a big portion of the Chicken

a la Success over the rice, neatly, since the gravy tends to run. Let your guests help themselves to peas and bread and butter. The salad can be served with the main course, or just after, depending on your own preference.

Success Salad —

Lettuce
Tomatoes
Croutons

Cut the lettuce and tomato up the way *you* like it in a salad bowl. Add croutons, about 1/2 cup, and mixed Italian dressing. (Buy the very best at the supermarket: Lawry's or Pfeiffer's are national brands which produce quality products. This is the quickest way. You can, of course, make a salad dressing by mixing oil and vinegar with salt and pepper. But the best bottled salad dressings will suffice. Remember, if you *like* to cook, you will experiment. You'll learn to make other things—add your own favorites. This is a first-time special meal recipe. Your guests will be flattered that you made the effort for them. The dish is one which appeals to a broad number of tastes, and usually goes over very well.

It will look more difficult to prepare then it really is.

Cherries Jubilee:

This is "easy as pie"—actually, even easier—and will impress everyone. Buy enough vanilla ice cream (the best quality) and two cans of *pitted* dark cherries. Pour the cherries in a chafing dish if you have one; if not, a small saucepan will do. Heat the cherries until they are about to boil. Then pour a half-cup of plain old brandy, any kind, into the cherries. Keep the heat high for less than a minute. Now, as your guests watch, drop a match into the mixture. Yes, it will light. Turn off the heat. Blow out the blue flame.

Sometimes this doesn't work, so don't make a big deal out of it if the thing doesn't light. It will taste the same without the theatrics. Remember, you are the choreographer . . . and nobody wants excuses, anyway.

Put the ice cream in dishes; pour the brandied cherries over it. Fantastic.

Serve coffee

And after-dinner drinks. If any of the women ask to let them help clear the table, graciously accept. But do help them yourself.

We will talk more extensively about wines later. But for our chicken dish we suggest you serve a chilled white wine. Since it is a "peasant" dish, an expensive French wine might be too sophisticated. A good California jug wine, or one of the new Italian dry white table wines will certainly complement Chicken a la Success, and should earn 100% approval from your peers and your boss.

Now for the Lyndon Johnson recipe. This one is for a more informal meal; again, it is very simple: just one dish and a salad. Beer can be served instead of wine—indeed, it may even be more appropriate. This dish is called Johnson's Chili, White House Style. It's really a very famous dish, since the Johnsons passed it out to everybody who tried it. It is one of the many variations of Perdenales chili that Lady Bird popularized. Lyndon

Johnson told one of the authors of this book that he made this dish in about "ten minutes." It's spicy, delicious, and always performs like a trouper.

JOHNSON'S WHITE HOUSE CHILI
Menu
Johnson's Chili
Grated Cheese
Sour Cream
Bread & Butter
Success Salad
Sherbet and Cookies
Coffee

This is what you'll have to buy.

Hamburger (enough to feed your guests)
1 can Old El Paso Chili & Beans for each two guests
1 can Old El Paso Pinto Beans
1 large onion (or bag of frozen chopped onions)
1 large container sour cream
1 stick margarine
A chunk of Swiss cheese or Jarlsberg
Spice Islands Chili Seasoning

1. Saute the onions in margarine, in the same kind of skillet you used for the chicken recipe, and in the same manner.
2. Put in the hamburger. Mash with a fork while it browns. Mix it with the onions. If it is too thick, add three-quarters of a cup of water.
3. When it is browned, add salt and pepper to your own taste. Then open the can of chili and the can of beans; add them to the mixture in the skillet. Let simmer until it begins to bubble. Keep stirring, so it all gets mixed together; the beans, chili, hamburger and onions.
4. Add the chili powder to taste. This is up to you, and depends on what you think your guests can handle. The Spice Islands Chili Seasoning is specially mixed for an American palate — hot without being oppressive. Use a capful: mix, and taste the sauce. That's the best way. If any of your guests wants it hotter, just give them the seasoning jar, and they can add all they want later.
5. Simmer for about 20 minutes.

This dish can be made in the morning before you go to work, and it's even better the second day. The rice is prepared the same way as for the chicken. The cheese is grated (you can buy a couple of packages of pre-grated cheddar or Swiss, or both, if you don't want to take the cheese and run it across the grater). The sour cream is served in a bowl. You serve the chili, piping hot, over the rice, in the same way you served the chicken. The guests can help themselves to the condiments of cheese and sour cream.

Use the same talk-through technique. Tell about Lyndon Johnson's recipe, given to you by a former TV newsman who got the recipe from the late president himself. When people seem surprised about the sour cream, explain that the section of Texas where the Johnsons lived was heavily populated by Germans who put sour cream on everything, including chili — because the combination is out of this world. Try it. Watch the hesitation of your guests as they take a dollop of sour cream, cautiously, and mix it with the chili. Then watch their faces. You'll know you've been successful with a very simple dish. Don't tell anybody about the canned chili you've spiked the dish with — that's your secret. Beer goes well with chili. Use the same kind of good bread. And the dessert is very simple: sherbet and some kind of cookie, then coffee. A winner!

SUCCESSFUL MEN SHOULD KNOW ABOUT WINE

"IT'S FUNNY ABOUT wine," claims *New York Times* columnist Frank J. Prial. "People who drink it become charming; people who write about it become pedantic." But the fact remains that men who are intent on occupying the executive suite should assimilate the habits of executives. In the case of wine, that is no hardship. Wine is not only important to good living; it is also quite wonderful. "A man's other faults may be overlooked," said the late *bon vivant* Lucius Beebe, "if he serves an excellent wine at dinner." Even The Bible (Psalms 104:5) exclaims, "Wine maketh glad the heart of man." And, according to Roy Bartolomei, manager of Sherry/Lehmann Wine and Spirits in New York, one of the most prominent retail wine operations in the world, "At the very least, wine never fails to make interesting conversation."

Bartolomei, who was an instructor in American History at Hunter College before his scholarly interest in wine superceded his academic pursuits, says that he "rarely meets a successful man who isn't interested, at least to a degree, in wine." He admits, however, that it is a complicated subject; like any other interest, it becomes more interesting as you learn more about it.

"Wine is with us," Bartolomei says, emphatically. "And it has become part of the American tradition of good taste." Wine sales now outnumber hard liquor sales in most parts of the United States. With so many wines to choose from, it is often confusing for the beginner to select a good one. "You go into the store and you are faced with a tremendous array of bottles," says Bartolomei. "The thing for the beginner to do is to find that liquor store in your city — every town has one — where someone on the staff has a real interest in wine. Let him know that you are interested, and he'll be a great help. A responsible wine merchant will be a steady source of pleasurable drinking. Tell him what you're having for dinner. Let him suggest a wine. Don't be embarrassed to admit what you can afford. And if you are dissatisfied with his recommendations, be sure to let him know. Little by little, you will begin to know the wines yourself."

Bartolomei suggests two books that can help a beginner: Hugh Johnson's *"Pocket Encyclopedia of Wine"*, or the *"Wine Buyer's Guide"*, by Sam Aaron and Clifton Fadiman — both in paperback.

He also believes that, in spite of rising wine prices due in part to inflation, there will always be good buys for those who seek them out.

Roy Bartolomei

"Especially in the new California wines, which are growing in popularity. They are served in Europe. And California Jug Wines are really much better than the equivalent priced wines sold in France."

Bartolomei offers the following "secrets of success" about wine.

GENERAL POINTS

The most important thing to look for, of course, is quality — but also try for variety and balance.

—Experiment with different styles of wine, so that you will always have something on hand to fit the occasion, the mood, the meal.

—Choose wines from a number of different countries and regions; this will give you a sense of the breadth and diversity of wine-making, and will help make the wine itself (its origins, its history, as well as its taste) a topic of conversation.

—Don't buy a bottle for every dinner. Have a small cellar on hand; wines in different price ranges — some serious and costly wines for important occasions, but lots of good inexpensive wines, too, for parties and daily use.

—Learn (and help your friends to learn) the gentle art of wine tasting. There's more to wine than the quick swallow. The color and brilliance of a good wine in a clear glass can be a pleasant introduction. The aroma of the wine (the "nose" as it's sometimes called) can often be more memorable than the flavor itself. And as for tasting, a good wine held in the mouth for a few seconds before swallowing can offer a variety of flavors that you would never find if you drank more quickly. There's no need to be pompous or theatrical, to swirl the glass and furrow your brow — but slow and careful wine-tasting provides a string of several pleasures. Try to cultivate it.

Some Suggested Red Wines ... With Approximate Prices

From California

   (a) One good Cabernet Sauvignon — e.g., Heitz, Mt. Veeder, Clos du Val ($8-14).
   (b) One good Zinfandel — Ridge, Clos du Val, etc. ($7-10).
   (c) One less expensive Cabernet Sauvignon — Parducci ($5-7).
   (d) One less expensive Zinfandel — Sutter Home ($5-7).
   (e) A good general table red like Mondavi Red ($3).

From France

   (a) One or two good estate-bottled Bordeaux from the 1970 or 1971 vintages if possible, though 1973 and 1974 are acceptable, too. Chateau Bouscaut (Graves), Chateau Gloria (St. Julien) $12-17 for the 1970 and 1971; $6-8 for the 1973 and 1974.
   (b) A good estate-bottled Burgundy, from a town like Nuits St. Georges — or from the Cote de Beaune or Cote de Nuits — 1976 vintage if you can find it. ($8-12) — Lichine, Jadot, Latour are good shippers here.
   (c) Rhone Valley — one nice Chateauneuf-du-Pape from a good shipper

($8-10). A good Cotes du Rhone, eg. from La Viele Ferme, at less than $3.50.

(d) Beaujolais — One of the best is a wine from Brouilly called Chateau de la Chaize (less than $7). Beaujolais Villages 1978 from Beaudet or Jadot, two very good producers ($5-6).

From Italy

(a) A good wine from the Piedmont: Barolo, Gattinara, etc. — 1970 and 1971 are good. Younger vintages might require more bottle aging ($7-10).

(b) Chianti Classico should be drunk young and fruity. A Chianti Classico RISERVA has more age and is a more serious wine. A good one — from Antinori, Ruffino, or Brolio — costs $7-10.

(c) Rubesco, a light fruity wine from near Perugia ($4-5).

From Spain

(a) A nice Rioja, like Marqués de Cáceres (less than $4).

(b) Torres Sangre de Toro, from the Penedés region south of Barcelona (around $4-$5)

Others

Good red wines are imported from many other countries. They are generally inexpensive, and are often good buys for daily drinking. Some suggestions: Andean Cabernet Sauvignon (Argentina); Concha y Toro Cabernet Sauvignon (Chile); Premiat Pinot Noir (Rumania) — all under $4.

NOTE ON RED WINE

Price is often an index to the type of wine you are buying. Bigger, more serious wines — which often require aging — cost more than lighter, younger wines intended for quick drinking. Inquire about "drinkability now" when you purchase. Gradually, you will want to put aside some younger bottles for maturing in your own "cellar."

Some Suggested White Wines

From California

(a) One expensive California Chardonnay — Chateau St. Jean Simi, etc. ($8-10).

(b) One inexpensive Chardonnay — Wente, or Pedroncelli ($6-7).

(c) A Fumé Blanc from Mondavi ($6-7).

(d) A Johannisberg Riesling from Firestone or Joseph Phelps ($4-8).

(e) A nice daily table wine like Mondavi White ($3).

From Germany

(a) The Riesling grape is the king here. Choose an estate-bottled wine from the Rhine or Mosel areas. For example, something like Piesporter Goldtropfchen from the Mosel, or Schloss Johannisberg from the Rhine — the 1975 and 1976 vintages are great, producing full, long-lasting wines. Choose a "Q.B.A." or "Kabinett" level for a fine wine to accompany food, and a "Spatlese" or "Auslese" for richer, sweeter wines to accompany (or replace) dessert. Kabinetts are $7-10 — Ausleses are $15 and up.

(b) Lesser vintages often provide light and refreshing table wines — e.g., in 1977 and 1978. Avoid the famous and heavily advertised national brands if possible, especially if you have access to a decent wine shipment. For instance, a liter of Riesling 1977 (von Kesselstaat) — a good estate-bottled wine — sells for only $4.49 in New York, and is better than famous Liebfraumilchs and Moselblumchens selling for more in smaller bottles.

From France

(a) At least one good estate-bottled Burgundy in a good vintage; let's say a 1976, 1977 or 1978 Chassagne-Montrachet or Meursault ($12-15). Good shippers are Alexis Lichine, Jadot, Latour.

(b) One or two less expensive wines from the Macon region, such as a Macon-Villages or St. Veran at less than $6 the bottle. Avoid the over-priced Pouilly-Fuissé.

(c) One or two wines from the Loire Valley — a Sauvignon or Muscadet, Marquis de Goulaine 1976 or 1978 — a Sancerre 1976 or 1978 — Muscadet: $4-6 — Sancerre, Archambault or Sauvignon ($8-9).

(d) A first-rate Sauterne, rare, delectable, expensive — served with a simple dessert, it will make the end of the meal a religious experience. The pinnacle is Chateau d'Yquem.

From Italy

(a) Pinot Grigio, one of the best dry white wines of Italy ($4-6).

(b) Corvo Bianco, produced by Duca di Salaparuta ($5-6).

(c) Save the Soave for drinking at those restaurants where the wine lists are without imagination. It's a nice wine, but often over-priced. Folinari Soave, however, is not a bad buy for parties at $3.00 a liter.

A NOTE ON WHITE WINES

With few exceptions, white wines should be drunk young, when only a few years old. Look at vintage dates; avoid antique Muscadets or 5-year-old Soaves.

Those white wines that do benefit from bottle age include a rare Sauterns from an estate like Chateau d'Yquem (which can last a human lifetime) or a good Barsac like Chateau Climens, the great dessert wines of Germany, and some dry wines, too, like the full-bodied Montrachet of a good vintage.

Serve white wines chilled, but not icy cold, since too much cold suppresses flavor. The best way to keep white wine chilled at the table is to put the bottle in a bucket of crushed ice and ice water.

Sparkling Wines

From California

Go for the best here: Domaine Chandon, Korbel ($8-10). For sparkling-wine punches, Gallo is not at all bad for less than $4.

From France

Champagne prices are going up. Lanson Black Label Brut is excellent and always at the lower end of the price spectrum ($12). For glamour, greatness and luxurious cost, try Perrier Jouet, Fleur de Champagne, in the enamelled-flower bottle (less than $40).

From Italy

An Asti Spumante from a good firm like Martini and Rossi is a nice accompaniment to dessert.

NOTE ON SPARKLING WINES

In France, the word "Brut" on the label denotes the driest of Champagnes. Puzzlingly, "Extra Dry" is actually sweeter. If the less dry taste is to your liking, try the Extra Dry of Moet et Chandon ($10-12).

A bone-dry Champagne makes a fine aperitif and accompanies many foods throughout the meal. For dessert, however, it tends to come across as too dry, too acidic: The flavor and sweetness of the dessert suppresses the subtle flavor of the Brut Champagne. That's why the sweeter grades of Champagne are best for desserts.

A COUPLE OF EXPERTS' PERSONAL TASTE

...from a letter from Roy Bartolomei

"... One thing occurred to me after you left. You asked what wines I personally enjoy, and I answered: a nice Macon or a lighter Chardonnay from California. If you include this in the text, I'd like to make the point that one has to distinguish between the pleasures of everyday drinking and those rare occasions when one has the chance to taste some of the best wines made by man. For daily drinking I like a dry white wine, on the order of a St. Veran or Macon Villages — Muscadet or Cler Blanc from the Loire — or a lighter Chardonnay from California. But a truly great wine is another matter. Drinking one has the effect of fixing the occasion absolutely — and in great detail — in the memory. I remember everything about the evenings I tasted an incredible Montrachet 1971, Laguiche — my first 1967 Chateau d'Yquem — and a 1949 Lafite-Rothschild ... "
Everybody will be happy with wine, as an aperitif. But keep scotch, bourbon, gin and vodka on hand for those who want it.

The Successful Martini

A successful man is supposed to know how to mix a martini.

Frank Valenza is the founder and proprietor of the world's most expensive restaurant, The Palace, in New York. Despite the high prices, it is almost impossible to get a reservation at The Palace; yet customers return time and time again.

"They save up for it," Valenza says. "The Palace is pure art. An animal feeds, a man eats, but only a man of culture can dine. I try to create dining, and I think I've been very successful."

Valenza says that perfect drinks are "ones that are measured using *pure* products, so that the *taste of the alcohol comes through.*" For a martini, make sure the glass is cold. Keep one in the refrigerator, if you know your guests will want martinis. *Good* gin is the secret. A gin flavored gin, not one of those cheap gins. Fill the glass with crushed ice. Pour in the gin. Pour in *very little* vermouth. Mix, then rim glass with lemon peel;

twist the rind across and drop the twist in. Serve. You can almost taste the vermouth, the gin, and the lemon . . . and the cold. A perfect drink. Natural taste. Tart and different.

"The key to success is balance." # INTERVIEW:

FRANK VALENZA

Frank Valenza started out to be an actor and became instead one of New York's most successful restauranteurs. Proof of the Pudding is a very popular restaurant on New York's upper east side, and The Palace is certainly one of the most expensive in the world. When he opened The Palace, many of his friends were worried that the high prices would scare off diners. Valenza had confidence in himself. "I planned. I knew what people wanted. I know what I had to offer. I had a goal. And it worked. I was versed in the arts," Valenza said. "Theater, music, dance. I wanted to be an actor or a producer, and I run restaurants instead. Life doesn't always work out exactly as planned, but it takes theatrical ability to run a restaurant. It is choreographed; there are actors, and bit players, and an audience, and drama. It is drama that makes a restaurant work. So, I consider myself successful.

"I think success also means being able to make other people's lives happier and easier, and I try for that. The key to life's success is balance. I learned that through seven years of analysis. What you put in your spirit, nobody can take away from you. I think it is very important to work extremely hard. The guy who works hardest gets somewhere. There's no doubt of that. My father was a hard taskmaster. I learned challenge from him. If I could swim a mile, he'd say I had to swim two.

"But I think there is a time to get away from your parents and your parents' ideas, psychologically at least, and use your training for yourself. You have to devote yourself to your own ambitions. You have to learn your business, whatever it is. You must put your time in. You must use all the things you learned, whatever you've studied, toward your own business. Take the Stanislavsky method of acting. I use it all the time. I can put myself in the place of my chefs, my waiters, the customers.

"You get out of something only what you put in. You have to do what you do, but do it well. Never take anything for granted. Test it. Do it yourself. Examine. Study. Successful men all do that. They work hard. They are committed. They throw themselves into their work with all eight cylinders.

"I don't think success can be achieved unless you keep yourself in good shape, in tremendous health. And you have to have a sense of humor. Did I say commitment? There is a difference between total commitment and killing yourself, you know. There's a time to relax; you need it, otherwise you'll have a heart attack at a very young age. You have to balance your life. Take care of your own natural resources. Make the money you earn work for you. Life might not be perfect; we might not reach our exact goals, but we can get fairly close. It's certainly worth the struggle."

SUCCESS IN SPORTS

If you are a lousy golfer, then no matter how much you like the game it's not going to do you much good as far as your career is concerned. From that particular standpoint, it is better not to play at all than to spoil others' enjoyment of the game. Ineptness is not a virtue.

There is no need to belabor the importance of sports in the United States. We have a number of national crazes. Running has become part of the national character. Tennis has grown from a rich boy's sport to our most popular participatory sport, next to golf. Racket ball and squash are coming up fast.

And there's skiing, which can only be enjoyed a small part of the year for most of us.

There is a good reason why successful men seem to involve themself in a given sport. One, it is good for you because it helps you to keep in shape, and just plain calesthenics every morning is dull as dishwater. Nobody enjoys exercising; it is one of those necessary things. Working out in some kind of sport is much more exciting. Besides, *successful men are all competitive.*

THE COMPETITIVE SPIRIT

Life is competitive.

Don't let anyone tell you different. One of the authors of this book was sent by loving parents to a school with an experimental program in which competition was looked upon as an evil. "You only compete against yourself," the well-meaning principal advised. The result was that, when the student couldn't keep up in math, for example, it was alright. "Everyone can't learn everything." Nonsense. All that happened was that the student was cheated out of learning math.

Competition helps you learn; it makes you work harder. There is a spirit, an edge that comes from competition. If you are going to make something of yourself you *must* compete. In some respects, our schools should be more competitive. And that is why sports have continued to be so popular. Few things are openly competitive; only in sports can we win or lose, and all of us must lose sometimes. The name of the game is to win more times than you lose. But sports teaches you that you always have a chance. Last year's team in the cellar might be this year's pennant winner.

Sports is a microcosm of real life. We play within certain rules. There are things that are totally out of line, and when we foul we are removed, at least temporarily, from the game. The man who has played sports has a better idea of how corporate life, for example, is lived and how it works. He understands that being a steady player is sometimes better than being a sporadic player who occasionally hits home runs.

Sports deals in rewarding excellence. That's why most successful men have a sport in which they are involved; sometimes more than one. And it's not only because deals are made on the golf course. It's more because a man who leads a competitive life at work also likes competitive life in his play. It is a very natural instinct, especially among Americans.

Being good in a particular sport is one good reason to become involved in that sport. It gives you another "group" in which to move. A tennis player usually joins a tennis club, and there meets other people who are at least moderately adept at tennis — a bunch of otherwise disparate people who are tied together by a single interest. A doctor and a mechanical engineer may have nothing much in common, except hitting a ball across a net. It is a marvelous means of communication.

Try many different sports. Pick the one that interests you the most, and take lessons. You will quickly discover whether or not you have an aptitude for the game. Running clubs have been formed, with fancy club houses in some parts of the country. Even the best country clubs have their "running faction" now. It is one sport in which even the obviously non-athletic man can excel. Of the 11,000 men and women who participated in the recent New York Marathon, over 8,000 were able to complete a grueling 26-mile course. Few of these runners would probably be champions on the golf links or on a tennis court, but in running they are certainly champs.

So choose the sport in which you do well — whether it be volley ball, croquet, or curling. And use the sport for your own good. If you really like it, get involved in it on an organizational level. There are clubs for every sport, in every town. Compete. Run dinners. Get your picture in the paper with your team's trophy. It is important to be a champion. Being a champion means that you are successful.

You are not going to be any kind of champion if you don't keep fit. Some people are lucky. They enjoy a natural proclivity toward keeping in shape; stretching their legs, doing sit-ups and push-ups are a great source of satisfaction to them. To most of us it's an ordeal, something we'd rather avoid.

GET IN SHAPE

Well, don't avoid exercise.

If it is unpleasant, so be it.

There are very few sloppy fatties in the executive suite. It's hard to have a sharp mind with a baggy body.

What we suggest is to develop a set of exercises which you can do, and which are good for you. But do them. And at least 5 times a week. At least 15 minutes a day.

There are over 500 books available on how to exercise. All of them are valuable. The exercise routines work . . . if you do them.

We do eight exercises every morning on the living room floor. It is made less painful because we listen to the morning news at the same time. Our particular regimen has developed over several years and is based on our physical needs. They are derived from modern dance. And it works for us. Every successful person we've talked to seems to have his or her own routine, which they've worked out for them.

It is important, as we said, to have a sport. But sometimes the pressures of business don't allow you the time to play tennis as often as you'd like, no matter how enthusiastic you are about the game.

You always have 15 minutes a day to exercise.

Exercise!

That's an order.

And it must be obeyed or you'll pay the consequence.

INTERVIEW *"By not keeping in shape you let the rest of the team down..."*

BOBBY DEWS

Bobby Dews made headlines a couple of years ago as the baseball manager who brought Jim Bouton back to baseball, as a pitcher for the Savannah team. Dews was named Southern Association Manager of the Year for 1978. In 1979, he was promoted from Savannah to be the Atlanta Braves bullpen coach. Dews is recognized as an extremely knowledgeable and capable teacher of fundamentals. For many years he was an infielder in the Cardinals' farm system. A native of Edison, Georgia, he played basketball for Georgia Tech and is the son of the distinguished 1940s baseball great, Bobby Dews, Sr. He is a strong advocate of keeping fit.

"I think the stretching exercises we use on the Braves are as good as any man can do," Bobby Dews says. "But any regimen of exercise every day, for twenty minutes every morning will work. There are about 300 exercise books on the market, and most of them have good exercises. The thing is to do them regularly. Just try to stretch out each muscle, like professional athletes do. The key areas are shoulders, joints, and stomach."

How about running?

"Oh, running can't be beat. I run myself every morning. Not a great distance, but every day. A mile. A mile and a half. It's doing it regularly that keeps you in shape."

You think keeping in shape is good for everybody?

"Not only good, but necessary. You can't live without personal pride. I'm forty years old. We are given this body and so many of us don't take care of it when it is so easy. It's like anything else you do. You have to work at it. Set a goal. Know how much you want to weigh. It takes a little discipline, but discipline's easy if it becomes a habit. I see twenty-five-year-old men who look fifty. They let themselves go. If they go too far, it's hard getting back into shape. If you get in the habit of exercise, it will go with you forever and it won't be a big deal. And you won't be letting anybody down."

Letting people down? Who?

"Let me explain. My reason for wanting to be in good shape is that I have a good feeling for my team. If I'm in bad shape, I won't function well. I would let the others down: the players; the manager and the coach. We're all parts of a team. I happen to be in baseball, but people who work for a

160

company are on a team, too. One weak cog in the wheel, and the wheel is slowed down. If you have an obligation to yourself, you also won't let down the people who depend on you. Keeping in shape means you'll do a better job. You will feel better. We're all sorry creatures if we let others down."

What do all successful people you've met, in baseball or in other areas of your life, have in common?

"They think they're the best. Every really fine baseball player I've known, for example — every man of championship quality — thinks he is the best player. You must have that sense of security; otherwise, you can't compete. You can't get out there in front of that crowd and perform. Successful people also have perseverance. In baseball, you can have one bad day, and people are ready to write you off. You have to live with that. You have to accept your defeats and keep on playing to the very best of your ability. Not just the very best. You've got to be even better. In baseball, only a star has to play every day. But in business, people have to perform every day, which means they are stars. And stars have to have terrific strength and endurance. It takes staying in shape."

We asked Dr. Donald O. McIntyre, a distinguished physician and student of executive health, to comment on how successful men can stay in good health. Dr. McIntyre is a partner in the Western Internal Medicine and Nephrology Group, P.C. in Lakewood, Colorado; the Western Dyalysis Center in Denver and is on the clinical faculty of the University of Colorado Medical Center.

Dr. Donald O. McIntyre

The people whom I have come into contact with over the years that I have practiced medicine fall into a variety of categories of "success." The ones who seem to enjoy their "success" the most have a number of things in common which gives them an appearance of health and relaxed alertness. The following is a list of items that I have noted which should help the successful to achieve that state of health and fitness.

(1) *Diet:* At the position of cornerstone of fitness is a person's diet. Proper caloric intake of nutritious food stuffs supplies the individual with all the necessary energy, vitamins, and minerals that are required and makes ideal body weight easy to maintain. If one is overweight, a reduction in calories with a balanced diet allows excess weight to be dissipated by the utilization of stored body fat for energy. For the overweight person this requires behavioral modification which is one of the most difficult tasks a person can embark upon. Help can be found at a nearby medical center which, through its Department of Dietetics, offers weight reduction clinics. There, for a nominal fee, individual diet information is given and motivation through group participation is achieved. Weight Watchers® and TOPS® are also useful avenues to take. Fad and crash diets should be avoided by and large because the behavioral modification is usually not attained. Mega dose vitamins are generally useless for health maintenance; the excesses are lost in urine and stool, and your money is lost to the vendor.

Ideal body weight maintenance allows the person to operate at maximum efficiency, feel well, and appear the best.

(2) *Exercise:* Regular exercise is important for achieving general well-being (weight control, muscle definition, digestion, and sleep) and fitness

(stamina, muscular endurance and strength, flexibility, and balance). It also helps to keep us alert, breaks routine and dissipates tensions. The forms of exercise which allow the best combination of promoting well-being and fitness in order of importance are as follows:

Jogging

Bicycling

Handball, squash

Ice or roller skating

Swimming

Regular exercise with balanced diet and achievement of ideal body weight contribute largely to the human operating at optimal efficiency, and ready the person for self-enjoyment, as well as adversity.

(3) *Relaxation:* As little as 30 minutes a day alone with the self can help produce a tranquility that is necessary in seeking harmony between work and family requirements. During this time recreational reading, studying a subject, pursuing a hobby or just self-reflection can help to relieve tensions from the pressures of succeeding. This tranquility allows one to focus properly on his total environment and to confront problems in a less hostile or defensive manner. Vacations, whether a weekend or longer, should not be for working at the routine work-oriented problems, but should be reserved for gardening, "do-it-yourself projects," traveling, family or friend(s) time. It should allow one to "throw it all out of gear" and coast. This kind of relaxation helps to broaden interests, allows more flexibility, heightens interest in work and family, and promotes emotional fitness.

(4) *Sleep:* You know when you have enough. Make sure you get that amount nightly. It makes problems more easily handled and enjoyment of life more easily achieved. The lack of adequate sleep produces irritability, reduces enjoyment, and makes problems harder to approach. In the name of fatigue, good dietary practices frequently are lost, exercise is skipped and relaxation is harder to achieve.

(5) *Attitude:* Promote your positive aspects and stimulate the positive in those around you. Be aware of your negative side but don't dwell on it; work at changing it (quietly). Don't blame others for your behavior or performance. Everyone has anger; don't be afraid of it or feel guilty because of it; express it, gently (if possible), and specifically. Your attitude expresses your emotional fitness and this is as important as your physical fitness. If this is a problem area that can't be worked out by yourself, seek professional counseling; it can enhance the enjoyment of your success and possibly save your life.

(6) *Smoking:* Don't!! This is one of man's worst self-abuses. When you smoke, you say to the world, "I want to live a shorter life than I might otherwise expect." The problems it produces are insidious and delayed but when they occur, catastrophic. Lung cancer is just the tip of a huge iceberg which includes coronary artery disease with myocardial infarction, chronic bronchitis, emphysema, generalized arteriosclerosis, carcinoma of the urinary bladder. Most medical centers have Stop Smoking Clinics if you need motivation (education, group participation). Smoking is suicidally negative and robs you of the benefits produced by proper diet, maintenance of ideal body weight, exercise, and relaxation.

(7) *Alcohol:* In the proper dose this drug has many uses and can help to produce relaxation. The proper dose is one-two ounces of distilled spirits or

its equivalent (two beers, two four-ounce glasses of wine) several times per week. Occasionally more can be taken and enjoyed, e.g., in a social setting over a number of hours. Excess alcohol ingestion, however, has many adverse effects. If taken at the noon meal, it causes "fuzz in the afternoon." At any time, excess alcohol interferes with reality perception and can contribute to, and deepen, depression that may be already there. It adds calories to the body, causes one to ignore proper diet habits, interferes with exercise programs, relaxation and sleep. Excess alcohol use does not promote fitness and like smoking is negative.

(8) *Health Maintenance:* With success one needs to establish a rapport with an accountant, a lawyer, as well as with a physician. Make a list of family or internal medicine physicians by asking friends, acquaintances, and neighbors, whose opinion you trust, who their physicians are, and then select several to visit. Explain to the appointment secretary that you want to make a routine office visit to meet the physician. Ask him during that appointment about his office procedures, whether he "runs late" often, how he handles his call schedule and vacation time (e.g., who covers for him), what his attitude is about telephone advice and periodic physical exams, what his charges and billing procedures are, and at what hospitals he attends. Select the one whom you like the best and who seems to satisfy your needs and return for a physical exam, so that the rapport is established. Make sure that you are aware of your family history so that inheritable diseases are noted and proper advice can be obtained.

The above list contains nothing new; advice like this can be obtained from any mother. Though simple, the list contains items requiring great effort to achieve. If a number of items in the list need attention, set your goals in a realistic way, go at an easy pace, but work steadily to achieve the goals. The effort may not guarantee success but will allow any success to be enjoyed in the fullest sense.

A WORD ABOUT STRESS

Ask any executive what keeps him from producing at all twelve cylinders, and chances are the answer will be *stress*. But *stress* is part of contemporary life; you can avoid it only if you want to drop out, live in a commune, watch the clouds go by, and dissipate into the obscurity of history.

On the other hand, if you want to make your mark you're going to have to live with some kind of tension, some kind of stress. Dr. Tim Johnson, who regularly gives advice on "Good Morning America," (ABC-TV) claims that there are two ways to relieve your stress. He suggests regular exercise. "It is a terrific way to relieve your tension," Dr. Johnson points out. "And there's some research now that seems to demonstrate that regular exercise produces some chemical in your brain which helps you feel good."

Dr. Johnson has also found that stress comes from doing things that are particularly unpleasant. "If you sort out your priorities," he advises, "and reorder them, eliminating as many things as you can—things you don't do well—you might feel a little better."

For example, you might find yourself working on a project with a committee, and it becomes your responsibility to put a list of possible clients together. This kind of administrative function might drive you up the wall, but wouldn't bother another person on the committee. So what you might do is talk to him and switch assignments. Both of you may be happier, each doing the task he does well, and the job will still get done. Of course, this can't happen all the time. There are unpleasant things that are part and parcel of every job, every life. On those occasions, however, when priorities can be re-ordered, life can be made a modicum less tense.

CHANGING YOUR LIFESTYLE

Very simply, the successful man must have an ability to change. There is a time to stop being a boy. The apartment of a serious young man can be somewhat frivolous. We would tend to consider it odd for a twenty-five-year old to have a very staid apartment. But some people never reach the pinnacle of success because they aren't able to change their lifestyles.

Nobody reaches the pinnacle of success without sacrificing something. As you pick up increased responsibilities and start moving with more conservative people, you will have to become — at least on the surface — more conservative. Metaphorically speaking, there is a time to throw away your jeans and don pinstripes. Some people establish a lifestyle in their teens and hang on to it for dear life, then wonder why they aren't doing better. It is simple. They remain boys when they should be men. The thing to do is to know when to change.

We hope that you will give serious heed to the words and ideas expressed throughout this book by people who have "made it." Whether or not you agree with all they say, at least come to realize the wisdom of learning from their combined experience.

PART IV:

FINANCIAL SUCCESS

SAVINGS MAY BE HAZARDOUS TO YOUR WEALTH

YOU DON'T HEAR much about John Peeples anymore, but he was an American household name during the early decades of the 20th Century. A Methodist minister from Indianapolis, Peeples authored a number of guidebooks advising young people on subjects as diverse as taking care of their old parents to rules for marriage. In a book called "Laws for Financial Security," the good Reverend stressed what he called one of "life's verities." There was great virtue, Peeples advised, in *putting a little bit of one's wages away each week in a saving account.* Peeples believed (as has almost everyone in recent years) that "money in a savings account would grow in value year by year. It is one of life's great laws."

The law of gravity is not likely to change, but *Peeples' advice is as old-fashioned* and *unrealistic as the five-cent ice cream cone* and *the four-dollar tennis sneaker.*

At a recent congressional subcommittee on financial problems, a woman named Hilda Cloud testified that for most of her seventy-five years she had believed she was doing right by saving money in a savings bank, so that as a retired person her savings would greatly supplement her Social Security income. But she has instead discovered that *unbelievable price increases have upended the world of anyone who tries to save.*

In 1973 the rate of inflation breezed past the rate of savings account interest and has remained there. The result is depressing. *The real value of savings*, even after the interest is computed on your passbook, *drops every year.* Mrs. Cloud attacked the federal government's limits on bank interest that can be paid on savings. At the committee hearings, Mrs. Cloud and others giving testimony wore buttons reading: *SAVINGS MAY BE HAZARDOUS TO YOUR WEALTH.*

Economic predictions are just that: Predictions . . . based on what happened yesterday, with a guess as to what is going to happen tomorrow. "You must always remember," says economist John Kenneth Galbraith, "that prediction itself derives from the fact that no one really knows."

We feel safe, however, in predicting that—for at least the next five years, as in most decades of adjustment—the entire idea of money and what to do with it will undergo a number of startling changes. That does not mean you won't be able to prosper. It will just take a bit more planning. This book cannot give you a proven formula for taking the money you earn

TO SPEND OR BORROW? THAT IS THE QUESTION

and spinning it into a fortune. No one can do that. What we *can* do, however, is discuss the attitudes necessary for success in personal finance; how you handle the money you earn is certainly part of that. And so is what you do with your discretionary income — money that is left over after essential expenditures for food, housing and other vital necessities.

There's another American "verity" that seems to be upside-down at the moment, and that is the concept of *borrowing*. Benjamin Franklin would be shocked; and Polonius' advice to Laertes, "neither a borrower nor a lender be," is no longer prudent.

As *Money* magazine reported recently, "Borrowing has become smart. So has spending." And the borrowing-spending habit is seductive because *tax laws (and inflation) favor the borrower.*

Let's look at an example which will show you why understanding today's financial picture is so important to your success. The old idea was to save money for an item and then buy it. That was the conservative, true-blue All-American way. *Money* gives an example proving how wrong that is in today's market.

Let's assume you want to buy a stereo that costs $300. If you save $25 a month, you will have the $300 at the end of the year. At 5¼% passbook savings rate, compounded quarterly, you will have earned approximately $8.50 in interest. If you are in the 36% federal tax bracket, you will owe about $3.00 in federal taxes—leaving $5.50 net interest after the tax bill is subtracted. Meanwhile, the price of the stereo—assuming a 10% rate of inflation—has risen to $330. So, you will have lost $21.50 by waiting to save for the stereo, and you'll have had to spend the year listening to music on your tinny old record player.

Instead, what if you had gotten a $300 cash advance from your Master Charge and were able to get that stereo right away? In most parts of the country, you would be paying 12% interest on the advance. Compute the minimal monthly re-payment at approximately $26.50, and total interest cost at year's end when the debt is paid off will be about $18. Since interest payments can be deducted in determining taxable income, the *Money* magazine experts say, the real after-tax interest payments will be less than $12 (the $18 reduced by your 36% bracket tax saving). You would also have avoided the $27 price increase on the stereo by buying it now. So, subtracting the $12 after-tax real interest that you paid, you can save a net of $15. And, of course, you will have had the benefit of enjoying your stereo for an entire year.

Just remember one thing: when you borrow, you must eventually pay back! So be cautious and responsible in your planning.

What all this proves is that, as in every other area of your life, you have to plan and set goals.

Ask yourself: What do I want out of life? What sort of financial success would really please me? Will I think of myself as successful with just a good job, some money in the bank and a few stocks in the old portfolio — or do I want more than that? Only *you* can answer these questions. ·

As a guide to helping you understand yourself, we offer Gail North's "Success and Money Quiz." Again, as earlier in this book, you can't pass or fail the test. You can only learn from it. If you answer *no*, for example, to the question "Do you keep yourself informed about investment possibilities?" ... and yet you claim to be interested in investments, there's obviously something wrong. Investments might not really interest you. There might be another road you prefer to take to make money. We are all different from one another, and it is only when you understand yourself that you can really get ahead.

Success and Money Quiz

Do you fully understand your own knowledge of, and attitudes about, money? You may *think* you know yourself, *think* you have a handle on your own patterns and habits of saving and spending, but how you behave and how you speak about finances will ultimately reveal your true financial philosophy.

1. When you hear the word 'money' in a conversation, do you speak up or shut up?

2. Which statement comes closest to your own feelings about money?
   a. I would like to have a lot of money in order to live any way I choose—fine home, car, clothes, country club living.

   b. I don't want to be rich, I just want to be comfortable.

3. Do you have a well-defined dream of your future?
   a. Do you have a plan to finance that dream?
   b. What steps are you taking to implement that plan?
   c. How much are you willing to sacrafice to attain your long-range goals?

4. Do you know how to make your money work for you?
   a. Do you have a high-interest savings account?
   b. Do you think about investing?
   c. Do you keep yourself informed of investment possibilities?

5. Are you susceptible to "quick-money" schemes?

6. Are you willing to take educated risks with your money?

7. You feel one way about money, yet what you project may be different. Do you recognize any of these types?
   a. Free, easy, generous—picks up tabs before anyone else does.
   b. Prudent, fair—picks up the tab, but asks for each person's share.
   c. Frugal, tough—lets someone else pick it up and waits to be asked for his share.

8. You're owed a sum of money by a client, company or friend, and it's way overdue. How do you handle getting it back?
   a. Wait until it's mentioned by the other person then ask?
   b. Make a clear statement for yourself by asking him when it's due?
   c. Turn it over to a lawyer?

9. Credit cards and charge accounts—do they work for or against you? What do they mean to you?
   a. Tax deductions—an account of expeditures?
   b. A way of dealing with easy spending?
   c. A contemporary tool?

10. Cash is the reality of money. How much do you carry with you?
    a. Enough to get through the day?
    b. A Montana bankroll—all ones?
    c. Ostentatious amounts?

FINANCIAL QUIZ

169

11. Do you know how many credit lines you have open to you?

12. Are you an over-extender?
    a. Do you fly now and pay later?
    b. Do you have a limit on how much you will owe?

13. Do you have an idea of how the economics of the country affect you personally?

14. Have you considered hiring an accountant or a financial advisor?

15. Do you honestly feel you have an informed attitude toward money?

INTERVIEW

"Many people make the mistake of confusing the idea of failing with failure."

WILLIAM MURPHY

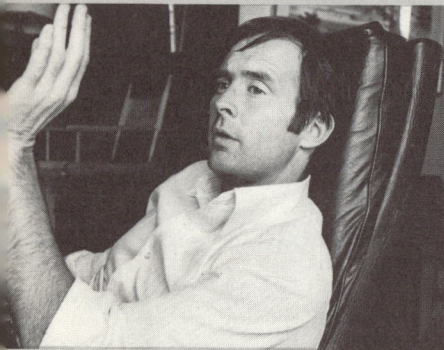

If you followed Ivy League football some years ago, the name Bill Murphy will have a special meaning. As an end on Cornell's team, he broke many records in the early 1960s. And before injuries forced him out of professional football, he was beginning to make a name for himself with the New England Patriots.

For the past five years, Murphy has been a commodities broker with Shearson, Hayden and Stone. When he started in the business, he earned a little less than $12,000 a year. This year, Murphy expects to bring home more than twice the income of the President of the United States. "I've done fairly well in the business," Murphy says with justified pride. "I like commodities. The business is a kind of thrill, like going to the races every day. In fact, it sometimes is almost too exciting. When you can make $100,000 in one day it can knock you out. The greatest thing is that everything that happens in the world affects my job, whether it's a war in Ghana or a new tax in Brazil. So I have to keep up. I am always taking a kind of constant crash course in current events. I have to keep alert. It's hard to take time off.

"I invest for myself and for clients. I am really pleased that my clients trust me; they leave the decisions to my discretion. But it's tough. I think any field is tough where you go all out to win. You have to give a lot of yourself. It's all in how much you give to the job. You have to keep in shape. I exercise. I play squash and tennis. I run. Maybe two and one-half miles. Right here in the city.

"Let me tell you about a running incident which proves how training makes you successful. I was once hit by a car while running. But from my football training I instinctively fell and rolled the way I would if I was hit while running on a field. I kept running and didn't realize how shaken up I was until I came home.

"Life can be great if you are able to control it. It's not fate. It's how you do things that counts. Life is habits. If you do enough of the right things enough times, chances are you'll make money. I think a successful man starts out early in life imagining the kind of person he'll be. You figure out what kinds of rewards you want. If you want a Jaguar, you think about how to earn that Jaguar.

170

"I was a skinny little kid but I made it into pro football. I didn't have any special ability. But I was able to catch very well. When I was playing football in high school, I'd constantly think about catching footballs. I was an end. I'd imagine myself catching it. The idea of catching that ball was always in my mind. It took over my thoughts. And when game time came, I did it easily. I think that if someone wants to be president of a certain firm, he has to start imagining himself in the role of the president—even if the dream won't come true for ten years. It's the same with money. If you want to have a great deal of money, think about it all the time.

"I try to be prudent, I guess, but I also take risks. There are two types of people: The achiever type and the security type. I can't think of one achiever I know who doesn't take a risk when it is absolutely necessary. I'm not saying to be foolhardy. The security-minded guy always thinks, 'What will happen if I fail?' Well, we all fail. I think the best advice I can give is that failing is not failure. Many people make the mistake of confusing the idea of failing with failure. We all have things we work on that don't win. Abraham Lincoln certainly failed more times than most people have even tried. Lincoln failed as a lawyer, a soldier, a businessman, and for some years he failed in politics. Also, we should try to take advantage of the future. Get involved in something where there's a whole lot of potential. Get into fields that aren't too crowded.

"I am in the minority on this one: Put away some cash. Everybody expects future income to pay for things. But the time to really make it is when you have cash handy during a national financial reverse, and that's going to happen. It won't be permanent. But if you have cash available during a buyer's market, you can pick up those bargains which will pay off in years to come.

"Don't get me wrong. I think the long-range future is going to be fabulous. But we are going to have a recession or two, and I think there's going to be a massive liquidation of certain properties—second homes, for example—that people have been buying during boom times. They'll need cash. If you have some cash, you'll be able to pick up the real estate less than at value, and it will pay off in the future. Dislocations always mean tremendous opportunities; those are times when strong people do well. Great fortunes were made in the South after the Civil War, by southerners who were able to understand what was happening and knew how to profit by it rather than sit around and cry.

"Have I mentioned enthusiasm? If you're not enthusiastic about a project, it's damn hard to make it work. Successful men are generally very enthusiastic about their work. But most of the time, I'll wager, it's not for the money. When you dream about something—and know exactly what you want to be, are enthusiastic and are willing to take the risks—you'll sure as hell get the money anyway. And you need a bit of luck, too. I was lucky to have two great parents who were on my side all the way."

HOW TO BUDGET YOUR MONEY

At least two hundred books and several thousand magazine articles have been written on the subject of budgeting. It is one of those necessary activities that most American men talk about and advocate — but avoid like the plague. None of us, even the most devoutly organized, enjoy the process of budgeting. Perhaps, psychologically, we fear and resent facing the fact of our financial limitations and learning what we have to do without. Yet, in the long run all facts are helpful; they are the information you need before you can begin to help yourself. Better to *know* your checking account is low, and not make out a specific check, than have the check bounce, spoil your credit and suffer a bank service charge to boot!

A budget is a financial plan, and as we have repeated again and again and again throughout this book, planning is necessary for success. Many men say: "Well, I'm pretty good with figures. I do all the budgeting in my head." *Don't* do it that way — even if you can. *Write it down.* When we write something, we tend to treat it as a commitment. It is like signing a contract with ourselves. As with exercise and diet, budgeting is unpleasant but necessary. And, like exercise, you feel better once you've done it. You know the exercise will strengthen your body. Similarly the budget will strengthen your financial future. Almost all the successful men we've interviewed stressed the importance of keeping a personal budget.

"It doesn't have to be complicated," advises Milton Van Rynn, a successful sales engineer and vice-president of Lapatronics, Inc., a medium-sized manufacturer of ultrasonic equiment for the medical industry. Van Rynn, who considers himself a very happy and integrated man, feels that his success comes from careful planning. He owns a $75,000 home (bought for $29,500 seven years ago), two cars, and has a thirty hour a week college student acting as nursemaid for his two children (ages 3 and 1) while his wife works as a math teacher in a nearby junior high school. The Van Rynns belong to two clubs. They lead an active social life. For the past six years they have put an annual average of $3,500 into stocks and bonds, out of Mrs. Van Rynn's salary.

"I picked my employer," Van Rynn explains. "There were two or three companies looking for someone with my capabilities. They were all in my area of the country (Iowa) and all had potential for growth. I chose Lapa-tronics because of the excellent fringe benefits. You can't imagine how much I save on life insurance and health premiums."

Van Rynn leases his car. "I use it for business, mostly, so I can write off a good part of its use." Until the gas crunch, he filled the tank according to octane rating. "Why pay for octane numbers not needed?," he asks. The Van Rynns wait for sales to buy clothes, and often save from twenty to twenty-five percent. As basketball fans, they spend about $120 for tickets to college games. "We don't think of ourselves as penny pinchers," Van Rynn stresses. "It's just getting a dollar's value out of a dollar."

The Van Rynn family has a system.

"We have a method of control. We looked at our lives and decided that our income should be allocated for (1) fixed obligations, (2) savings for the future and (3) current discretionary pleasures. "I come in contact with many successful businessmen," he says, "and next to our mutual business interests, the conversation often centers around money. In an inflation like the one we have, what else is on everybody's mind? It's the great common subject. What everyone agrees on is that *a system of control is necessary* for anyone who wants to feel comfortable with money."

Van Rynn doesn't suggest how anyone else divide up income. "If you want to defer savings until another year and concentrate your discretionary income on personal pleasure, why not? It's your life. Just make sure it's a lifestyle you have selected—not one you've drifted into because it's easy. *What you need is some kind of plan.* We don't even use the word 'budget,' because I don't think it's possible to keep a budget in the old-fashioned sense: sixty-seven cents for lighter fluid; $3.25 for shoeshines. Budgets like that look good on paper, but in practical use they don't work. People can't live by a minute-to-minute plan. Life is a series of fluctuations. But if you have some kind of master plan, you can withstand those fluctuations. If you are fat and keep to your diet, you can occasionally go to a restaurant and eat all the bread and potatoes you want. Just as long as you keep to the diet as a rule."

How to Prepare a Personal Budget

It's not really very hard to prepare a budget. The first thing you have to do is evaluate your assets.

1. What is your salary *before* taxes?
2. What is your salary *after* taxes?
3. What *other income* do you have?

Then —

Make a list of your fixed (unavoidable) expenses and your other regular expenses, in a simple chart like this one, using actual recent figures as a guide:

	Jan	Feb	March
RENT	$317	$317	$317
FOOD	262	194	236
NOTIONS (newspapers, tobacco, shaving cream, etc.)	81	101	78
GASOLINE	32	40	36
GARAGE (parking lot at work)	55	55	55
MEDICAL/ DENTAL	35	35	35
INSURANCE	16	16	16
ENTERTAINMENT	116	114	200
CREDIT CARD PAYMENT (personal—not business)	915	872	974

On the chart you see that your expenses average approximately $900 a month. You find that, after taxes, you take home $1,265 a month. That gives you about $365 a month in discretionary income—almost four thousand dollars a year. Out of that must come your luxuries, special entertainment, and savings. This also gives you a pretty good idea where you are financially, and where you are going. You know how much money you actually have. You can determine whether or not you can actually afford to stay in your present job. Ask yourself: Realistically, can you make more money in the near future? Will your next raise give you more discretionary income, or will it just cover the spiraling expenses? A simple little chart like this means an investment of less than an hour a month; it is certainly time well spent.

Every once in a while, it is advisable to really get into the heart of your expenses. It takes a bit more discipline, but only requires a few moments of your time. Buy a small 29¢ pocket notebook, and for one whole week (or, preferably, two) jot down every expense. We mean *every* expense. Write it so you can read it:

Date June 3, A.M.
Monday
  Newspapers   .25
  Breakfast $1.75
      Tip   .35
  Tip parking lot .25
  Coffee   .35
  Chinese Laundry $3.03
  Cigars $1.25
  Handkerchief $2.00

Joe's Birthday $1.00
Party (office) $1.50
  Stamps   3.00
June 3, P.M.
Lunch:
  Ajax Diner $4.75
      Tip   .50
Dry Cleaner $8.15
Time Magazine $1.25

You will soon see where your hard-earned dollars are going.

THE CREDIT CARD

Credit is very simple. It means —*buy now, pay later*. Living on credit has become so popular in America that it almost ranks ahead of baseball as the national sport. According to statistics compiled by the Survey Research Center of the University of Michigan, *almost eighty percent of young families (where the head of the household is age 25 to 34) are paying off an installment purchase or loan.* And so were sixty percent of the householders under age 54.

Not since the introduction of paper money has a financial innovation so changed the idea of paying bills as that piece of plastic known as the credit card. It is almost impossible to be in the business world today without owning a credit card of some kind. Try to rent a car without a credit card, even if you have a fistfull of hundred-dollar bills. And with the rising crime rates in most big cities, you wouldn't want to carry those bills even if you do have them. Credit cards are as good as cash in all parts of America and in most parts of the world.

A few years ago, a woman named Ann Foley tested the premise. She lived on a credit card for an entire month without spending a cent of cash. First, she spent two cashless weeks in her home town in California. She shopped for everything from handbags to groceries, had a tooth filled, and rented a bicycle. She rented a car and drove to Los Angeles. She stayed in a motel, toured the city, shopped, ate in the fanciest restaurants, visited

Disneyland and went to a baseball game. The only thing she was unable to charge on her credit card was a hot dog at Dodger Stadium.

Ask any salesman about the importance of a credit card. It is indispensable to anyone who has to conduct business outside his office. He can take a client to lunch in Omaha or Little Rock, pop out his credit card and sign the tab. He does not have to make inconvienient notes for his expense account, and nobody in the home office will question whether he really did spend $20.76, tax and tip, for a lunch at the Longhorn in Dallas on April 13th. It is also convenient to have a credit card with you on non-business occasions. (You're on Interstate 80, a tire blows and you have only five dollars in cash. What could have been a real mess diminishes as a problem when your credit card pays for both towing *and* the new tire.)

Now we come to that real "secret of success—" perhaps one of the top three secrets—which is really no secret at all: *Pay your bills.*

Your credit rating is more than just a badge of honor. It travels with you from town to town, job to job. If you lose your credit rating, it is difficult to get it back. *So, if you are having trouble paying your bills don't avoid your creditor. Let him know that you are having trouble. Write a letter to the credit department of the company you owe money to. Give them an idea of when you will be able to pay your bill. Or pay even a small part of it.* They will almost surely give you a chance if you let them know you are having trouble. If you avoid this responsibility, once they send your bill to a collection agency you are in trouble. It gets recorded in some credit bureau, and travels with you for life. Many companies send in names of delinquent accounts to the credit bureau, but then fail to let them know when the bill is paid, and the "bad credit notice" stays on your dossier.

Since you are going to have to deal with credit all of your professional and adult life, it would be wise to learn something about how your credit rating is prepared. When you apply for a charge account you force someone to judge the extent of your ability to pay the bill. The credit investigator has never met you; he probably never will. He uses methods so thorough that, by the time the people you have asked to give you credit approve (or deny) your application, the information supplied will tell more about you than you can possibly believe.

Take a look at a credit application.

They don't ask if you pay your bills on time.

They don't ask if you have a lot of money.

What they do is ask where you work; where you live; who you bank with; where you have other accounts. Your answers are clues necessary for the investigator to ferret out all the information about your character as it relates to paying bills. Usually, credit investigations are run by *credit bureaus* whose purpose it is to find out as much as possible about credit-seekers, circulate it among their clients (department stores, bank card companies, etc.) exchange the information with other credit bureaus.

Remember—your credit record begins the first time you make a formal request for credit. It doesn't end until you die. And over the years, every new request for credit will be noted, as well as your record of payment.

There are other things a credit bureau does, in addition to keeping an eye on how fast you pay Diners Club. They clip newspapers and study police blotters and court records. If your divorce comes to court, chances are it will be recorded on your credit record. Credit is a very big business; for it to work, it has to be a thorough business. If you get picked up as drunk and disorderly, or for a minor drug bust, it can go on your credit record. And as we have said, you can't get away from it. If you move to a new area, even the most remote corner of the globe and apply for credit, rest assured the local credit bureau will check with the credit bureau in the city you've just left, and your record will be forwarded.

There are consumer pressure organizations who feel credit bureaus know too much. In most states, it is possible for you to request a copy of your own record so you can see how you stand. It also gives you a chance to make sure all the information is accurate. Most of us never bother to check. However, if your credit has been good, you know you've paid your bills, and yet you *are* turned down—then do check! If you find any errors, it's up to you to prove them as errors, and then the record can be straightened out in a few days.

Everybody pays some bills late; this isn't what stores or credit card companies are after. They take the vicissitudes of contemporary life in stride. But if you are chronically late, watch out. Some prospective employers check your credit rating, too. So it's always wise to be in good stead with the credit bureau. If you decide *not* to pay a bill because of dissatisfaction with merchandise, be sure to contact the credit bureau in your area and let them know. They understand this kind of situation, and will give you a chance to work it out with the store before putting you down as a delinquent. It's ominous silence that makes creditors worry.

INTERVIEW *"Success is chance favoring a prepared mind."*

EDWARD HOGAN

Ed Hogan is vice-president of operations and security for the Interbank Card Association, the parent company for Master Charge. A former Naval officer and narcotics agent for the Department of Justice, Hogan joined Interbank as a security expert; within ten years he rose to a position of intensive responsibility. While we were interviewing him, he made a phone call which resulted in the cutting off of Master Charge credit for Nicaragua. Hogan is an advocate of the credit card.

"It has to do with more than the fact I am in the business," he assured us. "It is the wave of the future. We haven't begun to explore the ways the credit card is going to be used in the 1980s. The entire success in managing a credit card is this: *Don't let the card use you.* Too many people become prisoners of the card."

There is still some opposition to the idea of the credit card, even among top executives.

"It's diminishing. It's a cultural thing. Successful young people accept it without a blink. They've grown up with the concept. It's older people who still think it is sinful. In fact, I don't think it is possible anymore to conduct business in the United States, or anywhere in the world, without having a credit card."

Isn't a credit card a temptation? Even very conservative businessmen complain they spend more money with the card.

"It is a mature decision to keep within your credit line. Each card is good for an amount of money. Don't extend it if you can't handle it. It's easy to lose that credit rating, and without the card you really have trouble doing business. Have you tried to pay a hotel bill without a credit card? They won't even let you register. The card is *good*. It's people who abuse it. I think the young man on the go has to realize that *you don't use it just because you have it*. A credit card is a terrific privilege that makes life phenomenally more simple."

Simple?
"You are in a restaurant with two clients. Everybody want to pay the bill. You get stuck. Do you have $100 in your pocket? Probably not. Who carries cash? Only fools do. We live in a credit card society. If you are to be successful in this world, you've got to have credit cards. Your contemporaries will assume that you do. Prospective employers will assure that you do. A good credit rating is a handmaiden to responsibility."

What happens if someone abuses his credit card?
"A man can destroy his credit. And that tends to be very unhealthy. It affects other things. Employers often check credit records. A delinquent payer with a bad track record isn't the kind of man anybody wants to give responsibility in an important company. A credit rating tends to be an historical record, a document telling the kind of person you are. When you have a credit card in good standing it means a bank or credit institution is saying, 'We are entrusting Mr. X for so much money.' It is a badge of honor. It means you are a solid citizen. Let me go back to that business lunch again. You have invited someone to lunch. You think you have enough money. But your guest happens to order the special double filet mignon with champagne. You are embarrassed. Think what it looks like to him when you have to ask the waiter if the restaurant will take a check. It means that you *can't* get credit. You don't have credit cards. It means you aren't participating in your times. I read somewhere that there were three great inventions in history; inventions that changed ways of life: the wheel, fire and the credit card."

You obviously are convinced that the credit card is the cash of the future.
"Absolutely. That's why, to any young person who asks me about success, I stress that it is important to have them and use them responsibly. The 1980s are going to see a proliferation of cards. Credit cards are going to be used for greater amounts of dollars. They will replace the check at the point of sale. I can foresee where the credit card will take the place of the check. All the bookkeeping will be done by computer. The card will mean you have available credit and, as someone who is an achiever, what better asset is there? Using a credit card is a better way of doing business."

Don't you think the temptation to misuse the card is always with us?
"I don't know. It's very American to take chances. The idea of having more is what's made America great. The man with the large appetite, the large bite—he's the one who gets things done. If he spends a bit too much, it's his incentive to do better. Earn more. We're talking about success. And success takes work. The opportunities are always there, but you have to work like a son of a gun to get there. You always have to be prepared for success."

What do you mean by success?
"I'm not sure who said it, but I think I have a very good definition.
Success is chance favoring a prepared mind."

WHERE TO PUT YOUR SAVINGS MONEY

"Passbook savings accounts are obsolete, the buggy whips of the modern age. Inflation passed them by, and low government interest ceilings did them in . . ."

—Jane Bryant Quinn,
Newsweek
business columnist

Many economists have been predicting the demise of passbook savings for several years. How many stories have been read about old people complaining because the money they put in savings banks twenty-five years ago hasn't increased in value? The dollar certainly could buy a lot more in the 1950s than it can now. However, everybody should have some form of savings. All your money can't go into real estate, because we all need ready cash for upcoming expenses.

According to expert Jane Bryant Quinn, the smart money people are looking into mutual funds which are especially designed for savers. They are called *money market funds*. "If more people knew about them," Quinn says, "money funds could put passbook accounts right out of business."

A money market fund pools the cash of thousands of investors. It then lends the money, on short-term loans, to banks, big corporations, and also to the government. This is all done on free-market interest rates.

Because the quality of the borrowers is so blue-chip, and because the loans have to be paid back so quickly (some in a few days), the investor can expect a dollar back for every dollar invested—plus interest, of course.

As of mid-1979, the money funds were paying from 9 to 10% on deposits of $1,000 or more. Moreover, there are neither withdrawal penalties nor minimum time periods for deposits.

If you are in need of quick cash, you are permitted to write checks against the funds—generally in amounts of $500 or more. There is *no* sales charge.

Here are the names of some of the bigger money market funds:

SCUDDER MANAGED RESERVES (Boston)
KEMPER MONEY MARKET FUND (Chicago)
MERRILL LYNCH READY ASSETS (NYC)
MONEYMART ASSETS (NYC)
RESERVE FUND (NYC)
CAPITAL PRESERVATION FUND (Palo Alto)

INCOME TAX

Have you been overpaying your income tax? You don't think so, because you are so clever and have taken every deduction. Right? Well, you are in the *minority* if it is true. "It's our experience," writes Henry W. Block, president of H. & R. Block, Inc, the largest income-tax accounting firm in America (they prepare about six million returns yearly in the company's 4,000 offices) "that roughly three out of four clients have been overpaying, because they are simply unaware of all the credits to which they're entitled."

That's why you should get an expert to handle your taxes. *It's worth the money* because you'll save money. Don't just go to your friend, Bernie, because he happens to be an accountant, and a friend, and successful. Go to an accountant who handles other people in *your field*. An *expert*. Bernie might be great with his hardware and hard-goods wholesale clients. That's *his* specialty. But you're an executive in a wood products company. Ask around. Who handles your boss' account? Who handles other executives in the *industry*? That's the man who studies the tax laws with an eye on your profession. He will be the man who knows how to save you the most money.

Like preparing a budget, tax preparation is not only unpleasant (nobody wants to give money away) — it's *boring*. But the successful man can do a good job even when it is boring. The idea of doing a good job should be incentive enough. It's what gets you to the top, and should permeate every area of your life.

So, make records of your expenditures. Save all receipts.

Make it a habit. Xerox every bill and put a copy in a file simply labeled "Taxes." It only takes a minute, and when the time comes you will be *prepared*.

That's the *real* secret of success!

BUILDING YOUR FORTUNE

We went into a bookstore the other day and counted the number of books purporting to advise the investor on how to make lots of money. There were almost one hundred of them, written by everybody from a former movie star who did make a fortune on the stock market to a number of acknowledged security analysts. Every one of these books probably has good advice, specific advice. There were also books on how to make money in real estate, how to make money going into a mail-order business on the side, and all kinds of other guides.

All of these books contain valuable information. It *is* possible to make a small fortune, even in a side business. A California engineer made $300,000 in one year with a gimmick mail-order item called a "Feely." A twenty-nine-year-old Idaho chemicals salesman made $3,000 a *week* (according to an ad promoting a course on real estate sales) developing property — "with almost no investment." Folklore abounds with stories of bright young men who have built small investments into stock market fortunes. A thirty-four-year-old shipping executive salted away a half-million in stocks in the past ten years, by investing only part of his salary. (He made the headlines in 1979 when he was arrested for evading payment of his income taxes.) We know a man who invested $1,000 in Polaroid in 1958 and who sold it for $138,000 in 1968. Just about everybody has a friend or relative, or knows somebody who knows somebody who knows somebody, who had made a bundle by investing in an obscure electronics corporation. Stockbroker Bill Murphy says that fortunes can be made in days on the commodities market, and he seems to be proving it.

It's very important to have your money work for you. It is very wise to invest. But most people on the road to success have very little extra money. In the 1980s, discretionary income will be lessened even further by inflation.

179

What if you want to invest in the stockmarket?

So many questions arise: How risky is it? Which stocks should you buy? Are bonds the thing? After all, they're supposed to be safer. How much of your income *can* you afford to invest? Do you really know the difference between stocks and bonds? Or how they differ and how their prices are determined?

Do you *really* have an interest in stocks and bonds?

It is very important to *understand* how your money is working for you. When investing, you should choose an *expert* to advise you. You wouldn't go on a trip aborad without a travel agent. He or she is the expert, wise in the ways of the business, whose entire working life is devoted to travel and making your trip better. A *stockbroker* does this—he spends all his professional time (and most of his waking hours) thinking about stocks, bonds, investing. Generally, the company he works for has a department which analyzes all the business on the Exchanges, as well as the over-the-counter stocks.

It is his job to advise you. Putting it simply: *choose a field of investment in which there is an expert available to you*. And, most important, *you ought to be interested in the field in which you are going to invest*. Remember, no matter how little your investment it is your hard-earned money and you should know how it is being used.

If you can't generate an interest in the stock market (don't be embarrassed, many many top executives don't know *anything* about the stock market) then don't invest in the stock market. Invest in real estate, instead. Many young men are forming little side-business partnerships, putting money together and buying real estate as a group. It becomes a social as well as financial activity. Or, the same group may want to find a small business in which to invest. We knew a bright young man who began a service business, a small cleaning service for single people who lived in apartments, couldn't afford full-time maid service, but didn't have the time nor inclination to clean their apartments. The service would come in and spent no more than an hour in one apartment. Three men and one woman did all the work, and fast. They could do several apartments a day. The business was backed by three up-and-coming executives, each of whom put a small amount of money in the kitty. That was four years ago. Each now owns a third of a prosperous cleaning service company with twenty-five employees, two trucks, and a bright future.

Again, the secret of success in investing is to do it as professionally as possible (with the help of an expert—at least until you know enough to make decisions on your own) and in an area which sparks your imagination and has your interest and attention.

Also, if you are not prepared to possibly *lose* your money, then put it in savings banks or municipal bonds where you are assured of a regular income. There is nothing unmanly in being conservative. There is a cardinal rule in investing: You don't win all the time. There are as many "loser" stories as "winners."

Sometimes the slow, but steady, tortoise wins. If you buy two shares of a blue chip stock every six months, at the end of one year you will have four shares. In ten years, you could have shares in the hundreds, what with stock splits. Many conservative "fortunes" have been made by buying a small number of blue chips every year, letting them sit, and then reinvesting the profits in more stock. It's hard to go wrong with an American company which is in the top twenty of the Fortune 500 list (Fortune Magazine lists the 500 most profitable companies each year). Unless you have no faith at all in America's future — and in that case, you shouldn't be buying this book, since our plan is to help make *you* an important part of that future.

MARK H. FLEISCHMAN

Mark Fleischman is a man who not only takes chances, but truly thrives on challenge. The son of a successful New York hotel man, Fleischman graduated from the Cornell School of Hotel Administration and then spent his Navy career running an officers' club. Since 1964 he has: taken over, saved, and sold at profit a landmark New York inn; turned the financially troubled Executive Hotel into a profit-making operation, and opened and developed one of New York's most successful restaurants and supper clubs, *A Quiet Little Table In The Corner.*

He also acquired the principal interest in the Mon Ark Shrimp Corporation, a major importing firm that specializes in frozen seafood, and within two years increased sales by fifty percent to $12 million. With a group of associates, he acquired Davos, Inc., a small ski area in upstate New York with sales of under $400,000, and built it to a company with revenues in excess of $80 million. On top of all that he built Mt. Snow in Vermont into one of the largest ski resorts in the world.

Among his current interests are: restoring the bankrupt Virgin Isle Hotel (St. Thomas, Virgin Islands); running two unusual Japanese restaurants in New York (Robata and the SoHo Robata); producing films. Mark Fleischman was born in 1940.

A recent magazine profile of Fleischman described him this way: "quiet — not overly guarded or reticent, just listening quiet, weighing you as much as you're weighing him. 'It's important,' he said recently, 'to make people you're working with feel comfortable with you. To do this, you have to know what they want out of life; you have to listen.' "

Fleischman believes that the world is becoming more competitive. "In a competitive world, it is imperative to become more organized. I personally function best with many projects. At first I didn't know what my talents were, but I learned early in my career that one of my greatest pleasures was to create a space where people want to come; a hotel, a resort, a restaurant. It's what I love to do, and that's why I can devote all my effort to it. It's important to do what pleases you. Then your work becomes a vocation, not just a job. Something you must do. Not a nine-to-five job. Nobody who is really successful only works from nine-to-five. It's always with you. Even when you play. And why shouldn't it be?

"The successful businessman is very creative, I think. It's very easy to acquire something, if you can raise the money. What's terrific is to be able to make it work. That's the creative part. You take chances, and sometimes it doesn't work out as well as you would like. There are all kinds of factors. And you have to know how to deal with people. I don't want any of the people who work for me to do something just to please me. I want them to make decisions because they feel it's right. If we have a disagreement, I try to bring them around to my way of thinking through intelligent persuasion. I think that's a number one tool of the executive, to be able to do that. One thing you have to worry about is that people don't feel they have *lost* if things don't go their way. People are too much into this win or lose notion. People have to learn to respect themselves and each other more.

"And, you don't always win. We had a lot of trouble with Davos. I'm sure you read about it. We were right in the middle of the last energy crisis, in 1974. The ski business was really hurting, because of lack of snow, recession, the energy crisis, but I had faith in myself. Let me stress that: *having faith in yourself is one of the keys to success. Especially in bad times*. You also have to know your limitations and understand the gambles. We were losing money. We had employees to feed. The entire valley depended on the ski business. I had creditors calling me. But I did the right thing, I think, and I will give this as advice: I didn't run away. People in debt, even very legitimate ones, often run away. They don't answer their telephones and this is what gets people jumpy, nervous. I sat by the phone and explained the situation to everybody. If you confront your creditors directly, you preserve your own credibility in their eyes. I devised an alternate plan it was tough going, but Mt. Snow did not close down as it could have because of lack of maintenance funds.

"I told the story over and over about how we were *over-extended*, how the weather had been against us. And how I was going to Japan to get the money. If you confront your creditors and ask their advice, you will at least buy yourself some time. I went to Japan. If I had failed, I might have gone down the tubes myself. There was the responsibility of the whole town, depending on me. And I didn't want anything terrible to happen. I couldn't let go of myself for a minute. I had to be all confidence, all the time. I had to be calm and wait out the Japanese, who do business in a different way. I had promised the town that the Japanese would come through. I even had a group of people ready to picket the Japanese embassy if they didn't come through. But dealing with the Japanese is a waiting game. The Samurai spirit is still strong. I waited it out. They came through. It was tough going. But nobody sued us for money. Everybody got paid. *By planning, by being honest, and by following through, sticking to it, we won*.

"I have some advice for anybody who finds himself defeated, or at least temporarily in bad straits. Defeat involves other people. Clean up your mess as best you can. Do what you can to minimize losses. Let people know you're working the best you can. Ask them for their advice; it kind of forces them over to your side: 'Here's what happened to us. How would you handle it?'

"Find the specific reasons for your failure. Make sure you've learned every lesson. Be sure to look at all the fifteen levels of the downside. And if you have drive, you'll become successful again. You can't be successful in today's world unless you can cope with changes. You have to be self-motivated even under the direst circumstances. If that sounds hard, well, I personally don't know any other way. I'm married to the struggle. It's my life, and I make it wonderful."

GETTING OUT OF DEBT

It happens to all of us, even the most well-intentioned. We are only human, and we do err. Will it happen to you? We hope not. Credit lines seem inexhaustible, since it is readily available from so many sources. Let's hope you don't have to use this advice, but *preparation* is our keyword. *It is better to have a plan for an emergency*.

Your refrigerator stopped working while you were on vacation, water poured on the floor, ruining the linoleum and your neighbor's ceiling. You have to pay the plumber cash. You owe a thousand dollars and you only have two hundred in the bank. You can't borrow from any one person; and all your other bills are about to come due at once, and you don't want to lose your credit rating.

You can dash to Ecuador (better than Brazil nowadays, for non-extradition of Americans) or face the problem squarely and begin to climb the long ladder to solvency.

Remember, your "tragedy" is just another business problem to your creditors. Face them. Let them know what happened. Sit down with their credit managers and work out a plan. As in the case of credit card indebtedness, they will listen to *anything* that sounds like a solution. They want the money. They would rather have it in small payments over a long time than not at all. Keep in mind that, if you can't come up with a plan, creditors will take what steps are open to them. If you avoid them, they'll treat you with an equal lack of consideration; they will repossess your car, furniture, appliances. They may even force you into bankruptcy, in exceptional cases. But these are weapons of last resort. If you stay in touch with them and keep paying according to your agreement—even in small amounts—you can manage to reestablish your credit without the credit bureau ever having any notion of the situation.

There are professional credit counselors, but if you are really broke there's no way for you to pay their fees. If you are very friendly with your lawyer, perhaps he'll write letters to the creditors for you. There is a kind of confidence created when a creditor receives a letter from your lawyer (or accountant). It indicates that you are probably a responsible person who went off the straight and narrow by accident, and so there is a tendency on the part of creditors to give you the benefit of the doubt. *But while you are paying off these bills, don't run up others.*

If it's at all possible, get a consolidation loan from a bank. This arrangement involves getting one loan big enough to pay off other debts. One large debt is often preferable to several small ones, even when they total the same amount. Monthly payments are smaller, since the pay-back period has been extended. And the interest rate on a single bank loan may well be less than those on the combined overdue debts. But take care; don't count on this too much. Banks will listen to your plight, and if your job is good enough you might get the loan.

But banks are much happier about lending money to people who have collateral than to those who don't. It's a fact of life, despite all the bank advertising telling you how easy it is to get a loan for that trip to Bali or Timbuktoo.

The best advice is to be careful in the first place. Then, if you do get into financial trouble, be honest with your creditors—and concentrate on paying back your debts.

It's the great American dream: *to be in business for yourself*. Everybody thinks about it. Many try and many fail, for myriad reasons. The advice we've gotten from a number of sources is that *it will be difficult to go into business during the next few years because start-up money will be hard to find, especially for novices*.

There is plenty of venture capital around but, according to an article in *Newsweek*, most of it is tabbed for "bolstering established companies that

TRYING IT ON YOUR OWN

need expansion capital." This won't stop anybody who has a mind to go into business for himself. Nor should it. If you have the necessary confidence, a reasonable goal, and expertise in the field—and have enough money behind you—you have a fair chance of success. Of course, you may have to work seven days a week, three hundred and sixty-five days a year, take very little for yourself at first, and have to be able to meet payrolls and increased responsibilities since other lives will depend on you. You'll be totally responsible for the success or failure of the enterprise; you won't be able to put the blame on anybody else.

Many people think it is worth it. Some feel that the *only* way to be successful is to run your own company. But success is what you perceive it to be. If your idea of being successful is to be in business for yourself, you should consider it very carefully.

Steve Horn was one of the most successful commercial photographers in the United States and one of the most talented. His brilliant pictures have appeared in every major national magazine. His work has advertised scores of familiar products. There is a real feeling of relaxed elegance in Horn photos; they are individual, with his personal stamp clearly on them. He is now co-director of Steve Horn, Inc., together with his beautiful and talented wife, Linda. The company produces television commercials. Horn commercials win prizes. They also sell products. So the Horns are very busy, and are able to pick and choose among clients despite the fact that they have only been in business for five years.

Steve and Linda Horn

"Steve worked for me when I was running Vogue Patterns," Linda Horn says, "so we knew we could work together." Steve Horn had been part of a firm which produced TV commercials. Although the company title included his name, in essence "he wasn't more than an employee. He really was not able to do the kind of work that pleased him," Linda says. "Steve is an enormously talented man with goals. When he was an art director years ago, he found he could take better pictures than the photographers he was hiring. So he started taking pictures. He had faith in his ability."

Horn himself doesn't consider his situation anything special. To him, being a producer of commercials, or a successful photographer, is just another way of earning a living. Still it's one that is pleasing to him.

"I take two days off a week," he says, "like everybody else. But what else is there except work? If the work takes you over, and mine happens to be photography, you have a real chance to achieve. To make it. In business for myself, I am able to control the product completely. *When you are in business for yourself, you have control.* I don't say this is necessary for everybody; there are all kinds of happy, achieving people who don't run their own businesses. But those people who do go into business for themselves *have* to, because it is what satisfies them. They wouldn't be satisfied any other way. If you think that way, you just have to go into business."

Horn says that working with his wife is difficult, but both of them have a total commitment. "I don't have the need to be away from my wife. There are those men who have to separate themselves, at least during the working day, from their wives. Not me. I never have to do that. We are partners and we're always together."

Linda Horn claims that to be in business you have to have partners you trust. Many businesses fail because the partners don't have sufficient faith in one another. "We'll never have that problem," she says. "Moreover, we both have this tremendous capacity for work. And we enjoy working all the time. I don't advise anyone to go into business for himself unless he totally enjoys the work part. We compete with one another, yes. But what's wrong with that? Great things come from competition. I don't understand people who are afraid to compete. You have to respect one another. Partners must do that. And to be in business, you have to think about growing all the time. You cannot stand still. You must grow."

Steve Horn believes that it is imperative for a successful businessman, whatever his business, not to let others control him — neither creatively nor financially. "You must be organized," he stresses. "Businesses run on organization. And you have to be as good as the people you work with. You must train your people to be flexible. All of our people are flexible. I think that's a major reason for our success. In fact, most of our people are young and trained by us. We take chances on people we think can make it, and we've been right. You have to gamble. And to run a business, you have to be good. If you are *good*, you can switch from one thing to another. You can, as they say in the advertising business, wear many hats. Another thing I'd advise any person going into business is not to be afraid. Fear is a real no-no. *No one can be successful in anything if he is afraid.*

"If you believe something can be done, you cannot take no for an answer. There is *always* a solution."

Both the Horns agree that the best decisions are born out of security. "An insecure employee can water down an entire operation," Linda Horn warns. "And if the owner of a business is insecure, you can bet his business will reflect it."

"You can't stay in business playing it safe." **INTERVIEW**

Nobody has ever accused Gary Zeller of insecurity. His business would blow up—literally, if he didn't know what he was doing every minute. Gary Zeller is, among other things, an explosives expert, and with his wife Joyce Spector founded The Plastics Factory. The design and engineering firm creates one-of-a-kind props, breakaways, mechanical figures, electronic gadgetry, scale models, stunts, scenery, inflatables, weaponry, smoke, fog, rain, fireworks, pyrotechnical specialties and customized vehicles.

GARY ZELLER

Why did you go into business for yourself?
"Independence. I spent a great deal of lost time working for other people. Of course, I wanted more than a fixed income, but in jobs I was always assigned to special tasks. I never was able to do research. Everytime I worked for someone else, I never had sufficient time for pre-planning. I finally decided I had to have a positive base from which to work."

Had you saved enough money to capitalize yourself?
"No. I didn't have a lot of capital. I was a set designer at the Coconut Grove Playhouse in Florida, where I met Gypsy Rose Lee. She was starring in *Auntie Mame* and was very nice to me. I told her that New York scared me. When the play went on the road, she sent me $500. I came to New York and met Joyce (now Mrs. Zeller) and hit her up for money. I did work for other people and kept converting my earnings into starting a business. I acquired a few necessary tools through auctions. I went from

bank to bank and finally convinced one to lend me some money. I gave them a pretty good proposal about what the business idea was. You really can't start a business without capitalization."

How about credit?
"I had good credit. It's hard to start without that, and I kept building up a credit line. We borrowed small sums, even when we didn't need it, just so we could put it in our savings account and have interest to apply to the loans when we paid them back. I paid the loans back in short periods. I'll advise that: *borrow money from a bank a couple of times and pay it back quickly*. Small sums. But by the time we needed it, it was easy to say, 'Give me $10,000.' It had a great effect on suppliers, too, who got good references from banks. We built credibility. But we had people burn us, too. When you are in business, you find out how bad it is not to pay somebody for work they've done."

You took a big risk going into business.
"Everybody thinks about having money without having responsibility, but in fact it doesn't work. The big thrill in life is to have confidence. Dare to do. If you don't take the dare, you'll stagnate. The thing that bothers me most is costing out a project; anybody in business trying to make money has to know how to cost out his work. Many people are wonderfully creative or can 'build a better machine.' But we live in a competitive world, and *in the real world you had better be able to do a good job for the price you can get for the job, or else you are in trouble*.

"People always think I'm too expensive. It's a nightmare. I don't like costing jobs out. But I do it. Another thing. Someone going into business better be able to assess the value of his own time. If you can't put a dollar and cents value on your hour, you're sunk. You must know your value and how to price it accordingly. And if you see that you are going to cost more than you originally estimated, let your client know immediately. Don't spring it on him as a big surprise."

Has it been worth it to go into business? You sound a little diffident about it all.
"It's tough. Being in business is tough. Just ask any businessman. We've had every scheme played on us. We have had to become, in some cases, hard and cold. It isn't good to suspect every new client. But experience teaches you an awful lot. Still, I wouldn't change. There's phenomenal satisfaction in creating something that is all yours."

Is there a formula for success?
"I deal with chemicals to make explosives and there always are several processes to get the right mixture — in other words, several ways to get to the same place. But I would say that if an individual has a goal, he should start going through the ranks. This is the way to get certification. It's also a way to build clientele, if going into business is what you have in mind.

"When you think you have learned everything you can know about the business — have risen through the ranks — you just might be satisfied helping someone else run their company. So check yourself out; *make sure you really want to go into business*. If all the answers are 'yes', then you just have to try. The independent route has greater horizons, but you also make a lot of sacrifices. No one writes a paycheck for us. Pressure is always high. You have to be fantastically aggressive. That takes a lot of energy. You can't listen to others. *You can't stay in business playing it safe*. Competition is too tough. You have to burst forward. *If you can't be aggressive, don't go into business*. Nobody is just going to give you work. You have to keep knocking on doors. In a sense, even General Motors or Dupont is out there knocking on doors."

SOME GUIDES FOR GOING INTO BUSINESS FOR YOURSELF

Most businesses fail because they are undercapitalized. This is an absolute fact, and the first subject brought up by any business counselor with a client who has decided to go out on his own.

If you are planning to take the chance, be sure to stop in to your *Small Business Administration* office. Even if you don't seek the advice of one of their experts, they have scores of research materials available for the entrepreneur who needs advice on everything from putting his plan down on paper to finding the right financial lender. They also have a number of first-rate publications, among them: *Checklist for Going Into Business*, which is free: *SBA Business Loans*, also free: *Handbook of Small Business Finance*, only 75¢; *Starting and Managing a Business Of Your Own*, priced at just $1.35. If there is no SBA office in your vicinity, the material can be ordered from the Superintendent of Documents, Government Printing Office, Washington, D.C. 20402.

Other books available:

Tax Guide for Small Business
(Internal Revenue Service, Treasury Dept. Washington, D.C. 20224 (Free).

Business Planning Guide by David Bangs, Jr. and William R. Osgood. The Federal Reserve Bank of Boston, Boston, Mass. 02106 (Free).

The Bank of America's publications on how to start new businesses are highly credible. The most popular are *Steps to Starting a New Business* ($2.00), and *Financing Small Business* ($2.00); but there is a whole list available by writing to the Bank of America, Department 3120, P. O. Box 37000, San Francisco, California 94137.

Another very popular book is *Annual Statement Studies*, Robert Morris Associates, Philadelphia, Pa. 19107; it costs $15, and is available through your bookstore. (They'll order it if they don't have it in stock). Most bankers use this guide when analyzing *your* business plans.

There are two quite expensive books that are worth the money if you are serious and confident of some success in your venture. They are both published by Capital Publishing Company, Wellesley Hills, Mass. 02181, and cost $49.50 each (though if you buy both, you can get them for $80). One, *Source Guide for Borrowing Capital*, concerns banking, the SBA, major financial concerns and many unusual sources for borrowing capital. The other, *Guide to Venture Capital Sources*, includes names, addresses, officers and areas of interest of more than 500 sources of venture capital.

WHERE DO YOU GO FROM HERE?

At the beginning of this book, we stated that the 1980s will probably be among the most challenging decades of the century. Herman Kahn, head of the Hudson Institute and as celebrated a futurist as we have in America, believes that it is a turning point decade. In a way, it's the beginning of the 21st Century—or, at the very least, the start of a new economic era. It is a decade that projects both confidence and worries. Natural resources seem to be giving out. We will probably have plenty of energy—despite dismal prophesies from the Cassandras of the press—but it will cost us more money. The 1980s will certainly not be a decade of "cheap life". Yet, for the ambitious and clever man, there are always plenty of opportunities. He makes his own.

No matter what our national future, the rules remain the same: *If you are ambitious, work hard, plan wisely, do your best, take advantage of opportunities, use your intelligence, you will attain some sort of success.*

As we've seen from the interviews in this book, success means different things to different people. We know men who are happy as middle managment in small companies—they have worked very hard to get there and are proud of their achievement, as they should be. Other men will not consider themselves successful, unless they are presidents of large corporations.

Some would rather own modest businesses of their own than be Chairman of United States Steel. That is one of the great joys of living in a society where there are choices for everyone: the man who wants to get ahead has a real shot at doing so. The key: *know yourself, and understand what is likeliest to make you happy.*

But what sort of world will it be in the offices of the 1980s? Will new attitudes prevail? According to a study by Yankelovich, Skelly and White, the employee of the future will shift his focus to himself, and a belief that he is entitled to a fine lifestyle. He will also be concerned about meaningful work that provides not only financial satisfaction, but psychic rewards, as well. Only about thirteen percent of America's present work force feel their work is meaningful. This is resulting in a shift of energy and attention to leisure time activities: mastery of a sport, for example. Some experts say that this accounts for the intensity of interest in tennis, golf, boating. For many it supplants the goal of work fulfillment. Such a shift must inevitably result in less dedicated workers. And that in turn means *the dedicated and ambitious employee has a better than ever chance of getting ahead.*

Yankelovich also discovered that there appears to be, among most workers, a stepped-up sense of time—a move toward living for today, an increasing unwillingness to endure current hardship or deprivation. So in order to achieve some future benefit, again, *the executive who can endure some hardship and sacrifice will be the one whom management will watch, and promote.*

It's all there for you.

Not everyone will make it.

Nobody said it was easy.

It takes courage. Energy. Personality. Breadth of interest. Overall composure. Thoughtfulness. Drive. Not all of these intangibles can be learned—but planning and preparation can. That's what we have been emphasizing. The rewards are success, honor, privilege, and an extremely exciting and satisfying life.

Of course, there will be detractors. Most of your friends will ask, "Why bother? It isn't worth the effort. It means sacrifice and hard work, and missing that TV show or that bowling tournament." They will tell you that nobody can realize his ambitions anymore, that those days are over. Nonsense.

Take Irvin Feld, for example.

IRVIN FELD

When Feld was five years old, he found a dollar on a coal cellar door about a block from where he lived in Hagerstown, Maryland. Feld took the dollar home, and when his mother asked him what he was going to do with it, he told his mother, "I'm going to save it to buy a circus."

Most children have circus fantasies, but Irvin Feld made his come true. With a few million dollars added to that original one, he did buy a circus in 1967: the Greatest Show on Earth—Ringling Brothers and Barnum & Bailey. Feld says it was the most glorious, the happiest moment of his life. "The circus had always been my love. I loved everything about it."

He was an unusual kid. At thirteen, when other children his age were playing basketball or baseball, Irvin Feld was selling snake oil at carnivals with his brother Israel. "The oil cost us a nickel a bottle," Feld recalls, "and I was afraid to sell it for a dollar," so I worked up this routine whereby I said we were special representatives of the company. I told them that if they bought one bottle, I would give them a bottle free." Feld smiles at the thought of it all. "I think the oil was some kind of linament," he says with a twinkle. "I never really wanted to know. We told them it would cure everything from frostbite to colds. We sold $8,000 worth that summer.

"The next summer," Feld says, "we added another product. Imitation lemon and vanilla extract. I even bought a collapsible stand. Our pitch that summer was to sell the vanilla for a dollar and you would get the lemon free. We added personnel. Besides my brother and myself, two of our four sisters came along. Israel or I would do the pitch and our sisters would go through the crowd."

While still in high school, the Feld children kept selling, door to door. This time they had ten items: rubbing alcohol; toothpaste; aspirin. "The kinds of things that are needed around the house," Feld explains.

By the time he was in his early twenties, Feld was running a drugstore in Washington, D.C. Those who remember it say that the shop was very "circus," with a striped marquee and a man in the window doing tricks with a Gila monster. There was a background of blaring music. "I hated everything about the place," Feld says, "except the music. I found I had a kind of flair for forecasting which records would sell. I decided to go into the record business. But none of the big companies would listen to me." He finally found someone who would buy records for Feld to sell in his store. The records did so well that Feld franchised another store and another; before long he was running a string of music stores called Super Music City. He was also in the record producing business, cutting a smash hit in the 1940s called "Guitar Boogie."

Recognizing that rock-and-roll was the coming phenomenon, Feld promoted rock-and-roll tours and finally, when he saw that the Ringling Brothers circus was deteriorating, made an offer to buy it. John Ringling North turned him down. "I realized that the circus was out of touch with contemporary times," Feld says. "I knew I would keep trying to buy it.

"All through the 1950s I was promoting rock-and-roll tours," Feld said. "I booked Bill Haley, Buddy Holly, Paul Anka, Dick Clark, Sinatra, Fabian, Frankie Avalon. Everybody. Booking them into sports arenas. My idea was simply this: The era of the Big Top was over. I knew how many hard-top buildings there were in the United States that could contain the circus. I knew how many would be built in the next five years and where I wanted exclusive control of booking the circus." Finally, in 1968, after ninety-six years in the hands of one family, the circus changed ownership. Feld bought the circus and has run it ever since. (In 1971 he sold the circus to Mattel, Inc., but Feld still runs the show.)

What does success mean to you?

"Accomplishment. Fulfillment of desires. Making your fantasies come true. Financial success. Creative success. Lots of things."

How does opportunity come to a person?

"Opportunity doesn't knock. You make opportunity. More people out there are talented than there are opportunities. You have to take risks. You have to have confidence in yourself. You have to accept failure."

Failure?

"In a lifetime, you undertake projects which don't always work out. But the thing is to maximize your successes and mimimize your failures."

Do you fancy yourself as the new P. T. Barnum?

"Oh, no. I never sell the public short. I never try to kid. Whatever product you sell, you can't fool everybody all the time. Barnum couldn't make it today. If you think of people as suckers, you'll fail. Ultimately."

Most successful people claim dedication is important to success. Do you agree?

"Many people talk about dedication. It's conversation. You really have to be dedicated to your idea. Nothing comes easy. But everything is possible. Trying to accomplish something—that's good stuff. But there's something even more important than drive."

What is more important?

"A man has to be sincere with *himself*. He must put in an immense amount of work. You might be able to kid the rest of the world, sometimes. But you can't kid yourself. Most very, very successful men I've met have a great deal of integrity. Scoundrels who make it are in the minority. At least, they get found out eventually."

What else is important?

"Sacrifice. I don't take vacations, for example. I'm always working. I like to see everything *in* show business, since I'm *in* show business. I feel that my free time should be spent doing that. It's no hardship, of course. What would be a hardship would be *not* working. I've always had confidence in myself. I've never suffered from insecurity. There are disappointments, of course—but that's another quality a man needs to succeed. To be able to face disappointments. And crises. That's a fact of life in anybody's business. *A man who can't face constant crisis shouldn't be in a responsible position.* He won't be for long. My phone is liable to ring at three o'clock in the morning telling me that my wire walker fell into the cage of cats. You live by crisis. I don't know anybody who runs any vital organization who doesn't. And I've had my personal crises, as well."

You mean about your eyes?

"Yes. I was given a drug with a horrible side effect which eventually made me totally blind. I contacted a number of doctors and found one in Washington who operated. It was a big chance. But it worked. In a way, I was fortunate. Instead of brain damage, which this drug is capable of inflicting, I went blind. But the operation worked. And with special glasses I was able to see again. When I take them off I'm blind. But now, I see colors more intensely. A whole new world of color. I had other side effects. I lost my hair. I had some internal problems. Doctors and advisors told me I had better stop working, and that I should retire. But I couldn't. I felt that I could adjust to the limitations of my condition, and once I accustomed myself to the idea that there would be parameters within which I was forced to abide, I realized there was no handicap at all. There were only more opportunities."

What did you do?

"What do you think? What else would I do? What else *could* a man do? I went right back to work."

ABOUT THE AUTHORS

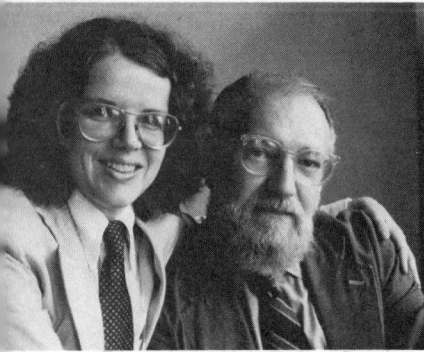

Photograph: Jules Siegel

J. Nebraska Gifford has built a reputation as both an artist and writer. She has had several one-woman shows in New York City and elsewhere and her paintings hang in museums and private and corporate collections from Ohio to California. She has worked as a magazine editor and her articles have appeared in many magazines, including *American Photographer*, *New Dawn*, *Ms.*, and has been architecture columnist of the *Soho Weekly News*.

Melvin B. Shestack is a veteran of the New York communications world. He has been an editor of the *old Saturday Evening Post*, editor-in-chief of *True* Magazine and a producer of television news and documentaries at CBS. He was written for a broad range of periodicals from *McCall's*, *Gallery* and *Playboy*, to *Science World*, *Harper's* and *Penthouse*. He is the author of "The Country Music Encyclopedia" and has just collaborated on a screenplay called "The Soul," and with J. Nebraska Gifford, on a mystery novel, "The SoHo Murders." J. Nebraska Gifford and Melvin B. Shestack have been successfully married for many years. They live in a converted New York factory with their daughter Victoria, and a herd of cats. Shestack's oldest daughter Lisa is a student at Ohio University.